Nazi-retro Film

▲▼▲

WITHDRAWN
FROM STOCK

Twayne's Filmmakers Series

Frank Beaver, General Editor

Nazi-retro Film

▲▼▲

How German Narrative Cinema Remembers the Past

Robert C. Reimer
Carol J. Reimer

Twayne Publishers ▾ New York
Maxwell Macmillan Canada ▾ Toronto
Maxwell Macmillan International ▾ New York Oxford Singapore Sydney

57736

Coláiste
Mhuire Gan Smal
Luimneach
Class No. 791.4
Acc. No. 563637
1454025
309430 86

Twayne's Filmmakers Series

Copyright 1992 by Twayne Publishers

All rights reserved. No part of this book may be reproduced or transmitted in any form or by any means, electronic or mechanical, including photocopying, recording, or by any information storage and retrieval system, without permission in writing from the Publisher.

Twayne Publishers
Macmillan Publishing Company
866 Third Avenue
New York, New York 10022

Maxwell Macmillan Canada, Inc.
1200 Eglinton Avenue East
Suite 200
Don Mills, Ontario M3C 3N1

Macmillan Publishing Company is a part of the Maxwell Communication Group of Companies.

Library of Congress Cataloging-in-Publication Data

Reimer, Robert C. (Robert Charles), 1943–
Nazi-retro film : how German narrative cinema remembers the past / Robert C. Reimer and Carol J. Reimer.
p. cm. — (Twayne's filmmakers series)
Includes bibliographical references (p.) and index.
ISBN 0-8057-9316-X (cloth). — ISBN 0-8057-9322-4 (paper)
1. National socialism in motion pictures. 2. World War, 1939–45—Motion pictures and the war. 3. Motion pictures—Germany—History. I. Reimer, Carol J. II. Title. III. Series.
PN1995.9.N36R45 1992
791.43'658—dc20 92-18054
CIP

The paper used in this publication meets the minimum requirements of American National Standard for Information Sciences Permanence of Paper for Printed Library Materials, ANSI Z39.48-1984.

10 9 8 7 6 5 4 3 2 1 (alk. paper)

10 9 8 7 6 5 4 3 2 1 (pbk.: alk. paper)

Printed in the United States of America.

For our families

Our children

Karl and Kirstin

And our parents

Charles and Leona Reimer

Arnold and Edith Jaeger

contents

▲▼▲

illustrations

▲▼▲

foreword

▲▼▲

Of all the contemporary arts, the motion picture is particularly timely and diverse as a popular culture enterprise. This lively art form cleverly combines storytelling with photography to achieve what has been a quintessential twentieth-century phenomenon. Individual as well as national and cultural interests have made the medium an unusually varied one for artistic expression and analysis. Films have been exploited for commercial gain, for political purposes, for experimentation, and for self-exploration. The various responses to the motion picture have given rise to different labels for both the fun and the seriousness with which this art form has been received, ranging from "the movies" to "cinema." These labels hint at both the theoretical and sociological parameters of the film medium.

A collective art, the motion picture has nevertheless allowed individual genius to flourish in all its artistic and technical areas: directing, screenwriting, cinematography, acting, editing. The medium also encompasses many genres beyond the narrative film, including documentary, animated, and avant-garde expression. The range and diversity of motion pictures suggest rich opportunities for appreciation and for study.

Twayne's Filmmakers Series examines the full panorama of motion picture history and art. Many studies are auteur-oriented and elucidate the work of individual directors whose ideas and cinematic styles make them the authors of their films. Other studies examine film movements and genres or analyze cinema from a national perspective. The series seeks to illuminate all the many aspects of film for the film student, the scholar, and the general reader.

FRANK BEAVER

University of Michigan

preface

▲▼▲

For almost 50 years, ever since the end of World War II and the collapse of the Third Reich, Germans have been trying to come to terms with the legacy bequeathed them by Adolf Hitler and the Nazis. The essence of the legacy is so powerful that single words can convey the hold the past has on the psyche: Auschwitz, the Holocaust. Probably no nation has tried to understand its past as much as Germany. *Vergangenheitsbewältigung,* the German word for "coming to terms with the past," is found prefaced to words like *novel*, *story*, *drama*, and *film*.

Coming to terms with the past has many points of entry. Some writers and directors who look at the past try to locate guilt and responsibility for the persecution of the Jews and other minorities that occurred during the Third Reich. Although film and literature do not always directly approach the pursuit by Nazis of what they referred to as the "Final Solution to the Jewish Question," Jewish persecution is present at least on the periphery. Other writers and directors, indeed most, concern themselves with other calamities of nazism: war, totalitarianism, and loss of identity. The many attempts to discover who was responsible and how responsibility carries over into later generations attest to the sincere desire of German authors and filmmakers to keep the past alive for their readers and audiences, to bring them to reflect on its lessons for the present.

The aim of this study is to describe the extent to which German filmmakers have focused their cameras on the Third Reich. Since 1945 over

100 German narrative films have been made for theaters and television. We cannot include them all in our study. The films we have decided to include fulfill at least one of three criteria: availability, historical importance, and commercial or critical success in Germany. We take as our point of departure three theses: first, viewers come into films about Nazi Germany with strong anti-Nazi feelings, which are activated during viewing of the films; second, directors employ strategies that shield viewers from identifying totally with what occurred in the past; and third, the tension created by the interaction of these audience feelings and director strategies creates a unique viewing experience for audiences at movies about Germany's past.

We have chosen the term "Nazi-retro" to describe the films in the book because it suggests both turning to the past and reflection on the past. The term is an adaptation of the French *mode retro*, which French critics use to describe entertainment films about fascist Europe. Although they use the term in the negative sense of being nostalgic about the past, or perhaps exploiting it for entertainment, we use it in a positive as well as a negative sense. Since most of the films we discuss were made for commercial release, their producers were striving to bring audiences into the theater. As a result, many are not as critical of the past as one might want them to be. On the other hand, the films were all made for audiences that, at the time of release, would have been able to understand the history behind them, even if the films themselves were sketchy about particulars. Consequently, the "look back" in these films is much harsher than their narratives might suggest. Nonetheless, some of the films are more successful than others at helping Germans locate responsibility for the past and helping them come to terms with history.

acknowledgments

▲▼▲

We wish to thank the United States Fulbright Commission, whose senior lecturer grant to Robert Reimer enabled us to spend 1984–85 in Germany, a time when the fortieth anniversary of the end of World War II was an occasion for a number of retrospectives of films dealing with the past. We also thank the Foundation of the University of North Carolina at Charlotte for its research stipends, which granted time to write and also paid for the rental of many of the films. Further thanks go to Wolf Rüdiger Grössl of Filderstadt, Germany, for lending us tapes of films that would have otherwise been unavailable. We owe a further debt to Ingrid Scheib-Rothbart of the Goethe House in New York, whose help in locating films aided our project once we got back to the United States. Thanks are also given to the Goethe Institute in Atlanta for supplying us with reviews and to Inter Nationes in Bonn for helping us locate stills. We would also like to thank the always helpful and courteous individuals at the National Film Archives in Washington, D.C., and West Glen Films in New York. Special thanks go to Robert Gleaves and Melvin Resnick, former chairs of the Department of Foreign Languages at the University of North Carolina at Charlotte, whose budget magic found money to rent films not covered by grant funds. We acknowledge the assistance received from Maryjim Whitlow, deceased, for her secretarial work. Our thanks also go to Angela Edwards, secretary in the Department of Foreign Languages, for her help with practical matters, to Edith Jaeger for her typing assistance, and to Kirstin Reimer and Kim Hewitt for their help with the filmography.

We also express our appreciation to the editors and publishers of the following publications, where some of the ideas presented in this book first appeared: *Journal of Popular Film and Television; Holding the Vision: Essays on Film, Sex and Love in Motion Pictures,* and *Varieties of Filmic Expression,* Proceedings of the First, Second, and Seventh Annual Conferences on Film, respectively, all edited by Douglas Radcliff-Umstead; and *The Third Reich in Recent German Films.* For the use of the many stills that appear in the book we wish to thank Inter Nationes, Tobis Filmkunst, Filmverlag der Autoren, WDR, Vogelmann, ZDF, Edgar Reitz, SFB, and Cine International.

Finally, we wish to thank our children, Kirstin and Karl, for their patience and their understanding of why we were not always available and for their tolerance of film talk at the dinner table.

chronology of historical events

▲▼▲

1919–1933	The Weimar Republic—Germany's attempt at democratic government is marked by internal squabbling among moderates and increasingly violent clashes between the extremists on the left and right.
1933	Hitler named chancellor of Germany 30 January. Reichstag burns 27 February, an event used by Nazis to solidify their power. Enabling Act grants Hitler absolute power 23 March.
1935	Series of laws designed to disenfranchise the Jews enacted. Known collectively as the Nuremberg laws, these decrees declare Jews to be noncitizens and forbid marriage between Jews and non-Jews. Jews can also no longer employ non-Jews in domestic service.
1938	Germany annexes Austria 13 March. England, France, and Czechoslovakia cede the Sudetenland to Germany 29 September. *Kristallnacht* (night of broken glass) takes place 9 November. Using as an excuse the assassination in Paris of a German diplomat by a distraught Jew, Nazi party members burn synagogues, destroy and loot Jewish shops, and physically abuse Jews.
1939	Germany moves into Prague and occupies Bohemia and Moravia 15 March. Nazis stage attack radio station in

	Gleiwitz, on the German-Polish border, 31 August. Accusing Poles of provocation, Germany attacks Poland 1 September.
1940	Germany establishes Auschwitz as a concentration camp for Poles and later for Soviet POWs.
1941	Auschwitz becomes a death camp for Jews. Germany attacks the Soviet Union 22 June.
1942	At a 20 January conference of Nazi officials at Wannsee, a Berlin suburb, the topic of discussion is European Jewry. Liquidation of Jews begins on a grand scale.
1943	German Sixth Army surrenders 31 January. More than 100,000 Germans lose their lives in the siege of Stalingrad.
1944	Allies land at Normandy, France, 6 June. Attempt on 20 July to assassinate Hitler fails. Colonel Stauffenberg and his co-conspirators are summarily executed.
1945	Hitler commits suicide 30 April. German armed forces unconditionally surrender 7–8 May.
1949	Creation of two German states, the Federal Republic of Germany (West Germany) and the German Democratic Republic (East Germany). Germany will remain divided until reunification in October 1990.
1951–1958	The *Wirtschaftswunder* period—West Germany's economic miracle.
1954	West Germany joins NATO. The West German team wins the soccer World Cup in May.
1956	Both German states build up military establishments.
1970–1977	Years of strong terrorist activity in West Germany, culminating, in the fall of 1977, in the kidnapping and murder of Hans Martin Schleyers, the storming of a hijacked plane in Mogadishu, and the suicide of three members of the Red Army Faction held in Stammheim Prison: Gudrun Ensslin, Andreas Baader, and Jan Carl Raspe.
1979	American miniseries "Holocaust" plays on German television (first broadcast in the United States in 1978).
1986	*Historikerstreit* (historians' conflict)—Jürgen Habermas attacks revisionist attempts of some historians, such as Ernst Nolte, and sets off a national debate on Germany's past.

1988	West German parliament president Philipp Jenninger's speech, delivered 10 November, during the fiftieth anniversary observances of the Kristallnacht pogrom, raises such fervor, owing to its content and tone, that he resigns two days later.
1990	West and East Germany reunified 3 October.

chronology of films

▲▼▲

1946	*The Murderers Are among Us* (*Die Mörder sind unter uns*), Wolfgang Staudte.
1951	*The Lost One* (*Der Verlorene*), Peter Lorre.
1954–1955	*08/15*, parts 1–3, Paul May.
1955	*The Devil's General* (*Des Teufels General*), Helmut Käutner. *It Happened on the 20th of July* (also, *Jackboot Mutiny*) (*Es geschah am 20. Juli*), G. W. Pabst.
1958	*Dogs, Do You Want to Live Forever?* (*Hunde, wollt ihr ewig leben?*), Frank Wisbar. *Rommel Calling Cairo* (*Rommel ruft Kairo*), Wolfgang Schleif. *Aren't We Wonderful* (*Wir Wunderkinder*), Kurt Hoffmann.
1959	*The Bridge* (*Die Brücke*), Bernhard Wicki. *Night Fell on Gotenhafen* (*Nacht fiel über Gotenhafen*), Frank Wisbar.
1960	*Brainwashed* (*Schachnovelle*), Gerd Oswald.
1961	*It Doesn't Always Have to Be Caviar* (*Es muss nicht immer Kaviar sein*), Geza von Radvanyi.
1965	*One Day* (*Ein Tag*), Egon Monk.

1966	*Cat and Mouse* (*Katz und Maus*), Hansjürgen Pohland.
1967	*I Was Nineteen* (*Ich war neunzehn*), Konrad Wolf.
1970	*Class Photo* (*Klassenphoto*: Erinnerungen deutscher Bürger), Eberhard Fechner.
1973	*The Pedestrian* (*Der Fussgänger*), Maximilian Schell.
1975	*My Country, Right or Wrong* (*Tadellöser und Wolff*), Eberhard Fechner.
1976	*Lost Life* (*Verlorenes Leben*), Ottokar Runze. *Mama, I Am Alive* (*Mama, ich lebe*), Konrad Wolf.
1977	*Girls' War* (*Mädchenkrieg*), Alf Brustellin and Bernhard Sinkel. *Winterspelt*, Eberhard Fechner.
1978	*Between the Tracks* (*Zwischengleis*), Wolfgang Staudte. *David*, Peter Lilienthal. *The First Polka* (*Die erste Polka*), Klaus Emmerich. *The Marriage of Maria Braun* (*Die Ehe der Maria Braun*), Rainer Werner Fassbinder.
1979	*The Tin Drum* (*Die Blechtrommel*), Volker Schlöndorff. *Germany, Pale Mother* (*Deutschland, bleiche Mutter*), Helma Sanders-Brahms.
1979–1980	*The Children of No. 67* (*Die Kinder aus No. 67*), Usch Barthelmess-Weller and Werner Meyer.
1980	*The Yellow Star* (*Der gelbe Stern*), Dieter Hildebrandt. *The Boat Is Full* (*Das Boot ist voll*), Markus Imhoof. *Lili Marleen*, Rainer Werner Fassbinder.
1981	*Mephisto*, István Szabó. *The Boat* (*Das Boot*), Wolfgang Petersen. *Charlotte*, Frans Weisz. *The Axe of Wandsbek* (*Das Beil von Wandsbek*), Horst Königstein and Heinrich Breloer. *Raindrops* (*Regentropfen*), Michael Hoffmann and Harry Raymon.
1981–1982	*It Went on Day and Night, Dear Child: Gypsies in Auschwitz* (*Es ging Tag und Nacht, liebes Kind: Zigeuner [Sinti] in Auschwitz*), Katrin Seybold and Melanie Spitta.
1982	*The White Rose* (*Die weisse Rose*), Michael Verhoeven. *Five Last Days* (*Fünf letzte Tage*), Percy Adlon.

	Veronika Voss (*Die Sehnsucht der Veronika Voss*), Rainer Werner Fassbinder.
	God Does Not Believe in Us Anymore (*An uns glaubt Gott nicht mehr*), Axel Corti.
1984	*My Father's War* (*Der Krieg meines Vaters*), Nico Hofmann.
	Heimat, Edgar Reitz.
	Angry Harvest (*Bittere Ernte*), Agnieszka Holland.
	Fellow Travellers (also, *Following the Führer*) (*Die Mitläufer*), Erwin Leiser, Eberhard Itzenplitz, and Oliver Storz.
	The Wannsee Conference (*Die Wannseekonferenz*), Heinz Schirk.
1985	*Welcome in Vienna*, Axel Corti.
1986	*38—Vienna before the Fall* (*38—Auch das war Wien*), Wolfgang Glück.
	A Minute of Darkness Does Not Blind Us (*Eine Minute Dunkel macht uns nicht blind*), Susanne Zanke.
1987	*Sansibar* ("*Sansibar oder der letzte Grund*"), Bernhard Wicki.
1988	*Autumn Milk* (*Herbstmilch*), Joseph Vilsmaier.
	Country of the Fathers, Country of the Sons (*Land der Väter, Land der Söhne*), Nico Hofmann.
1989	*The Spider's Web* (*Das Spinnennetz*), Bernhard Wicki.
	Hanussen, István Szabó.
1990	*The Nasty Girl* (*Das schreckliche Mädchen*), Michael Verhoeven.
1991	*Europa Europa* (*Hitlerjunge Salomon*), Agnieszka Holland.

The Bridge (1959). The seven 16-year-old Nazi soldiers in Bernhard Wicki's classic antiwar film stand on the bridge that costs six of them their lives when they try to defend it. Courtesy Inter Nationes.

chapter 1

▲▼▲

defining the genre

Since the Second World War many directors have made films concerning the Third Reich in Germany (1933–45), its antecedents, and its legacy. The designation *Nazi-retro* refers to these films. Like the French term *mode retro* from which it is adapted, Nazi-retro carries a faintly negative connotation: these films have a morbid fascination for a time and place that scarred a nation's psyche and from which Europe has not yet fully recovered. The term implies exploitation and trivialization for commercial purposes of the suffering caused by fascism. Furthermore, it points to the nostalgic allure of the past for those who lived through it and for the post-war generations who did not. It suggests history shot through a colored lens, showing the period not as it was but as the audience would like to remember it. On the one hand then, Nazi-retro refers to retrograde thinking, which at its most innocent leads to indulgence in nostalgia and sentimentalization of the past. At its most insidious it leads to a revisionism that sanitizes and thereby falsifies the past.

We have constructed the term Nazi-retro rather than use mode retro because we want a word that also carries positive meaning. If the term suggests retrograde on the one hand, on the other it refers to retrospection, the act of thoughtfully surveying the past. Directors of films about Nazi Germany have, for the most part, made these films with a sincere desire to help viewers understand and come to terms with the past by means of the cinematic experience. Filmmakers look back not to exploit the sensational aspects of Germany's history but to uncover the reasons that history happened as it did. The German term for coming to terms with the past through film, *Vergangenheitsbewältigungsfilm*, implies that film can be used as a means for reflection on and judgment and internalization of the past. In Nazi-retro films the past is presented as an object of study. Viewers are asked to reflect on what occurred, to form moral judgments about what people did, and to internalize the lessons of the consequences. This goal is clearly quite a responsibility for the lowly commercial film, and it is therefore not surprising that many fail to accomplish it. For in combining serious intent with commercial enterprise, the films create a duality that often introduces unwanted messages or subtexts. Some examples: when focusing on ordinary citizens and the strategies they used to cope with life during the Third Reich, the films sometimes suggest that the average citizen was completely separate from the government; when showing how the Nazis victimized the world, they sometimes show Germany too as a victim; when re-creating everyday life in the Third Reich, they create nostalgic reminiscences of a false normalcy; when acknowledging the Holocaust, they may avoid implicating anyone but high Nazi officials, while ignoring the virulent strain of anti-Semitism in central Europe that supported Nazi policy; and finally, when marrying serious historical questions with the formulas of narrative cinema, Nazi-retro films may divert viewers' attention from matters of importance and substance to those of a trivial nature. In spite of these pitfalls, however, Nazi-retro films provide a positive film experience.

The term "Nazi-retro" then covers any feature film made after World War II that focuses on the events leading up to the Third Reich, on the Third Reich period, or on the aftermath or legacy of nazism in Germany. We mean it to suggest the nostalgia of mode retro and the seriousness of the *Vergangenheitsbewältigungsfilm*. Since the end of the Third Reich in 1945, directors have made over 100 such films, and more are made every year. For the most part, the directors are native Germans who have made the films for German audiences. A few non-German directors, however, have made Nazi-retro films. Moreover, although few of the films have been made available for general release in the United States, many have won international acclaim and enjoyed commercial success in non-German-speaking countries. In the following pages, we concentrate on films that are available to American viewers, although we also include films available only in Germany that have special historical, cultural, or aesthetic importance.

▲▼▲

Nazi-retro films offer viewers a cinematic experience similar to that of other genre movies. The film scholar Robert Stam, drawing on the literary theories of Mikhail M. Bakhtin, describes the ability of genre to "evoke the existence of a life/world independent of the text and its representations."[1] Film noir, for example, creates "a cinematic space/time in which the postwar crises in cultural values and in economic and sexual identity found vernacular expression" (Stam, 12). Nazi-retro films likewise create a particular space-time. Their world is at once familiar, because viewers know the historical time and place to which the signs refer, and inviting, because the world has been structured to be nonthreatening—that is, the films' moral issues are clear. Nazi values are located in an "other" against whom the heroes and heroines—and through identification, the spectators as well—are placed in an adversarial position. Yet Nazi-retro films also ask viewers to judge what is occurring. The real space-time is too charged with political value to allow viewers to ignore the actions of the characters and the choices they are making. Like film noir, which offers a cynical urban landscape that directs viewers to experience a pessimistic world, and like Westerns, which construct worlds that allow viewers to accept a fantasy of unbridled individualism, Nazi-retro films also create their own space-time relationship. Their world is more influenced, however, by the space-time to which they refer. Viewers are thus drawn into the film through familiarity with form and content that extends from film to film. They are also given distance from which to judge what is occurring.

To bring viewers into their films, directors use sympathetic characters with whom viewers can identify. Of course, other narrative film genres do likewise, but in Nazi-retro films the creation of sympathetic characters presents a dilemma: if the characters are shown as part of the Third Reich, then the film asks the audience to identify with supporters of the Nazis, clearly an unacceptable prospect for most viewers. Yet to keep the characters divorced from the regime suggests that the Nazis and their supporters remain some vaguely defined "other." Rather than risk loosening the bonds of identification between viewers and characters, most directors choose to protect their creations from the Nazi label. Characters in Nazi-retro films either are completely separate from the Nazi regime or have an excuse for having supported Nazi policies; but even when shown in support of the Third Reich, they are shown to have opposed the atrocities of this criminal regime. In this way, viewers are allowed to keep a safe psychological distance from nazism, just as the characters with whom they identify are allowed moral distance due to noninvolvement, fear, youth, and so forth. The heroes and heroines of Nazi-retro films represent the foot soldiers and average citizens of Germany. According to the narratives, they are ordinary soldiers who follow a universal code of war. They are officers who protect their men by defying the edicts of Hitler and the high command. They are clerks whose only intent in following the Nazis is to protect their families. They are housewives who are struggling to run their households and therefore have no time or energy to worry about the ideological underpinnings of their society. They are young people who are coming of age in a time they do not fully comprehend. The one facet of society they never represent is national socialism. The Nazis in these films are clearly somebody other than the heroes and heroines. They are either peripheral characters who do not engage the sympathy of viewers, or monstrous villains whom the viewers and protagonists oppose together. In this respect, Nazi-retro films are similar to all formula films in which the viewer sides with good characters in their battles against evil.

Nazi-retro films are different from typical genre films, however. They depict the specific time and place of a world that activates associations or awakens memories in viewers. It is doubtful that most viewers have a strong opinion about the world to which Westerns and films noir refer—the mythical wild West and the urban jungle, respectively. The opposite is true of the effect of Nazi-retro films on audiences. On the one hand, the history in these films may function in the sense that Christian Metz has in mind when he refers to familiar material as a signpost in which "certain articles of the cinematic codes or sub-codes . . . are made responsible for suggesting to the spectator the vector along which permanent identification with his own look [gaze] should be extended temporarily inside the film."[2] History helps viewers recognize and thus enter the world of the narrative, bringing them into contact with sympathetic characters. In short, history contributes to the cinematic illusion when it helps make the fictional narrative more familiar. On the other hand, it is probable that national socialist Germany as a time and place is part of the field of knowledge of most viewers, most of whom also have a strong reaction to that world. These memories and reactions may be reflections of first-hand experiences with the policies of the Third Reich; this would certainly have been a common experience for those spectators viewing the first postwar Nazi-retro films during their initial release. Today, however, most viewers' knowledge of national socialist policies and life under Hitler comes from books, lectures, television, oral accounts, and films. Whether the knowledge is from primary or secondary experience, it is certain that viewers know something about the Third Reich, and that the world portrayed in the films is familiar to them or at least not strange.

The texts that Nazi-retro films communicate are very much determined by the prejudices and biases that viewers hold. That is, reception of the films is dependent on what reception theorist Hans Jauss refers to as a "horizon of expectations," which he defines as a certain abstract level of factual and emotional knowledge that readers have about the literature they are reading.[3] Applying his concept of a "horizon of expectations" to Nazi-retro films, one could expect that the films will affect viewers to the degree that they hold opinions about Hitler, nazism, and the Third Reich. Given the ubiquity of references in Western culture to this period, it is fair to assume that most viewers of a Nazi-retro film would be able to offer an opinion about nazism if they were asked. If one doubts that the Third Reich has found a permanent place in popular culture, one has only to think of recent films in which it has played a prominent role—Steven Spielberg's movies about Indiana Jones and the television miniseries "V" (1983) and "War and Remembrance" (1989), among other works. Or one has only to be reminded that even Pres. George Bush relied on the public's knowledge of the past by referring to Iraq's Pres. Saddam Hussein as another Hitler.

It is a valid assumption that if viewers know about the Third Reich, Hitler, and the Nazis, they will be predisposed toward a negative opinion of them. Probably no other government in the twentieth century calls forth as universal a condemnation of its official policies as does the Third Reich. Probably no event of the twentieth century is more repugnant to more people than the Holocaust. These strong and negative reactions to nazism—one need only remember the public outrage over Pres. Ronald Reagan's visit to the graves of SS men at the Bitburg, West Germany, cemetery in 1985, the forced resignation of Philipp Jenninger, president of the West German parliament, after he delivered a speech on the normalcy of the ordinary German's positive reaction to Nazi policies, the initial reservations of some in the West and the East about Germany's reunification—must influence the way a Nazi-retro film is received and understood by viewers, who experience the fictional world of the narrative against a backdrop of actual history.

All narrative films, of course, create their meaning through the tension between what is fictional (the narrative) and the world to which the fictional narrative refers. Indeed, such tension is part of narrative structure; it causes viewers to anticipate, to worry or relax, as they watch a film. But in most films the emotional involvement is not very high. As pointed out above, spectators usually do not care deeply if the white hats win over the black hats, regardless of how well the cinematic narrative is constructed. Narratives constructed from the emotionally charged events of history, on the other hand, evoke intense emotions. Viewers react more strongly to material about which they have formed opinions. For example, it is probable that films about the Vietnam War strike an emotional chord in viewers that is independent of the quality of the film and the intensity of its story. In like fashion, films about Nazi Germany call forth a reaction that is influenced as much by what viewers think about the era as by what is shown on the screen. In fact, response to Nazi-retro films may be even more universal and more uniform, for although the senselessness of the Vietnam War is widely accepted, the belief is not universal. In addition, viewers may feel that the war was senseless but recognize that the experience of soldiers in Vietnam had meaning. The reaction to films about national socialism is more monolithic.

Of course, not all viewers have had the same experience with nazism or share the same opinion of its policies. Among German and other Central European viewers, there are political, regional (Austrian, Silesian, Bohemian), racial, religious, and generational differences. An older German responds differently than an individual from the second or third postwar generation. If the viewing audience is expanded beyond ethnic Germans, the responses will vary even more. Surely Americans respond differently to a Nazi-retro film than do the French or Russians, for example. And all three nationalities respond differently than the Germans. Furthermore, those who were victimized or whose ancestors were victimized—Jews, Communists, Poles, Gypsies—may make associations that those who themselves or whose groups were not victimized do not, or cannot, make. Regardless of differences in response, all viewers will recognize that the values of the world in which the characters are acting threaten their own (the viewers') system of values. Moreover, they will recognize this even if the films avoid showing the more negative aspects of nazism. Thus, criticisms such as Tony Pipolo's—that German films about the Third Reich tend to ignore the "twin evils, Nazism and the Holocaust"—or Margarethe von Trotta's—that "we were quick to push aside guilt and responsibility"[4]—although accurate, do not necessarily reflect the power of the movies to call forth critical responses from viewers. Indeed, it may be that by the very omission of the criminal activities of national socialism the films cause informed viewers to reflect on those activities. In other words, for most viewers nazism is synonymous with evil to such a degree that they will have a heightened intellectual and emotional response to what they see. This is true whether the films graphically depict Nazi atrocities, merely suggest them, or avoid them altogether.

▲▼▲

History is present as both background and foreground in Nazi-retro films. As background the historical figures, prominent events, and other well-known allusions lend atmosphere to the films and help viewers orient themselves in the narrative world. It allows them to say, "I know this time, I know this place." Because the historical background can call forth value-laden associations, however, it becomes foregrounded at the appearance of direct references: historical figures (Himmler, Goebbels, Hitler), actual events (the attack on the Gleiwitz radio station, the march into the Sudetenland), specific icons (marching boots, the Nazi swastika, the Nazi salute), remembered sounds (familiar melodies, freight doors closing), or statistics (6 million Jews gassed, one hundred thousand dead at Stalingrad).

Thus foregrounded, calling attention to the horrors of the past, history alienates viewers from the narrative. It functions like a Brechtian strategy, distancing viewers from the screen in order that they might reflect on what they see and feel. Film theorists have long alluded to the dreamlike quality of the cinematic experience. Amos Vogel, for example, has written that when the lights go down in a theater, viewers enter a trancelike state and experience events on the screen as in a dream.[5] If so, then the appearance of history in Nazi-retro films is a scream that awakens us from a nightmare. It is an intrusion into the otherwise illusory film world. History calls attention to itself by referring beyond its purpose in the narrative structure. The phenomenon is similar to what Kristin Thompson describes as "cinematic excess." Thompson has written that colors, costumes, backgrounds, and so forth, can comment on a narrative by creating "a materiality of the image [that] goes beyond the narrative structures of unity in film." When this occurs, Thompson concludes, "excess comes forward and must affect narrative meaning."[6] History could be added to Thompson's list of elements, for it functions in Nazi-retro films to remind viewers of something beyond the narrative, which then influences the way they understand the narrative.

But history's ambivalent role in Nazi-retro films, as both background and foreground, causes the excess of historical material to affect narrative meaning in contradictory ways. Viewers are simultaneously entering and leaving the fictional world. They are identifying with, and yet feeling distanced from, the protagonists. The effect of this viewing paradox is twofold. Like a Gestaltist figure, the film presents viewers with an attractive face that seduces them into accepting the values of the world they have entered; but the film then exposes the falsity of the values to which the protagonists subscribe. For example, in a war film such as Wolfgang Petersen's *Das Boot (The Boat*, 1981), viewers see both a film that condemns war and a film that praises the virtues that lead to war. Similarly, spectators see the title character of Rainer Werner Fassbinder's *Lili Marleen* (1980) as both an opportunist and a modern heroine.

By simultaneously creating and destroying cinematic illusion, Nazi-retro films produce a state of equilibrium in which viewers are free to become a part of the narrative world and yet pass judgment on it—unlike in real life, for seldom is one able to pass judgment on a value system with which one identifies. These films, however, with their power to pull people in and push them out, give the spectator this very experience. This phenomenon is not unique to Nazi-retro films. Thomas Elsaesser, for example, writes about Fassbinder's "audience-getting" and "audience-frustrating" techniques, which both fascinate and repel viewers.[7] But Fassbinder and other directors use formal techniques to prevent the cinematic illusion from becoming too strong. In films about Nazi Germany, formal means of alienation are not needed to break the illusion. The very presence of the historical material is sufficient to break the hold that the narrative has on viewers. The same history that helped them accept the political system on the screen now allows them to judge that political system and the protagonists—sometimes historical figures and at other times fictional characters—who subscribed to it. In other words, Nazi-retro films provide a vehicle for understanding the appeal of systems that viewers would otherwise find abhorrent, for they make viewers a part of the system and then bring them to judge it. Nazi-retro films help viewers experience how easy it is to succumb to the values of nazism, how easy it is to overlook or to ignore dangers in a political system. Because viewers have come to identify with the heroes and heroines of these films, the judgment that they pass reflects back on themselves. At the end of the film viewers are left with an important question: would they have acted differently?

Nazi-retro films are a mirror, allowing viewers to see themselves in the characters and yet also allowing them to recognize that what they see is a virtual image, placed before them for judgment. The camera and characters of Nazi-retro films bring viewers into the imaginary world of the screen by reflecting a familiar world. Viewers know these characters, locales, and events from other movies, from literature, from family albums, and from oral histories. Reflected back are the faces of concerned fathers, troubled youths, and struggling artists; the theaters of Berlin and Vienna, the boulevard apartments of the upper middle class, the fields and countryside of Bavaria and Silesia, and the battlefields in Russia; the annexation of Austria, the march into the Sudetenland, the attack on Poland, the winter campaign in Russia, the final defeat and occupation of Germany, and the liberation of the concentration camps. But the reflection startles viewers. It helps them recall the blemishes of the characters, the truth about the comforting locales, and the consequences of the events. The reflection makes viewers aware that they are identifying with characters who act in support of a regime whose actions have been universally judged as immoral. On the one hand, spectators identify with the characters, see themselves in the characters, and come to understand why the characters act as they do. On the other hand, spectators are free to judge—as they might judge themselves in a mirror—the actions of the characters in light of what they know of nazism and the Third Reich. This is the unique experience afforded by Nazi-retro films: they provide a means for viewers to experience the choices that the films' characters make and also to pass judgment on those choices.

Narrative films set in a real historical past face a dilemma: as documents of the past, they are responsible for showing historical truth; yet as fictional constructs created to entertain as well as enlighten, they are constrained by the requirements of the medium. Nazi-retro films in particular tend to distort the past to create dramatic conflict where none may have existed, to romanticize the subject matter and emphasize individual, heroic actions, and to emphasize conventional values: valor, commitment to family, concern for one's neighbor, and love for one's country. Many of these films examine the period 1933–45 through a filter that subjectivizes, thus distorting the object of interest. Whatever the films focus on is transformed beyond its historical reference into something that will appeal to viewers, something more suited to cinematic narrative: films about resistance become spy capers; those about the battlefront show viewers comrades-in-war; and those about Jewish persecution are about martyrdom. Judging from Nazi-retro films, one would assume that every German family had a Jewish friend whom it sought to protect. By relying on filmic conventions (suspense, stereotyping, sentimentalizing) and cinematic themes (war heroism, unbeatable will, courageous resistance), Nazi-retro films open themselves up to the criticism that they trivialize the past and distort the truth. By resorting to formulaic structures and melodramatic narratives, the films create worlds that do not reflect historical truth.

Indeed, history becomes a mere backdrop for a mystery, a political intrigue, an adolescent problem, a love story. These formula plots, in turn, can distract from the seriousness of the period; by making viewers comfortable with the screen world, they can suggest that the real world of the Third Reich was not as evil as previously perceived. By concentrating on the heroics of war, formula plots can hide the reasons wars have been fought. By focusing on the courageous struggle of good against evil, they can reduce a real-life tragedy that had no dramatic cause to a melodramatic good guys–versus–bad guys confrontation. In short, the formulas of cinema that bring viewers into the films and open the way for them to pass judgment on what they see also introduce undesirable subtexts into the films.

Whether Nazi-retro films produce unwanted subtexts or bring about critical judgment is dependent on many factors, among the most important being whether the film allows itself to be seen as a construct. That is, even though history, by its very presence, calls attention to itself and interrupts the cinematic illusion, the interruption does not always allow viewers to respond with critical judgments. Sometimes the camera films history in such a way as to subsume it into the narrative, incorporate it into the illusion. It dissolves or obscures the artifice of the narrative and changes the screen from a mirror reflecting the past into a window looking onto the past. As a mirror, the screen reflects the artificiality of the virtual image back to the viewers; as a window, it suggests to viewers that what they see is the way things really happened.

Of equal importance in leading viewers to critical judgments is the degree to which the films show the characters in control of their lives. In effect, the narrative has to show that the characters are engaged in making choices and that these choices lead to situations that are threatening, although the film may be vague about the nature of the threat. For example, in films that depict normalcy, nazism becomes part of the scenery, no more dangerous than any other element in the lives of the characters. Indeed, in extreme cases viewers may wonder whether nefarious Nazi policies really happened or whether the Nazi threat was part of a collective dream.

Finally, the predisposition of the audience is important in fostering critical judgment. As noted earlier, the expected viewers for a Nazi-retro film have sufficient knowledge of nazism and its effects on history to help them judge what they see. That all viewers will be so prepared, however, cannot be taken for granted. When Bernhard Wicki's *Die Brücke* (*The Bridge*, 1959) was released in South America, for example, it was entitled *And the Brave Die Lonely* (authors' translation), suggesting, as Martin

Osterland points out, that the distributors viewed the potential audience as one for a traditional war film, not one for an antifascist film.[8] The film's antifascist message only works for viewers who know that the young men who died did so in the service of Hitler.

▲▼▲

Whether made one year after the war or 45 years later, Nazi-retro films give viewers a world that asks to be judged. The first of these films, the so-called *Trümmerfilme* (rubble films), were made when war memories were still fresh in viewers' minds. Reminders of the war were everywhere: in bombed buildings, in scavenging refugees, in returning soldiers, in black market activities, and in occupying armies. In addition, part of the Allies' policy of reeducating the populace included the forced viewing of documentaries about Nazi atrocities. One such documentary, a 22-minute film entitled *Die Todesmühlen* (*Death Mills*, 1945), showed Germans footage from their country's extermination camps. The text of the narration speaks of the criminality of the former regime and describes the camps as "death mills every one. 20 million men, women, and children died, murdered by the Nazis. Few survived the camps, and for many survivors help came too late."[9]

The physical and psychic dislocations experienced by Germans became the focus of the rubble films, perhaps as a way to rid the country of its ghosts. And even though these films do not portray the country's crimes as vividly as the films of denazification, they hardly allow viewers to escape into a fantasy world on the screen. *Trümmerfilme* take place, as their name suggests, amid the rubble of bomb craters. Scenes shot on location, reminiscent of Italian neorealism, reflect back to viewers a destroyed world and ask, how did this happen? Perhaps even more critical, given the circumstances, they ask viewers how they can live with what occurred. Less frequently the films depict the actual crimes, and even less frequently they deal with questions of responsibility. Their main goal was to help viewers cope with the present that the past had produced. Only secondarily did they try to help viewers cope with the past itself. The films are structured, however, to induce spectators to judge the choices the characters make as they rebuild their world.

A few years later, in the 1950s, material conditions had improved, at least in West Germany. Films to help people cope with the present were not as necessary. At the same time there was enough evidence of the lost war—occupying armies, pockmarked buildings—to suggest that moviegoers wanted to see something besides reminders of their past. As a result, most of the films from this period are light entertainment. Those films that do focus on the war for the most part avoid questions of guilt and responsibility. Many of these films are battlefront films that, even while questioning war, emphasize the virtues of bravery, patriotism, and comradeship. It is as if the filmmakers wanted to help viewers find meaning in the deaths of their friends and loved ones. Many critics see these films as an ebb in Germany's effort to come to terms with the past, since the films as a group seem to revise history. If rubble films set Germans apart from the Nazis, these films seem to set the military apart from the government as well. Coming at a time when West Germany was rearming for NATO, the 1950s films come across as an apologia for the military, an attempt to rally support for rearmament. Meanwhile, East German films were portraying Germany's fascist past. In these films, too, however, fascism was an "other," which the Communist regime was able to defeat.

After this brief hiatus in the 1950s, when Germans may have been too intent on rebuilding to want to answer questions about former times, filmmakers began to focus more and more on the past and to ask who was responsible for what happened. The films from the 1970s, in particular, seem preoccupied with locating the root cause of nazism. Some of these films seem motivated by a sincere effort to understand what went on during the Third Reich, how a seeming madman could have captured the hearts and minds of an entire populace. An entire group of film narratives from this period are told by those who were adolescents during the Third Reich. These protagonists witnessed what went on but were hardly in a position to stop what was occurring.

In the late 1980s such films gave way to those told from the perspective of protagonists who were not born until after the war. In this fashion, the question of guilt and responsibility has been brought into the present. Another trend in recent years has been to focus on the normalcy of the Third Reich, to show that life went on as usual under the Nazis and that most people were too busy trying to cope with daily existence to worry about the government and politics.

▲▼▲

Nazi-retro films deal with a variety of themes and provide a litany of questions for viewers to consider. Some focus on the callous and rational ways in which Nazis formulated policies, and others focus on the bravery of the resistance groups inside Germany that sought to overthrow the government. Some treat the persecution of the Jews under Hitler or show how the Nazis relentlessly pursued the policy of the Final Solution. Others focus instead on the hardships that war imposed on German citizens. All of these films initiate a dialogue with the audience. They ask viewers to determine who was responsible for what happened, and how universal the responsibility is. They also ask whether nazism was an aberrant movement that took hold of the German psyche for a short period of time, or whether it is still present in German institutions. Finally, the films ask whether nazism could rise once again to power and prominence.

Lili Marleen (1980). Willie (Hanna Schygulla) performs for an audience of Nazis. Courtesy Tobis Filmkunst and Inter Nationes.

chapter 2

▲▼▲

searching for the culprits

Wolfgang Staudte made *Die Mörder sind unter uns* (*The Murderers Are among Us*, 1946), the first German postwar film about coming to terms with the past, out of a personal desire to atone for not having done anything to oppose Hitler and national socialism. Asked why he had made the film, Staudte responded: "I asked myself that question often, especially since I had not been politically active in the Nazi era. [Rather] my thoughts were about making it through the period alive. . . . The fact that I made it through gave me an obligation and I had a feeling of guilt which I have not lost and which occupies me to this day."[1]

Joe Hembus and Christa Bandmann report that Staudte got the idea for his movie from a personal experience he had before the war ended. He had been threatened at gunpoint by an SS officer. The screenplay he wrote in response to this act of aggression was apparently a way of avenging it. Although the director could not win approval from the Allies for his movie, he had little trouble getting the support of the Russians, who wanted to nurture an indigenous film product. Shortly after the war they established the East German production company DEFA, which used the facilities at the old Babelsberg studio in the East Zone of Berlin. Staudte's film was one of its first productions. Staudte did have to make changes, however, in order to realize his film. The Russian cultural attaché, to whom Staudte showed his script, liked his idea but insisted on changing the original ending, in which the protagonist Mertens kills Bruckner, an ex-Nazi officer. The attaché was worried that this ending would encourage those Germans who felt they had been victimized by the Nazis to carry out personal acts of revenge. "At the time I was full of anger . . . but I saw that the change was correct" (Hembus and Bandmann, 153).

Staudte's film was popular with German audiences, attracting 5 million viewers by 1951 (Hembus and Bandmann, 153). This response may at first seem surprising considering that the reminders of the war were not only fresh in the memories of viewers but were physically present in the rubble outside the theaters. But *The Murderers Are among Us*, in spite of reflecting the conditions from which viewers were perhaps hoping to escape when they came into the movie house, offered them a chance to feel optimistic about the future and to assuage their feelings of guilt. Perhaps the members of the immediate postwar audiences could do little to atone for any collective guilt with which the Third Reich had burdened them. *The Murderers Are among Us*, however, assured viewers that those who could do something were actively hunting down those responsible for the crimes and bringing them to trial.

The story revolves around the postwar lives of Susanna, an idealistic young woman who has been released from a concentration camp; Mertens, a cynical doctor who is tormented by memories of the war; and Bruckner, an ex-Nazi officer and now an increasingly successful industrialist. Bruckner murdered women and children in a Polish village, a crime that Mertens witnessed, and the doctor is now intent on killing Bruckner, thereby making him pay for his past. Susanna's love for Mertens cures him of his cynicism. She also helps him to realize that his plan to punish the industrialist without the benefit of a legal trial would not serve the future. With Bruckner behind bars, the story ends on the statement that only a trial conducted in the full light of a free society will bring justice to the people who were wronged.

Staudte involves viewers in his narrative by using the classic cinematic strategies—camera angles, lighting, portentous symbolism, music, and melodramatic twists of fate. These strategies, together with a hero and heroine with whom viewers can easily identify, allow viewers to experience the physical and psychic scars that prevailed in 1946. For contemporary viewers these conditions would have been reminders of what they were actually escaping from, and for later audiences, reminders of an ever dimmer past. The film's happy end, also a mainstay of classic cinema, takes viewers beyond the scars and helps them recognize that brighter days lie ahead.

By disguising the message of his film in a formulaic narrative, Staudte clearly made it more appealing to general audiences; but critics, especially those outside Germany and those of later generations, were not as pleased. One British critic found that its style reflected German consciousness, with its "UFA heritage of camera angles, heaviness, neurosis, sentimentality and deviations into dim and fleshy cabarets." The *New York Times* found Staudte's film noir style to be "stilted and old-fashioned," and the film to be a "confused and rambling study of disillusionment in postwar Germany . . . presented in heavily stylized fashion."[2] Later critics have tended to excuse its camera style as "close to the dark pessimism of the pre-war films [showing] echoes of the film noir genre as practiced in Hollywood during the 1940's by German emigrés."[3] The German film historians Anton Kaes and Eric Rentschler both point out the similarity of the film's shadows and oblique camera angles to those in *Cabinet des Dr. Caligari* (*The Cabinet of Dr. Caligari*, 1919).[4]

The strength of *The Murderers Are among Us*, however, lies not in the homage it may make to early German film or to the films made in Hollywood by German emigrés, but in the way it allows history to speak directly to the audience. About a third of the way into the movie, the camera briefly captures a headline of a newspaper in which Bruckner, the industrialist, has wrapped his lunch: "2,000,000 People Gassed." This intrusion of history into the fictional narrative jolts the audience into watching the movie differently. A film that starts out as a nonthreatening story about coping with the problems of postwar recovery has become a film about coming to terms with the past. Staudte uses Bruckner to suggest that those responsible for war crimes were being integrated back into German society.

Staudte's film is much different from Gerhard Lamprecht's *Irgendwo in Berlin* (*Somewhere in Berlin*, 1946), also made by the East Zone's DEFA studios. In this film, which is about a returning soldier's difficulties in overcoming his cynicism and pessimism so that he can help to rebuild Germany, the horrors of the past are never visible. The city of Berlin may lie in rubble, but the film ignores the reasons that the city was destroyed. Staudte, on the other hand, reminds viewers of why German cities and lives were in ruins. Moreover, he confronts viewers with how horrible the crimes of the past truly were. As brief as the headline's appearance on screen is, it is the key to understanding *The Murderers Are among Us*, for it is a reminder of the historical reality that lies behind the movie's fictional narrative. Without the reference to the gas chambers, the narrative would include only the one fictional murderer, whom the film's hero is able to catch. Equally as important in broadening the scope of the film beyond its fiction is the understanding of history that viewers bring with them into the theater. If they do not understand the reference to the Holocaust or the other historical references, however, the film will provide little more than an evening of entertainment.

That the film would have been received as mere entertainment at its release is unlikely, of course. *The Murderers Are among Us* takes place amid the ruins of bombed-out Berlin, a setting that would have been indistinguishable from the scarred world viewers had left out on the street. When the train pulls up to the station at the opening of the film, the camera is clearly capturing everyday reality, in the fashion of Auguste and Louis Lumiere's *L'Arrivé d'un train en gare* (*Arrival of a Train*, 1895). Hildegard Knef, who played Susanna, writes that "the extras hung like bunches of grapes around the furiously snorting locomotive, intent only on protecting their places on the crowded footplates and handles" (Ott, 240). Here is a perfect example of reality being used to create fiction, which, in turn, is used to create the illusion of reality, much like the opening sequence in Roberto Rossellini's *Roma città aperta* (*Rome Open City*, 1945). But this intrusion of reality, a cinematic illusion that makes the fictional world immediately accessible to viewers, is also a reminder of the real world outside. The opposition of film narrative and real-world references activates memories in viewers of what they and their relatives and friends may have done during the war. And as the title suggests, they may have been murderers. The title implicates everyone. On the one hand, it conjures up visions of an infiltrating enemy—the Nazi "other" as opposed to the "good" Germans—but on the other hand, the title implies that the murderers are within, not outside, society. The guilty are not easily recognizable criminals with the mark of Cain on their foreheads. They could indeed be one's neighbors, friends, even lovers. In one of postwar cinema's ironies, Ernst Wilhelm Borchert, the actor who played the conscience-ridden Mertens, was himself one of the guilty. It was discovered after the release of the movie that he had been a minor Nazi. He was subsequently arrested and spent three months in prison (Ott, 241).

The Lost One

▲▼▲

The Murderers Are among Us was just one of the *Trümmerfilme*—feature movies, set in the ruins of German cities—about how the dispossessed and dislocated are cured of their cynicism and feelings of malaise and begin to rebuild their lives and Germany. As conditions outside the theater improved the popularity of the rubble films declined. One could interpret the decline as a reluctance on the part of audiences to be reminded of the past. But one could also interpret it as a loss of importance of those films that deal with healing the immediate scars of the past.

When Peter Lorre's *Der Verlorene* (*The Lost One*, 1951) appeared, it was apparently already too late for a rubble film to succeed commercially. In some respects, the film is very much like other rubble films. Its main character is filled with cynicism and pessimism, and its story is, at least in part, set amid the desolation of immediate postwar Germany. But *The Lost One* offers no hope that things will get better. The protagonist experiences no epiphany that would cure him of his malaise. Instead of pointing to the future, the film points backward as the protagonist commits suicide. *The Lost One* also offered no consolation to a postwar audience that wanted to be forgiven, if not totally to forget, past crimes. Lorre, who had emigrated to Hollywood in 1933, returned to Germany in 1949 to make this film, the only one he ever directed. He had heard a story about a doctor who, shortly after the war was over, had killed his assistant and then jumped in front of a train. Both men had incriminating pasts from their activities during the Third Reich, and the doctor believed that his new identity might be discovered.[5] Lorre fashioned this murder-suicide into a morality play about the horrors that had just transpired in the Third Reich. He himself played the lead, Dr. Rothe, a doctor in a postwar refugee camp who is tormented by a series of murders he committed during the past. Lorre's role as a psychotic killer is, of course, a reprise of the role that had brought him worldwide fame, the child murderer in Fritz Lang's *M: Mórder unter uns* (*M*, 1931). Lorre is drawing a parallel in *The Lost One* between the crimes of the doctor—who, except for his uncontrollable urge to murder, is portrayed as a decent individual—and the average German's involvement in the murders committed by the Third Reich. As one critic wrote, the film "would lighten Germany's conscience by making the doctor's crimes understandable."[6]

Lorre was attempting to help viewers come to terms with the legacy of the Nazis, but his complex movie is ultimately unsuccessful. He took a classic tale of a mass murderer, set it in the Third Reich, and added a frame set in postwar Germany in which the mass murderer is now a sympathetic doctor. As suspenseful as the film is, and as meticulously informative from the historical data Lorre added, *The Lost One* confuses more than it enlightens. Its greatest problem is that its narrative perspective is fuzzy. Although Dr. Rothe is a murderer and the film is structured like a classic thriller, viewers are never threatened by him. Much of the story is told from his perspective, and viewers thus come to identify with him. Moreover, he is portrayed as a kindly old doctor with whom it is difficult to associate the murderer in the flashback scenes. It is clear that the man telling the tale, if he did indeed commit the murders, has had a complete change of character and is no longer responsible for what he did. Other parts of the story are told from the perspective of the former assistant, Hösch-Nowak, who attempts to blackmail the doctor. These moments of the film, when the assistant relates the story, are perhaps meant to create distance between viewers and the doctor. In actuality, however, they merely delay identification with the doctor until he returns to tell the tale.

A second problem of the film is that the parallels it draws between the psychopathic killings of the doctor and the murderous activities of the Gestapo are both too tenuous to be convincing and too facile to be accepted. Yet these parallels must be convincing and acceptable if they are to help viewers come to terms with what they represent in the past. The film asks viewers to equate the murders of a serial killer with the sanctioned mass killings of the Nazi state when it interconnects Rothe's first murder and the Gestapo's aid in having it hushed up. This parallel not only places undue emphasis on the murders of an isolated madman by equating them with the sanctioned crimes of the state, but far worse, it trivializes the crimes of the state by reducing them to the level of crimes of isolated

The Lost One (1951). Peter Lorre and assistant Karl John. Courtesy Inter Nationes.

individuals. One has to ask, is the film suggesting that the German state was under a compulsion to kill its millions of victims?

The resolution of the conflict between the doctor and his assistant is also problematic. Although the final shoot-out and suicide may provide the melodramatic touches required by a thriller, they also deflect audience attention from the discomfort of coming to terms with the past. Instead of focusing on the moral issues of guilt and responsibility, viewers are concerned about the safety of the doctor. In a scene fraught with suspense, the former assistant threatens Dr. Rothe, commenting that the doctor is incapable of defending himself. The doctor wryly tells the assistant he had better step to the side, then shoots him. Dr. Rothe's suicide is just as melodramatic. As he walks along the railroad tracks, his figure fills the center of the frame from top to bottom. The screen then reveals an approaching train; the doctor covers his face; the screen goes black. The doctor's demise by a deus ex machina offers reassurance to an audience that may be looking for a closure to the past. But it is ultimately unsatisfying and unhelpful to those trying to understand the past.

Both *The Murderers Are among Us* and *The Lost One* illustrate the hesitancy that directors may have felt in confronting viewers directly about their role in the period that had just ended. Rather than focus their narratives on the Nazis directly responsible for the war crimes, they allow those crimes to be committed by third parties against whom the protagonists can mount a moral crusade. In this way, viewers remain unthreatened as they identify with good.

But at least Staudte and Lorre addressed the past. As film director Margarethe von Trotta commented in 1980, Germans were quick to forget (Pipolo). For almost two decades after Staudte's and Lorre's films were released, German directors either totally ignored the Third Reich or focused on issues other than those of guilt and responsibility. Although some films of the 1950s and 1960s could be seen as ones about coming to terms with the past, none touched upon crime itself, as did the films of Staudte and Lorre. They relocated the problem by asking, instead, why was the war lost? and why did the general populace go along? These questions were also examined in the shadows cast by the precursors and antecedents to nazism. Even the films from the East, for which fighting fascism became an obsession, did little but separate the East German regime from the Nazi past. This is not to suggest that films made in the 1950s and 1960s are dishonest, but only to show that they are concerned with matters other than locating responsibility.

By the late 1970s, however, as memories of the Third Reich were becoming more distant, directors found renewed interest in locating responsibility for the crimes of the Nazis. How far-reaching the interest in Germany's past was can be seen in two films whose narratives are really concerned with other issues: von Trotta's *Die bleierne Zeit* (*Marianne and Juliane,* 1981), and Werner Herzog's *Nosferatu—Phantom der Nacht* (*Nosferatu the Vampyre*, 1979). Von Trotta's film is about terrorism in Germany in the 1970s. Yet she includes flashback scenes of the main characters (two sisters) watching documentaries about Nazi atrocities, thus tying Germany's problems in the 1970s with terrorists to the country's Nazi past. Herzog's film about Dracula, a faithful remake of F. W. Murnau's *Nosferatu* (1922), begins by slowly panning across scenes of Hell carved into sarcophagi. Besides setting the mood for a film about the living dead, the scenes of tortured bodies also seem to refer directly to the Holocaust. In contrast, the 1970s films whose main focus is the Third Reich or its aftermath do not address the past and make connections between it and the present as forthrightly as do the brief references by von Trotta and Herzog. Instead, they continue where Staudte's and Lorre's films left off—allowing stories of personal guilt and atonement to stand in for questions of collective guilt and responsibility.

The Spider's Web

▲▼▲

Although the early films focused rather tightly on the need and responsibility to identify the guilty, the films of the 1970s and later cope with guilt and responsibility for the past in several different ways. Some look to the precursors or antecedents to nazism to assign guilt. Several films portray individuals who went along with or even benefited from the Nazi regime. Others look at the debilitating effects of guilt and blame. Some focus on German rehabilitation and forgiveness, and a few films reflect on the consequences of exposing former Nazis and Nazi crimes.

Bernhard Wicki's *Das Spinnennetz* (*The Spider's Web*, 1989), is set in 1923, before Hitler came to power. Lieutenant Lohse, one of two main characters, is an unexceptional servant of the state. His average nature makes him a sympathetic and dangerous character. Injured while defending the government during a rebellion of Communist sailors and workers in Kiel, the young lieutenant gains the admiration of a right-wing political party. At first he is used unscrupulously by the right in its efforts to undermine the fledgling Weimar Republic. He gradually learns how to insinuate himself into its higher circles, however, and after further ingratiating himself with the conservatives by ruthlessly putting down a peasant rebellion in Poland, Lohse begins a political career, which will clearly be successful. Throughout his climb to the top, Lohse is opposed by Lenz, a cynical Jew, played by Klaus Maria Brandauer. After playing opportunists in *Mephisto* (1981), *Oberst Redl* (*Colonel Redl*, 1984), and *Hanussen* (1989), Brandauer here plays a character whom Wicki feels deserves to win the audience's sympathy. "The public must have a role it can identify with. Lenz is the positive figure, the sympathy carrier. You can identify with him sooner than with Lohse."[7] Yet Lohse, too, through his ingenuity and vulnerability, gains the affection of viewers. As Wicki admits, Lohse "is not merely a figure that repels."[8] Moreover, Lohse's transparent opportunism is often a welcome relief from Lenz's political cynicism.

The Spider's Web, based on Joseph Roth's novel of the same title, is the fifth film in which Wicki treats some aspect of the Third Reich or World War II. (The others are *The Bridge*, *The Longest Day* [1961], *Kennwort: Morituri* [*Morituri*, 1965], and "*Sansibar oder der letzte Grund*" [*Sansibar*, 1987].) With the exception of *The Longest Day*, a Hollywood production about the Allied landing at Normandy, the films all examine the role of the individual vis-à-vis the totalitarian state. Whether Wicki's films are exclusively German or Hollywood productions, they all combine the trademarks of Hollywood films—high production values, attractive and larger-than-life characters, melodramatic twists, sex, and violence—with the themes and concerns of "art house" cinema—locating responsibility for the past, restructuring of cinematic clichés, avoidance of the happy ending, and criticism of politics. Wicki involves viewers emotionally in the stories and lives of his characters. Like his Hollywood counterparts, he seldom breaks the illusion his techniques create. In *The Bridge* he re-creates the agony of a group of 16-year-old youths. The strong identification that viewers feel with the boys, however, interferes with the film's antiwar message. Attention is focused instead on the positive nature of the values of war, which the film is trying to discredit. In *Morituri* viewers are likewise distracted from any antiwar message the story may convey and become transfixed instead by the mental duel between two of Hollywood's major actors, Marlon Brando and Yul Brynner. In *Sansibar* the suspense of the escape genre overwhelms the story of political and individual sacrifice. Yet in all these films the illusion is eventually broken, not by external references to the reality outside of the narrative but by the force of the historical material itself. The close-up of the face of the 16-year-old youth that closes *The Bridge* awakens viewers to a sense of the waste of war. In *Morituri* the dissolution of the idealistic Nazi, played by Yul Brynner, weakens the hold he has on viewers. Finally, the many examples of personal sacrifice in *Sansibar* remind viewers of the importance of the suspenseful escape.

In *The Spider's Web* Lohse and Lenz are different from the characters who usually populate Wicki's movies. They lack the values—bravery, honesty, idealism—of the heroes of *The Bridge*, *Morituri*, *The Longest Day*, and *Sansibar* and are characterized instead by cowardice, deceit, and cynicism. Whereas the usual heroes are ready to sacrifice themselves for the good of the group, Lohse and Lenz serve only themselves, although Lenz's work in behalf of Jewish refugees mitigates his cynicism somewhat. In spite of their negative attributes, however, these characters gain the attention of viewers. They are the viewers' entry into a world filled with sex, violence, intrigue, romance, and treachery. Through them, viewers experience the moral and political corruption of the Weimar Republic that contributed to the rise of nazism.

Lenz and Lohse vie for the sympathy of the audience. Because he is morally superior to Lohse, Lenz usually provides viewers the perspective from which to witness events. Nevertheless, even though Lohse's opportunism is at times repellent, he is a more interesting character because he is more dangerous. Thus, viewers can identify with him in spite of his credo that might makes right. With Lohse, Wicki has created a character who gives viewers a disturbing film experience. His vulnerability and disarming manner put viewers on his side. This otherwise ordinary man arouses curiosity about what lies behind his cold demeanor. The audience's attraction to him has a parallel within the movie in the two women who love him. The one, Rachel, a rich Jewess, loves him in spite of his professed anti-Semitism. The other, a daughter of a baron, is attracted to him only after she recognizes his ruthlessness.

Nowhere in the film does Wicki provide viewers any distance from which to judge Lohse. There is no frame, no disembodied narrator commenting on the story, and no obtrusive historical allusions. Since the story takes place before the start of the Third Reich, even the usual icons of the period are missing. Only the reference to the 1923 beer-hall putsch, a flash of a swastika pin, and the presence of anti-Semitism remind viewers of the history behind the narrative. Yet these brief reminders are sufficient to dispel any illusion created by Wicki's classic film strategies of close-ups, characterizations, and suspense. When Lenz is on-screen opposite Lohse, his moral superiority may produce a shift in allegiance among viewers. Nonetheless, it is primarily the viewers' knowledge of where the episodes depicted in the film are leading that creates a distance from which to pass moral judgment on Lohse. In other words, the only way for viewers to distance themselves from Lohse is to remember that this attractive yet ordinary man, in all his attractiveness and ordinariness, is a precursor of the Nazi regime.

The Spider's Web offers a disturbing but insightful look into pre-Nazi Germany. Although the film is set in 1923, ten years before the Nazis' rise to power, it shows that at this early date there had been more than a seed of fascism planted by Hitler's putsch. By 1923 the plant had begun to grow. The few historical allusions in the film indicate that ruthless power was used to put down the Kiel rebellion in 1918 and the uprising of the Polish peasants in 1923, and that violence against the Jews existed already. The pogrom that the workers stage at the instigation of some government officials anticipates the *Kristallnacht* pogrom of 1938. The trains on which the Jews are being deported back to Poland are soon to become transports that carry Jews to the concentration camps. These scenes, which take up only a few minutes of the three-hour film, are powerful enough to remind viewers that the Final Solution did not develop in a vacuum. This indeed seems to be a central theme of the film. As Bernhard Wicki states in an interview with Wolf Donner:

> Although the film is set in 1923, it has an uncanny relevance for us. It's about the time before fascism. The tendency to the Right, which has never been eradicated in Germany, unfortunately, and which I have sensed repeatedly over the years, has been confirmed by the elections in Berlin [in which the right-wing Republikaner won representation for the first time]. The atmosphere of those years seemed to be relevant to today. And besides this prefascist era has not been handled on film: Before Hitler came to power the decisive things had already occurred. (Donner)

The power of Wicki's film is that it not only lets viewers see that the decisive things had already occurred, but also lets them experience, with dangerous and disturbing fascination, the growth of nazism.

Hanussen

▲▼▲

Like *The Spider's Web*, István Szabó's *Hanussen* also takes place during the Weimar period. It is the third film of Szabó's trilogy about the beginnings of the Third Reich. *Mephisto*, the first in the series, takes place during the Third Reich. The second film, *Colonel Redl*, is set in pre-World War I Austria. *Hanussen* falls in the middle period, 1918–33, the years of the Weimar Republic. The film tells of the career of the clairvoyant Karl Schneider from the waning days of World War I until his death shortly after the Reichstag fire and the coming to power of the Nazis. Schneider is

563632

a sergeant who receives a head wound in the war and is treated by a Dr. Bettelheim. From the beginning his charismatic powers are evident: he hypnotizes a wounded soldier and talks him out of exploding a grenade and killing himself and those in his barracks. Schneider's doctor interprets Schneider's powers as the gift of being able to transfer his will to others. Since Bettelheim is interested in hypnosis, he initiates a friendship with Schneider that continues after the war, when Schneider has joined a fellow officer in a show as a clairvoyant. He changes his name to Hanussen and achieves almost overnight success when he correctly predicts the sinking of a ship. As his fame spreads, Hanussen gets into trouble with local authorities and eventually moves to Berlin. His partner leaves him in the belief that Hanussen is allowing himself to be seduced by Nazi power. Hanussen eventually lands in trouble with the Nazis, who, perhaps sensing that he could be dangerous to them, have him killed.

Hanussen is a tour de force of historical narrative. In the film nothing historical is nailed down or is what it seems. Except for the names Hanussen and Hitler, for example, all names have been changed—but not to protect their real-life referents, whose closeness to the characters only calls attention to them. The real-life filmmaker Leni Riefenstahl becomes photographer Henni Stahl. Walther Rathenau's name is changed to Reittinger. Dates are also shifted. Szabó telescopes, stretches, and otherwise distorts the iconographic historical information viewers remember. Secretary of State Reittinger is assassinated in 1932, whereas Rathenau's death occurred in 1922. Germany's period of hyperinflation, as depicted in the movie, is off by several years. Finally, the ship that Hanussen predicts will sink goes under in 1922 on its way to the United States, not in 1916 on its way to Europe, as the *Lusitania* did. Dr. Bettelheim is also an allusion to Bruno Bettelheim, the German psychologist who left Germany before the rise of the Nazis, not after, as in the film.

Szabó seems intent on refuting Siegfried Kracauer's assertion that historical films cannot be successful films.[9] In *Hanussen* he makes history work for him by activating the knowledge viewers bring to the film. The historical associations give Hanussen's predictions an ominous quality. The difficult and wrenching decisions that Jews were actually having to make during this period make the questioning of the clairvoyant by many characters—will they, should they, leave Germany?—serious, even chilling. Hanussen's predictions have the ring of truth for spectators because they know his predictions will be fulfilled. The acceptance and respect given to his pronouncements by his audiences, the press, and both the Weimar and Nazi governments become believable. Once the credibility of Hanussen's abilities is established through the association of

Hanussen (1989). Hanussen (Klaus Maria Brandauer, far left) shortly before his murder by Nazi police. Courtesy Tobis Filmkunst and Inter Nationes.

historical reality with the narrative, the sense of truth in the reasons he advances for Germans' acceptance of nazism is also enhanced. Being able to read people's souls, Hanussen claims that Germans will readily give up freedom and accept Hitler and nazism in their desire for order with which to drive out the chaos engulfing Germany.

Szabó does not provide transitional dates as superimposed titles to help audiences orient themselves to his historical narrative. Instead he alludes to historical events to tell viewers when the action is taking place. These are sufficiently distorted that viewers remain disoriented, continually having to put together a puzzle whose pieces have been altered. The historical confusion leads to a sort of Brechtian alienation that brings viewers to reflect on the issue of power and the rise of Hitler and the Nazis without having to consider the history books. Focus is shifted from the power of politics to the power of charisma, from how Hitler rose to power to the qualities that allow an ordinary man to capture the minds of even intelligent people. Hanussen is a stand-in for Hitler in this study. He has the same birthday and the same birthright as Hitler. The question that the film asks is whether or not "a person can transfer his will to another." The answer is unclear. At times the film seems to answer yes, as when Hanussen talks the young man out of murder-suicide, and when he talks a young lady into setting fire to a curtain. But when he fails to talk his lover into jumping from an open window, the implication is that he can make people do only what they really want to do. In yet another scene, however, he persuades a young Nazi to make a fool of himself in front of a crowd of people. Would the young man have willingly submitted to humiliation? Such obvious ambiguity helps viewers reflect on the historical references of the film. It suggests that Hitler accomplished what he did not merely because of conditions in Germany but also because the people wanted to believe in him. The people invited him into their house and perhaps even knew what they were getting. The film seems to say that Germans knew that Hitler would suspend some of their freedom, if not all of it.

Lost Life

▲▼▲

Postwar atonement for transgressions against individual lives is the subject of Ottokar Runze's *Verlorenes Leben* (*Lost Life*, 1976). This film, like Lorre's *The Lost One*, could have taken place at any time in any country. Indeed, the main story is set in pre-Nazi Germany. It avoids allusions to Hitler, national socialism, and the coming historical tragedy and is linked to nazism only through a narrative frame, which opens and closes the movie. This frame transforms a universal tale of friendship and betrayal into an examination of guilt and responsibility for what occurred in Germany under the Nazis.

The almost total separation, however, between the narrative and the frame creates a confusing film experience. On the one hand, Runze's use of a genre formula for the main story creates a suspenseful mystery. The characters are likable and easy to identify with; therefore viewers easily become more interested in the outcome of personal relationships than in the historical events being depicted. On the other hand, Runze's frame thwarts the complete fulfillment of the viewing experience. It introduces material that is extraneous to the narrative and whose function it is to lead viewers to a deeper understanding of the story. This is, of course, the function of framing in a narrative, whether film or play: to provide the audience with distance from the main story, which is then experienced on a different level. But in *Lost Life* the frame alludes to more than its place in the film; it also alludes to a historical reality outside the film: Germany

Lost Life (1976). A moment of suspicion about a telephone call mars the growing friendship between Marius Müller-Westernhagen and Gerhard Olsschewski. Courtesy Inter Nationes.

during the Third Reich. It turns a story of betrayal into an exploration of what transpired in the past, to locate responsibility and assign guilt.

The main narrative of *Lost Life* is set in 1928 in a small town in Silesia and in Berlin. The frame places viewers in an air raid shelter in 1944. The man who narrates the story has been asked by a youth to explain why he became a priest. The frame thus directs viewers to understand the coming story in light of the boy's question. Moreover, the question itself is colored by the fact that it is asked by a member of the Hitler Youth, who poses his question in a shelter during a bombing raid on Nazi Berlin.

The priest tells a simple story of loneliness, friendship, and betrayal from his own past. A Polish gardener, Cioska, is suspected by a zealous district attorney of having murdered a small girl in a Silesian village. The attorney has no proof, only his own prejudice against outsiders. When the gardener moves to Berlin, the attorney hires a Polish student (the priest in the frame) to befriend him and to wrest a confession out of him. The student's task is easy since Cioska is shy and lonely. Gradually the student grows to dislike his assignment, but he continues it, having been convinced by the attorney that the man is a child murderer. When Cioska believes that he is about to lose the friendship of the student, he confesses to a murder, hoping the confession will bind the student closer to him. The police have been monitoring the conversation of the two and arrest Cioska, who is tried, convicted, and executed. Whether the gardener is guilty or not is unclear. Runze so successfully reflects the man's loneliness in the drab rooming houses and decaying streets of Berlin that viewers easily believe he confesses to a murder he did not commit to keep a friend.

Clearly the story of *Lost Life* would be compelling even without a frame. And in truth, the film deserved much wider attention than distributors gave it. Runze gives his film the feel of the gardener's desolate life by overlaying a sepia tone onto sharp black-and-white cinematography. At times he uses back projections of archival film footage of Berlin, a technique that brings the lonely, desperate condition of an individual in a big city to life. The friendship between the two men grows naturally so that the betrayal by the student of his friend leads to an emotional catharsis that would have made a perfect end to the movie. The closing frame, however, changes the movie's direction. It reminds viewers of the priest's words in the opening frame: that the worst fear in the world is not of war but of "doing evil, of having done evil, of doing it again." On one level this comment refers to the main story and the student/priest's fear of perhaps destroying another life through betrayal of trust and friendship. On another level the priest is referring directly to the question of guilt and responsibility for what occurred in Nazi Germany. Runze underscores the broader message of his movie in the closing frame. As the priest finishes his story, he remarks that the only thing the gardener said at his trial was to answer no when asked if he regretted the crime that had excluded him from human society. The priest interprets this to mean that "maybe he did not want to belong to such a society." At this point in the film, the air raid ends and the priest and the boy in his Hitler Youth uniform come out of the shelter and face the camera, which then surveys the scene of desolation around them.

Runze uses the narrative frame to turn a simple mystery into a film about coming to terms with universal guilt. The "lost life" of the title refers to several lives in the narrative—the little girl, the Polish gardener, the student turned priest—and a fourth referent is added in the frame, the Hitler Youth member. The frame and narrative span two governments, the Nazis and the Weimar Republic. The frame, given the significance to history of the system it portrays, focuses attention on the governing system in the narrative. With hindsight, it implies that "justice" as practiced by the Nazis was present in pre-Nazi Germany. The frame and narrative taken together propose questions about post-Nazi Germany. The film suggests that the zeal of the prosecuting attorney in protecting the state from outsiders destroyed the values of friendship and trust. Furthermore, this loss led to a system that destroyed human values even further and eventually cost human lives. The film thus takes on a political dimension that reflects the concerns of intellectuals in 1975, the year the film was made. The 1970s in Germany were a decade in which the German state, in the eyes of many on the left, ruthlessly trampled individual freedoms in the name of societal good. This is the theme of Volker Schlöndorff and Margarethe von Trotta's *Die verlorene Ehre von Katharina Blum* (*The Lost Honor of Katharina Blum*, 1975), based on Heinrich Böll's novel of the same name. It is also the theme of von Trotta's *Marianne and Juliane* and the multi-directed film *Deutschland im Herbst* (*Germany in Autumn*, 1977–78). The efficiency with which the prosecutor in *Lost Life* deals with outsiders finds a parallel in the efficiency with which the German government was dealing with its dissenters, as reflected in these other 1970s films.

Mephisto

▲▼▲

Once the Nazi party came into power, many people either passively supported the regime or actively sought to rise under its aegis. Hendrick Höfgen, the protagonist of István Szabó's *Mephisto*, is not a murderer of the same ilk as Lohse in *The Spider's Web*. Indeed, he never murders anyone. He is, however, as described in Klaus Mann's novel on which the movie is based, "a clown for the diversion of murderers."[10] Klaus Mann based the figure of Höfgen on the legendary actor Gustav Gründgens, whom he viewed, for personal as well as political reasons, as a stooge of Heinrich Himmler, the model for another figure in the book and film, the prime minister of Prussia. Szabó shares Mann's antipathy for Höfgen and emphasizes in his film the complicity of his hero in the policies of the Third Reich. Szabó commented in an interview, "I maintain that Hendrick Höfgen became guilty even though he never was on the front, he never shot at soldiers, he never murdered, on the contrary in some cases he helped people [who were in danger]. Nonetheless he became guilty because he helped Fascism become acceptable, brought it into the parlor, so to speak."[11]

The central issue of *Mephisto* is whether or not Höfgen is guilty of political crimes. His only role in the government is to give speeches, as head of the state theater, about the growth of culture in Nazi Germany. Szabó and Klaus Maria Brandauer, who played Höfgen, do not offer an unequivocal answer. Under Szabó's direction, Brandauer's portrayal of Höfgen transforms the arrogant, clearly opportunistic, and negative protagonist of Klaus Mann's roman à clef into a likable fellow. He may compromise his ideals occasionally, but he almost as immediately finds them again. The ambivalence in the character is intentional. Szabó remarked in the interview quoted earlier that his Höfgen is "more complicated, more dramatic and more nuanced. The viewer can therefore better identify with the film hero" (Fenyves, 44). Since it is doubtful that viewers would want to identify with someone who is clearly guilty of collaborating with murderers, Szabó and Brandauer have made Höfgen's function under the Nazis ambiguous. He is the liaison between the Nazis and the intellectual world. As a representative of the Nazis, he enjoys the perquisites of his

Mephisto (1981). Celebration of Höfgen's triumph as Hamlet. Courtesy Inter Nationes.

office, namely, fame and fortune. But Höfgen is also portrayed as a good man. The bouts he has with his conscience over what he is doing are sincere. He clearly does not subscribe to Nazi ideology.

Szabó uses camera distance to increase identification with Höfgen by the viewer. The director uses close-ups of the actor's face whenever Höfgen is agonizing over the choice between furthering his career and betraying his friends. In this way, the director increases sympathy for this man who wants so much to remain an actor that he is willing to compromise his principles. Moreover, as Höfgen's dilemma intensifies and his story approaches its climax in the stadium, the camera shows him in more favorable poses. That is, as the true extent of Höfgen's compromise becomes clear to viewers, the camera enhances his stature and makes it more difficult not to identify with him. Early in the film the camera stays at a distance. It captures Höfgen in bizarre poses, reveals his moodiness, and exposes his frequent tirades. The camera distance and what the camera shows keep the viewer from identifying with the character. In later scenes he is less agitated. His tranquillity seems to be that of a man who has found happiness. The close-ups used in these scenes enhance any viewer identification brought about by the change in the character.

It is an irony of Szabó's mise-en-scène that as the camera captures Höfgen in more positive poses, it also captures him in closer proximity to Nazi symbolism. As the bond of identification that viewers have with him deepens, the character becomes more and more associated with nazism. By the penultimate scene which precedes Höfgen's breakdown in the stadium, he is at his most appealing and yet is also closest to nazism. Höfgen has just had a great success in a reinterpretation of Hamlet that incorporates Nazi ideology. Viewers of the movie are meant to share the enthusiasm of the audience that has witnessed his triumph. At a postperformance ceremony, Höfgen is welcomed into a huge hall festooned with Nazi banners. As he begins to speak, praising nazism, he shares the frame at this moment of success with only one object, a huge Nazi banner that runs the length of the screen from top to bottom behind his centrally placed figure. The scene is a disturbing shock, for it reminds viewers, who have grown to like Höfgen and have identified with him, that they have been as seduced by the lie of his success as he. Until this scene it is easy to overlook all the Nazi symbolism and to believe that maybe Höfgen has kept his integrity in this, his greatest acting achievement. Nothing breaks the illusion of identification with Höfgen until this scene in which the swastika dominates the screen.

After speaking to his admirers, Höfgen is driven by the prime minister to a mysterious tour of the Berlin stadium. Here, after an ominous and

Mephisto (1981). The General (Rolf Hoppe) praises Hendrik Höfgen's (Klaus Maria Brandauer) performance as Mephisto. Courtesy Inter Nationes.

disturbing speech by the prime minister, Höfgen slowly walks to the center of the field. The final scene of the movie reveals to what degree Höfgen has compromised himself and become a puppet of the regime: standing in the middle of the Berlin stadium, in the spotlights that the prime minister has focused on him, Höfgen whispers, "What do they want from me? I'm only an actor." The confused and frightened actor is a prisoner within the beams of light. In spite of himself he has fallen victim to a carefully orchestrated plan of the Nazis to use his high standing in the world of the arts. He has given the Nazis the respectability they are seeking. This scene affects viewers all the more strongly because, until this moment, they have been as beguiled by success as he. In this scene they finally see that the devilish face Höfgen wore as Mephisto—the role that first brought him fame and ignited his career—a face mirrored by the face of his protector, the prime minister, was no mask after all. Szabó has remarked: "Fascism did not always appear in a devilish form. Therefore we have to depict and investigate those manifestations of fascism in which it won people over and bound them to itself through various means and ingenious and well thought-out methods. We have to expose these methods with which it . . . perverted human thinking and feeling in order to make it serve its goals" (Fenyves, 44). Is Höfgen guilty? Yes? But the film suggests, by forging a close bond between viewers and Höfgen, that the viewers might not have acted any differently.

Lili Marleen

▲▼▲

Like Hendrik Höfgen, Willie Bunterberg, the heroine in Rainer Werner Fassbinder's *Lili Marleen* (1980) becomes a pawn of Nazi propaganda because of her desire to be a star. And like Höfgen, she asserts her innocence by protesting that she does not serve Nazi interests. Midway through the movie, Willie's Jewish lover, Robert, has a secret rendezvous with her in a bombed-out building in Berlin. He rebukes her for supporting the Nazi cause with her performances, to which she replies, "But I only sing a song." Stung by his criticism and perhaps recognizing the feeble nature of her excuse, she engages in espionage for him. She is captured, but the Nazis need her to perform. She does so to save her lover, but inevitably her performance helps the Nazi image as well.

The character of Willie is based on the singer Lale Andersen, whose autobiography, *Der Himmel hat viele Farben* (*The Sky Has Many Colors* [authors' translation], 1972), chronicles her overnight success with the soldier's ballad "Lili Marleen." In her book, which is a not very veiled apologia for her career under the Nazis, Andersen deemphasizes the perquisites that "singing for the Nazis" brought her and emphasizes instead how, in spite of singing for the Nazis, she remained decidedly anti-Nazi. The persona that Andersen creates for herself in her autobiography is very much like the fictional Höfgen. Like him, she is convinced that purity of heart and good intentions will keep her free of Nazi domination. Fassbinder, who claimed not to have read the book closely, if at all, used Andersen's tale of success among the Nazis to reveal how easy it is to succumb to self-deception. Using his usual strategies for distancing the audience, he exposes the singer's story for the apologia that it is and makes clear that it was not just a song she sang.

Fassbinder's film is a stylized tour de force that forces Willie's complicity in the Nazi propaganda machine into the consciousness of viewers. In this big-budget movie, the director used more of his stylistic gimmickry than usual: mirror reflections, shots through multiple layers of glass, low-angle and high-angle camera shots, bizarre lighting, and vibrant colors. In addition, Fassbinder directed the players to overact, punctuated dramatic scenes with satirical musical accompaniment, portrayed the members of a

Jewish organization as Gestapo-like agents, appeared himself in a cameo role as a mysterious underground agent, and employed a poorly synchronized and highly manneristic voice track. (The film was originally shot in English, then poorly dubbed into German and released in English-speaking countries with the German voice track and subtitles.) Furthermore, he mixed a variety of film genres in telling the singer's story—espionage thriller, music biography, love story, war film, and gangster movie. The stylistic potpourri of *Lili Marleen* caused Vincent Canby of the *New York Times* to describe the story as "wildly melodramatic and sentimental," and yet the film itself as "cold as death."[12] His is an apt description, for the film is indeed sentimental but cold, dramatic but understated. The film alternately involves viewers and pushes them away, wanting them to identify with the central character and yet also wanting them to judge her harshly.

Louis Skorecki, a French film critic, describes the confusion built into *Lili Marleen* as intentional. Skorecki finds that Fassbinder's style helps viewers evaluate everything they see more critically. The mixture of genres in the movie perplexes viewers and distances them from the melodrama. The film's Brechtian alienation thus takes viewers out of the film, where they have identified with the characters, and places them back in the theater, where they are free to reflect on the meaning of historical events. "Each spectator, manipulated, put into a scene, must accept being at war with himself, split between emotion and reflection, free. Free to say yes, no, perhaps."[13] For Skorecki, *Lili Marleen* creates tension in viewers by suspending them between the movie's melodrama and its background. And in this suspended state, viewers think about what they see.

That Fassbinder's alienation techniques cause tension in viewers cannot be denied. Numerous Fassbinder scholars have recognized the director's penchant for mixing identification, which is a mainstay of classic cinema, with distancing, the mainstay of art house cinema. Yet the alienation techniques and stylistic breaks of *Lili Marleen* cannot alone cause viewers to reflect on what they see. For one, the desire of viewers to identify with the heroes and heroines of the films they watch is strong. Moreover, Willie herself is so appealing that Fassbinder's mannerisms do not by themselves keep viewers from identifying with her. If viewers are brought to reflect on the degree to which Willie is an opportunist, they do so because of what they know about history and about the Nazis before they enter the theater. Fassbinder's mannerisms simply activate that knowledge. They then distance themselves from the illusion.

Perhaps it is more accurate to say that what viewers already know about the Nazi regime influences the way in which they experience the melodrama. If this is the case, the film may never rise above being a melodrama for many viewers, in spite of the techniques of Brechtian alienation employed by Fassbinder. Viewers not already possessing a critical view of history will succumb to the sentimentality of the film, will identify with Willie, and will accept as excusable the contradiction that her emotional confusion causes in her life. They will agree that it must indeed be difficult to forge a career in a "system that holds her lover prisoner." Viewers without an opinion about history would applaud her success and overlook the system in which she has that success. For them, *Lili Marleen* functions as a movie about the sacrifices one must make if one wants a career in show business. In spite of the techniques of alienation with which historical background is presented, history would function as little more than a backdrop for a singer's biography and would do so regardless of camera angles, acting styles, color schemes, or the mixture of genres.

For viewers who know about history, however, and for those who know about the horrors of the Third Reich—in other words, for the knowledgeable viewer, and it is for the knowledgeable viewer that Fassbinder made his films—Willie's self-deception about her role in the Third Reich is exposed. In a pivotal sequence from the movie, the camera follows the heroine around the room of a newly decorated apartment with which Hitler has rewarded her success. The camera follows her movements from the perspective of her accompanist and a Nazi officer. Each glance Willie throws in the mirrors she passes on her walk, each brush of an opulent object—despite the apparent parody of the scene—entices viewers more and more into applauding her success with her schmaltzy ballad. Spectators are no longer voyeurs in this scene. The accompanist's perspective has given way to Willie's. Viewers have now become fellow narcissists, savoring every moment as much as Willie does. Heavenly music and a majestic view from a picture window bring viewers further into the film so that they experience with Willie her astonishment at having made it to the top.

In the next scene, viewers are seduced into further involvement with the film's characters as Willie and her partner tease each other, make fun of their success, and playfully confess their opportunism in an extemporaneous parody of their hit song. By the time Willie falls down on a bed and seductively kisses her image in an oval mirror she has removed from a wall, identification with the heroine has reached its peak. Viewers join in the singer's narcissistic embrace of her mirror image. Then Willie goes off-camera, and her reflection is replaced by that of her accompanist giving a Nazi salute. His bizarre image shocks viewers and breaks the illusion of success and happiness. Suddenly viewers are outside of the film's illusionary world, reflecting on historical referents. They have been averting their eyes from the truth, choosing to focus, like the heroine, only on success and not on how it was bought. Thus jolted by history's look back at them in the form of the Nazi salute, they now pass judgment on Willie's success and sense that it was more than a song that she sang. The look back from the screen that the mirror image offers reflects the look back that Höfgen gives when the spotlights fall on him. The same effect occurs after the countryside sequence in Bob Fosse's *Cabaret* (1972), when an idyllic scene is followed by the face of the master of ceremonies. In his Mephistopheles makeup, he smiles malevolently out at the audience, reminding them of the evil that lurks behind the sentimental images.

Fellow Travellers

▲▼▲

The question posed by *Mephisto* and *Lili Marleen* is also asked by *Die Mitläufer* (*Fellow Travellers*, 1984), a feature-length documentary made for German television. Were all those who knew about Nazi policies and did nothing to oppose them as guilty as those who actively supported the Third Reich? The films of Szabó and Fassbinder certainly implicate Höfgen and Willie as responsible to some degree for what happened under the Nazis. After all, they profited from being part of the Nazi cultural apparatus. *Fellow Travellers* has an even more inclusive definition of those bearing responsibility for what occurred during the Third Reich. The film is a combination documentary and "you are there" docudrama. The documentary footage shows the official Nazi version of events in the Third Reich. The fictional segments comment on this official version by dramatizing how ordinary people coped with day-to-day life under Hitler. Together, documentary and fiction seek answers to the questions, how was Hitler possible? and who bears the responsibility for what occurred? The Nazi footage is commented upon further by a narrator who deconstructs the images the Nazis are creating. In one scene, for example, shots from a Nazi propaganda film show people lining up for food. The government's intent was to impress on its audience that the Third Reich was taking care of the populace. The commentary points out the political agenda behind these pictures of caring.

The dramatic reenactments of private lives affected by the events of the Third Reich are more insightful than the documentary material, for it is in these reenactments that the complicity of the average citizen in those events is explored. For example, reenacted segments portray a working family and a bourgeois family as they hear the news that the Reichstag has been burned. In both families the immediate reaction is to stay uninvolved. The same reaction to outside events is depicted in a conversation between women in a breadline. One woman remarks that a politically active neighbor is missing, and another woman reminds her that she ought to be quiet or she might also disappear. In another scene a man rebukes a cleaning lady for working for Jews. This scene is juxtaposed with scenes of the Kristallnacht, suggesting the eventual outcome of acquiescence to political intimidation.

But not all citizens are shown complying. The cleaning lady, for example, continues to work for the Jewish family. In an air raid shelter an old man refuses to stop his mockery of the Nazis in spite of threats from the shelter leader. Finally, in yet another scene of defiance, two soldiers are overheard discussing desertion. These moments of individual bravery could be seen as pandering to viewers who may be tired of feeling responsible for the past and may be looking for release from Germany's burden of guilt. Were it not for scenes critical of how ordinary Germans responded to nazism, this would certainly be the case. The film, however, contrasts the Germans who made right choices with those who, out of cowardice or callousness, made incorrect ones. In one scene a woman is angry because her husband ruins Christmas with his reports about the deportation of the Jews. In another, a teacher allows himself to be coerced into supporting the Nazis.

These scenes have their own problematic subtext, however, suggesting that people went along with the Nazis out of fear. While there is certainly truth to this idea, it is also true that someone must have supported the government. Yet *Fellow Travellers* shows only people opposed to Hitler or those who reluctantly went along. In a recent essay delivered on public television, Roger Rosenblatt asked the question, "How was a man like Hitler possible?" and suggested that Hitler came to power because "people invited him in."[14] Although such an idea is surely an exaggeration as well as an oversimplification, it seems closer to the truth than the answer suggested by the subtext of *Fellow Travellers*—that the people had no choice but to acquiesce to Hitler and his terrorism.

The Axe of Wandsbek

▲▼▲

One of the more successful films about guilt and responsibility for the crimes of the Third Reich was made for German television and released abroad as a 16mm film. *Das Beil von Wandsbek* (*The Axe of Wandsbek*,

1981), directed by Horst Königstein and Heinrich Breloer, is based on the Arnold Zweig novel of the same name. The novel was first made into a movie in 1951 by Falk Harnack. Whereas Harnack followed classic cinema strategies in his film, Königstein and Breloer place their fictional narrative within the framework of a documentary. While the fictional narrative tells the story of Teetjen, a butcher whose livelihood is destroyed after he becomes an executioner for the German government, the documentary searches for the historical antecedents behind this story. The film seeks to discover and uncover "what events in the fiction are fabricated and which are based on historical facts and persons."

The directors begin *The Axe of Wandsbek* outside the fictional narrative with a newsreel of a political rally in 1932 when 7,500 Nazis marched into the socialist workers' district in Hamburg. In the riot that ensued a police officer was among those killed. Eventually four Communists were sentenced to die for the deaths. The execution of one of them, a young man named Bruno Tesch, is the focus of the directors' investigation into historical truth. At the same time his execution provides a springboard into the story of the fictional butcher, Teetjen, and his wife. For it is Tesch's execution, which occurred at the hands of a substitute executioner, that leads the film to ask, was this substitute executioner the model for the butcher in Zweig's novel being fictionalized here? To reconstruct Tesch's history, the directors interview his friends and witnesses of the riots, read from his diary, and employ stills and newsreels. At one point, as an offscreen narrator reads Tesch's diary, the film cuts to 1937 and begins the fictional story—Teetjen is writing a letter to a wealthy friend, asking for help in finding a job.

The structure of *The Axe of Wandsbek* is complex: the documentary reconstructs the trial of Bruno Tesch by using archival material from 1932 as well as interviews with eyewitnesses and historians conducted in 1985, the year the film was made. The fictional narrative sets the Hamburg events of 1932 in 1937. There are many points of similarity between history and the fiction of Zweig's novel, but more important, the film allows viewers to see how history has influenced that fiction. Moreover, *The Axe of Wandsbek* makes it clear that the past, both as it really happened and as it has been fictionalized, still reverberates 50 years later.

By employing the documentary form as they do, the directors give their fictional narrative a solid grounding in historical reality. Interviews, letters, newspaper accounts, photos, and newsreels are introduced outside of the fiction. This intrusion of non-narrative material into the story distances viewers from the narrative and offers them a short history. It also serves to make the fiction "history"—that is, it creates the illusion that the fiction is an authentic reenactment of the past. In its turn, however, the narrative fiction affects how viewers see the history within the film. As they watch *The Axe of Wandsbek*, viewers are drawn ever deeper into the fictional story. As the narrative progresses, the interruptions from a reality outside the fiction become less frequent. In this way the film builds suspense and interest in its characters—the ostracized butcher and his wife. These two are made more attractive and vulnerable, and by the end of the fictional part of the film they have won the sympathy of viewers. But the directors are careful to expose as a delusion Teetjen's sense of victimization. At one point in the film the butcher takes down a portrait of Hitler and asks, "Did you cheat us, or were you fooled, too?" The utter absurdity of his feeling of victimization is even clearer at the end of the fictional story. Teetjen throws his wife's body into a construction site, but before he shoots himself and lets his body fall in after hers, the narrator recites his thoughts: "Adolf had thrown him on the rubbish heap. Why him?" The fictional narrative ends here, and the documentary continues telling the history of Bruno Tesch, thereby refocusing viewers' concern toward the true victims of nazism.

Königstein and Breloer use documentary inserts, offscreen narration, and eyewitness interviews to interrupt the effect that the cinematic illusion might otherwise have on the audience. Teetjen and his wife are sympathetic characters. Their financial struggles and conservative values work together to make them vulnerable to exploitation by the powerful. Their very ordinariness makes them appealing. The critic Fred Gehler describes the way Teetjen was portrayed in the 1951 version: "The most frightening aspect of such a person is his averageness and interchangeability. The effect he produces is not unsympathetic. On the contrary, there is a trusted everyday quality about him, as well as the smell of one who is normal. The truly monstrous thing about a figure like this is that he grows 'normally' into his role as executioner. He seems made for the everyday task of killing, for the axe of Wandsbek, but also for the ovens at Auschwitz."[15] But will viewers see the executioner's deeds of blood in so sympathetic a character? Will they recognize how this ordinary man contributed to the killing under the Nazi regime? Or will their sympathy for him allow them to see only his struggle for economic independence, his adherence to conservative values, and his mistreatment by the powerful? The continuous interruption of cinematic illusion in Königstein and Breloer's film ensures that viewers are given the opportunity to make a judgment.

Between the Tracks

▲▼▲

Late in his career, with the release of *Zwischengleis* (*Between the Tracks*, 1978), Wolfgang Staudte returned to the themes of guilt and responsibility. In *The Murderers Are among Us* Staudte stresses exposing guilty individuals; here he examines the guilt of individuals. *Between the Tracks* was a commercial and critical failure, owing as much to the vicissitudes of timing as to weaknesses in the film. It was released in the same year as Fassbinder's *Die Ehe der Maria Braun* (*The Marriage of Maria Braun*, 1978), at a time when German film was enjoying a renaissance among intellectuals. In comparison with the films of the "New German Cinema," *Between the Tracks* seems anachronistic in both content and style. Moreover, where the films of the New German Cinema were tackling political issues of the day and showing how contemporary problems were a result of the legacy of the past, Staudte's film merely added historical color to a well-worn story: the search for the truth about a person who has died. In the opening scene of *Between the Tracks*, Anne, a woman in her thirties, jumps off a railway trestle. The remainder of the movie seeks to unravel the mystery behind her death. The narrative is set in the time immediately following her suicide in 1961, in the days preceding her decision to jump, and in the immediate postwar years when she was a refugee from the East. In addition, in a flashback within a flashback, Anne remembers pushing a boy off the transport train that brought her and her family to the West. That act is the "crime" on which Staudte focuses in this study of the nature of guilt and atonement.

Because of her sense of guilt, which the movie suggests is exaggerated, Anne commits suicide. After her death, Anne's brother excuses her act on the train as necessary self-defense, since "it was either push or be pushed." From the perspective of Anne's personal tragedy, this comment is justified. Anne was 14 when the incident on the train occurred. Moreover, as the recurring flashback indicates, the boy was trying to push Anne and in the struggle fell from the train. Anne's inability to forget the past eventually leads to her self-destruction.

The brother's comment refers to more than Anne's act on the train, however. He is suggesting that, in general, personal conduct is based on circumstances, not on universal principles of right and wrong. Such relativizing in a film about Nazi Germany is problematical. On the one hand, the film suggests that there were reasons that people acted as they did. One such reason is indicated, for example, during a confrontation between Anne's lover, a Jewish colonel in the occupation forces, and her mother, an alcoholic. The mother's drinking suggests that she is trying to forget the past, but it is unclear whether she wants to forget her personal responsibility for what occurred under the Nazis or whether she wants to forget what she has lost. She confesses to the colonel that she, too, was anti-Semitic; she nonetheless adds, she was always friendly to the Jews around her. Furthermore, although she admits that she did nothing to stop the deportation of the Jews from her neighborhood, she reminds the colonel that no one stopped her deportation from the East after the war, "as if we were all equally guilty." The mother clearly tries to justify her victimization of others by making herself into a victim. Her alcoholism and general depression suggest that she is only partially successful; they suggest that the best way to cope with the past is to forget it. To dwell on history, the movie seems to be saying, is to risk self-destruction.

Welcome in Vienna

▲▼▲

One of the themes in Axel Corti's *Welcome in Vienna* (1985), the last in his trilogy on the war years, *Wohin und zurück* (*Whereto and Back*), is the relative ease with which many Germans—indeed, many former Nazis—were rehabilitated and reintegrated into the German infrastructure. The title of Corti's film refers to the homecoming of a young Jewish emigré returning to Vienna with the American army after the war. He experiences a personal crisis when he discovers that the return to which he had been looking forward since first fleeing Vienna seven years earlier was not what he had anticipated. He realizes immediately that anti-Semitism has not disappeared, and that if he plans to stay in Vienna he will have to come to terms with being a Jew in an environment even more non-Jewish than before he fled. As the film progresses, he becomes politically enlightened and comes to realize that his welcome in Vienna is decidedly cooler than that accorded to former members of the Nazi government, including those who worked in concentration camps. Rather than leave, he decides to stay and work through his disillusionment.

Welcome in Vienna is a love story that never develops the potential of its historical material. The emotional involvement we experience in the movie comes through three main characters: Freddy, the young Jew whose naive perspective receives most of the viewer's attention; Adler, an idealistic Jewish sergeant who returns with Freddy, has a conversion to postwar cynicism, and becomes Freddy's rival for Claudia Schuette; and Claudia, an Austrian actress whose father is an important ex-Nazi now serving the Americans. While these three individuals are personable enough to engage us in the film, their personal problems are perhaps too engaging. They tend to overwhelm the historical material that Corti has put into the film and that should be part of this film's viewing experience.

For example, one of the movie's historical themes is that it was easy for ex-Nazis to insinuate themselves back into society. This theme is the central focus in films such as *Wir Wunderkinder* (*Aren't We Wonderful*, 1958) and *The Murderers Are among Us*, but here it serves only to highlight Freddy's dilemma: deciding whether he should stay in Vienna or return to America. No one else in the film shares his concern about ex-Nazis. Indeed, by locating in the naive Freddy all the objections to so easily reintegrating Nazis, the film suggests the problem is his personal crisis to resolve, that it is within the accepted scheme of things for the ex-Nazis to rebuild Vienna and reestablish themselves in its institutions.

The film could also be seen as a prescient comment on Austria's readiness to forget its past. A year after the film was released Kurt Waldheim, who had served as secretary general to the United Nations from 1972 to 1981, was elected president of Austria on 8 June 1986 amid allegations that during the war he had served as interpreter and ordnance operator in Greece in a unit that was responsible for sending thousands of Jews to their death in concentration camps. In spite of the controversy surrounding Waldheim's role in the war crimes in Greece, he was elected with 53.9 percent of the vote. Apparently the majority of Austrian voters was as unwilling to consider Waldheim's past as an obstacle to gaining a position of power as are the fictional characters in *Welcome in Vienna*.

Moreover, Corti does not portray the Viennese as uninvolved in the crimes of the Nazi regime. For example, General Schuette, Claudia's father, remains a virulent anti-Semite. The woman who "bought" the house of Freddy's family is adamant that she will not relinquish it. In addition, the degree to which she remains unreconstructed and unrepentant is manifest in her belief that Freddy escaped the hardships she had to endure when he ran off to America. Comments such as these do not portray the Austrians as blameless, but the film excuses them as the reactions of a people desperate to survive. In a scene central to the film Claudia performs in Thornton Wilder's *The Skin of Our Teeth* (1942). In an unheated theater she performs to a sold-out audience, which gives an ovation to her claim that it is either "eat or be eaten."

Country of the Fathers, Country of the Sons

▲▼▲

The question of what individuals did to support or to stop Hitler comes up again in Nico Hofmann's *Land der Väter, Land der Söhne* (*Country of the*

Fathers, Country of the Sons, 1988), a film in which a son tries to discover, in 1981, the truth about his father's suicide ten years earlier. In a flashback about two-thirds of the way through the movie, the father, Eberhard Kleinert, is sitting in a movie theater immediately after the war, in 1945, watching *Death Mills*, the Allied reeducation film (see chapter 1). As the camera shows both the atrocities depicted in the Allied film and the faces in the audience, a narrating voice intones: "I was there. What did I do against it? Millions of Germans cheered evil: drunken with hate and revenge, who swore death and destruction to free speech and free spirit, who helped to attack and kill innocent defenseless people, reaping as they had sown, crosses [death]." Kleinert gets up and tries to leave, the film's images and message having been apparently too much for his conscience to bear, but an American MP blocks his exit, forcing him to return and watch the rest of the film. In the sequence that immediately follows, Kleinert is found "guilty of minor infractions" but is otherwise declared sufficiently innocent of Nazi crimes and is given back the right to manage his factory. The scene continues the motif found in other Nazi-retro films, from *The Murderers Are among Us* to *Aren't We Wonderful*, to *Welcome in Vienna*: the relative ease with which men like Kleinert were rehabilitated and welcomed back into German society, even if their crimes were serious. Kleinert's crime was profiting from a Polish factory, which he took over from a deported Jew. The factory used labor from a nearby concentration camp; during this time Kleinert had never bothered to inquire why he continually received new workers. Moreover, to get the machinery to rebuild his factory in the West after the war, he requisitioned troop transport trains that were meant to carry the wounded to hospitals.

Country of the Fathers, Country of the Sons is not about hunting down Nazi war criminals. Eberhard Kleinert is already dead as the film begins. Rather, the movie is about reconciling present and past, about accepting responsibility for Germany's past without burdening the young with guilt. In the films made in the immediate postwar years it was possible to believe, with the hero of *The Murderers Are among Us*, that the first responsibility of Germany after the war was to pursue justice. The sight of the industrialist Bruckner reduced to a pathetic figure behind bars at the end of the film was an apt comment on what seemed to be the agenda of the day for German society. Forty years later, however, a new approach was needed to deal with the murderers of the Nazi regime. The hero of *Country of the Fathers, Country of the Sons*, Eberhard Kleinert's son Thomas, is in his twenties. He does not bear the same responsibility as his father for the past. Yet as a German he cannot forget the past either. In the film Nico Hofmann asks two simple questions: Who is responsible for

Country of the Fathers, Country of the Sons (1988). An American officer overlooks Eberhard Kleinert's (Karl-Heinz von Liebezeit, second from left) use of a troop transport to smuggle machines from Poland into the Western Zone. Courtesy Filmverlag der Autoren.

Nazi Germany? What responsibility does the present have in remembering what occurred?

The deeper Thomas digs into the past, into his father's life, the more he discovers that is troublesome. In a search occasioned by the bankruptcy of his father's factory in 1981, the young man discovers that his father committed suicide in 1972. He wants to find out why. Through confrontational conversations with his mother, interviews with his father's colleagues, a trip to Poland to visit the factory his father "purchased" from a Jew during the war, and an interview with a former worker at that factory, Thomas discovers the crimes of his father that are enumerated above.

Hofmann's film neither excuses the father for his activities nor burdens the son with the sins of the past. It never becomes an apologia, never resorts to breast-beating, and never allows a cathartic confession to cleanse the collective soul of guilt. What the movie accomplishes is reconciliation of the present generation with the past without excusing the young from their responsibilities vis-à-vis the past. The film offers an experience of healing, which culminates in a dream sequence after Thomas discovers his father's crimes. The young man goes to the hotel room where his father committed suicide. Sitting on the bed, he imagines he hears water running in the bathroom. The camera pans to the sink and shows a man washing his hands, having just taken out and loaded a revolver. Viewers know from a scene at the beginning of the movie that the man is in the room to commit suicide. Suddenly a second pair of hands (Thomas's hands) appear, gently caressing the father's hands, as if trying to console him for whatever is leading to the suicide. Thomas cannot change the past. He can neither prevent the suicide nor wish away what his father did during the Third Reich. But he can forgive his father for both acts, which he does in this scene.

Hofmann does not let this tender scene turn the film into an apologia. Thomas may understand, and he may forgive his father, but he nonetheless exposes his father's past in a newspaper article that he entitles "Country of the Fathers." Commenting on the article, a veteran reporter acknowledges its conciliatory tone: "It's fairer than my report. I would have written an indictment, even of my father. In 1968 we pretended we were not writing about our fathers. But this is more like an attempt to understand something." His words can stand as a comment on Hofmann's movie. It too is fair. It presents the charges against the father in an objective manner. Eberhard Kleinert is not depicted as a Nazi ogre in the flashbacks. He is a conscientious businessman, but he is also a Nazi. Moreover, the scenes set in the past make it clear that he was not simply a fellow traveler; he believed in the Nazi ideology. That his crimes occurred 45 years earlier does not diminish their magnitude. Guilt remains and must be remembered. Nonetheless, the film suggests, life continues. After all, the country of the fathers is also the country of their sons. While the sins cannot be forgotten, nothing is to be gained from passing them on.

The strength of Hofmann's film is that it reconciles the apparent contradictions in wanting to remember and wanting to forget. All the main characters of the film vie with this problem. Eberhard's wife, Thomas's mother, confesses that the only way she was able to survive was to ignore the contradictions. Being more immediately guilty, the father could not ignore them and killed himself. The editor of the newspaper where Thomas works is a member of the war generation. He is so tired of the past that he tells people to blame him for it and then to get on with other matters. On the other hand, the veteran reporter, a member of the late-1960s generation, which blamed every problem Germany had on its fascist past, is unwilling to be reconciled. A young schoolteacher whom

Thomas interviews hopes to build a bridge to the past by having her students visit the places where the crimes were committed. Her superiors, wanting to hide the past away, refuse permission for the trips. Thomas is willing to face both past and present honestly. He neither hides from the past nor uses it in self-righteous recrimination. Making no excuses for what took place, he nevertheless accepts what occurred, writes about it, and makes it a part of himself. Perhaps he hopes that making it a part of his memory will somehow prevent another Third Reich, or a similar situation, from arising again. Meanwhile, he can get on with his life.

The Pedestrian

▲▼▲

The protagonists in many Nazi-retro films have been concerned with exposing Nazi crimes and their perpetrators. From Staudte's *The Murderers Are among Us* to Verhoeven's *Das schreckliche Mädchen* (*The Nasty Girl*, 1990), various German postwar films have attempted to deal with how such exposés affect individuals and the community. How debilitating for a country and for individuals the unsolved contradictions of the past can become is the theme of Maximilian Schell's *Der Fussgänger* (*The Pedestrian*, 1973). The film was released 15 years before Nico Hofmann's film, at a time when Germany had not yet found the distance to deal with the past. Consequently, *The Pedestrian*, which is a study in how failure to come to terms with the past destroys lives, yields answers that are not completely satisfying. The movie tells the story of an important industrialist named Giese, who is being vilified in the press for his actions in a Greek village during the war: he reportedly fired on a group of women and children taking refuge in a church. The press, ignoring evidence that another man actually pulled the trigger, goes after Giese because he is a well-known industrialist; and the other man is an obscure professor. Flashback scenes reveal that Giese's oldest son discovered his father's purported crime from someone investigating the case for the newspaper. Believing that his father should pay for his crimes, and unable himself to live with the knowledge of his father's past, the young man grabs the wheel of the car his father is driving and in which he is a passenger. The son is killed, but the father survives. The movie is about how the industrialist copes with the press, his son's death, and his own past.

Schell's film asks the same questions as Nico Hofmann's: what responsibility do individuals carry for their actions during the Third Reich, and what are the responsibilities of present generations in keeping memories of the past alive? As if in answer to these questions, Gustav Rudolf

Sellner, who played Giese remarked in an interview: "I decided to play the role of Giese in order not to forget. And I can only hope that the public through this film will understand the necessity of not forgetting. That it will be led to an active historical consciousness."[16] The film itself is not as clear in its resolve to keep the past alive as Sellner was. Its treatment of the theme of memory is instead ambivalent. Although it is clear that *The Pedestrian* wants viewers to be aware that not all war criminals have been punished, that Staudte's warning, "the murderers are among us," is still applicable, the press, which exposes the crime, and those who vilify the industrialist are not kindly drawn. The film also implies, especially in the opening and closing sequences, that perhaps Germany's past is a relic and belongs in a museum rather than in people's consciousness.

The confused message that *The Pedestrian* gives can be attributed to the portrayal of the main character, Giese. Schell allows no distance to develop between the character and the audience. The camera and the story both treat Giese kindly and sympathetically. His acquaintances and workers like him. He relates well to his grandson, daughter-in-law, and wife. Although he has a mistress, her role seems necessary only to drive the plot and to make the hero more sympathetic to viewers. For example, in one scene calculated to make viewers see Giese even more favorably, the old man, in a mood of extreme depression, rejects his young lover's bed in favor of the bed of his lifelong partner. The only people around Giese who dislike him are depicted as leftist agitators who demonstrate not out of personal conviction but because they have been incited to do so by the fanaticism of a hysterical press. In short, the film asks viewers to judge a man who has won their sympathies.

Schell's film offers several disturbing subtexts. One of these results from the film's readiness to diffuse guilt by drawing parallels between what happened in Germany and what has happened in other countries. For example, during a crucial scene on a streetcar in which the sight of Giese triggers an old Greek woman's memory of the massacre, Giese is shown reading a paper that contains a photo of the My Lai massacre. Although the massacre in My Lai was a crime, and America's presence in Vietnam was as uninvited as was Germany's presence in Greece, the suggestion of similarities between the two situations relativizes Germany's crimes. Moreover, the headline accompanying the news article has the effect of diverting guilt, of suggesting that the massacre in Greece was within the bounds of legitimate war activities engaged in by other countries also. The lawyer who defends Giese makes this point more directly. He suggests that in war entire villages are sometimes the enemy and that, in any event, wars are fought to be won and therefore entire villages may have to be sacrificed. Schell relies solely on the camera to dispute what the lawyer says. While he speaks, the lawyer is filmed in a grotesque close-up. His mouth looks as distorted as the sentiments he proclaims. Furthermore, the message is presented as a verbal harangue, which further alienates viewers from the lawyer and his philosophy. And yet, the defense is uttered in support of Giese, a man with whom viewers identify and whom they know is innocent of the actual act of killing. It is therefore difficult to totally discredit the lawyer's defense.

Viewer responses to the film collected by Evan Pattak after an American screening suggest other subtexts. One viewer said, "I thought the point was to show that people had lives that went on, and that they continued and that they were people, and that even though they had past experiences, they tended to forget them if they were unpleasant and leave them behind." Another commented, "It's about an ex-German officer who is constantly reliving the guilt of his past—the war crimes, the atrocities of the war that he is taking personal blame for and punishing himself for and cannot allow himself to be absolved for. . . . It shows what guilt can do to a person, how it's one of the most horrible things anybody can suffer."[17] In neither of these comments is there any indication that the viewer felt the film was about acknowledging past crimes, about remembering the past and thereby perhaps preventing its repetition. In the movie one character comments about Giese's part in the killings, "Even if he did not pull the trigger, he could have pushed the rifle aside." Another philosophizes that "if one person is guilty then we are all guilty." The viewers quoted have overlooked these sentiments in favor of one expressed by another of Giese's sons: "I am tired of being the bad German. I am tired of being the son of a bad German. That's all past, all over with. It must end."

Finally, the most disturbing subtext is created by the concluding sequence, in which Giese's grandson comes to him with an artifact he has found that he wants to take to a museum. He asks why people bring things to museums. Giese answers, "So that we do not forget." The film tries to underscore what it is that should be remembered by closing with Greek folk music on the soundtrack. The subtext, however, suggests that the way to remember the past is to enshrine it in a museum, to make an artifact of it, upon which people can focus at will. People can choose to think about what a museum contains, or they can choose to ignore what is there, just as they choose to reactivate memories by looking through old photo albums. But the inconvenience of visiting a museum makes its artifacts even more removed than the photos in an album. Thus, while bringing the past to a museum may preserve history, it also diminishes the importance of that history in people's daily lives and consciousness.

The Nasty Girl

▲▼▲

Movies dealing with Germany's past must help viewers to both externalize and internalize memory. The films discussed in this chapter all do that, with varying degrees of success. They give visible form to what viewers may already know about the past and remind them of the importance of what they are seeing. That is, like a photo in an album or an artifact in a museum, they help viewers to recall why the photo was taken or to reflect upon the culture to which the artifact in the display case belonged. But these films also give a visible form to what viewers know about the past and help them have a virtual experience of the past. That experience, in turn, allows viewers to make the past a part of their psyche, a memory they can then recall without outside stimulus.

Eight years after making *Die weisse Rose* (*The White Rose*, 1982), the story of the White Rose resistance group, the writer-director Michael Verhoeven revisited the struggle against nazism—this time in the present. *Das schreckliche Mädchen* (*The Nasty Girl*, 1990), differs in perspective and tone from the other films discussed in this chapter. Like *The Pedestrian* and *Country of the Fathers, Country of the Sons*, *The Nasty Girl* examines attempts by young people to uncover what occurred in the past and the equally zealous attempts by adults to hide the facts from the investigators. Unlike Schell's and Hofmann's films, however, Verhoeven's work contains no historical images from the Nazi period: no iconography, no flashbacks to that time. This film, although it deals with the Nazi past, gives no visible form to the past, nor does it create any virtual experience of the past for the audience. Instead, it is located completely in the present. The attention of viewers is never diverted to the atrocities that occurred. The film never seems like an attempt to achieve a personal catharsis in order to exorcise the sins of the past. Rather, the film's focus remains on the current status of Germany's ability to reconcile its past in a meaningful way. That is, Verhoeven asks whether the apparent willingness to admit what occurred under the Nazis is not a subterfuge to sweep the past under the carpet once again.

In addition to the different focus, the movie also gives a different tone to the past. It is part fact and part fiction, part documentary and part comedic farce. *The Nasty Girl* is based on the life of Anja Elisabeth Rosmus, a German woman born in 1960 and raised in Passau, who entered an essay contest in 1980. The topic of her essay was her town's past during the Third Reich. She ran into opposition from the townspeople during her research, became known as "the Nasty Girl" for poking around where she was not wanted, published a book on her findings in 1983, and was accepted by the community once it recognized that her international fame made it likely she could not be quieted. Verhoeven does not deviate from Rosmus's story. Although he fictionalizes the material—Passau becomes Pfilzing, Anja Rosmus becomes Sonja Rosenberger—the experiences his heroine undergoes are those Anja Rosmus went through. Rosmus remarked after seeing the movie: "It was an enormous surprise that somebody who hadn't been with me, having no knowledge of this time, shows me exactly as it was."[18]

The film stars Lena Stolze, who portrayed Sophie Scholl in both Verhoeven's *The White Rose* and Percy Adlon's *Five Last Days*. In this latest film she plays a young woman who, encouraged by her high school teacher, enters a national essay contest centered around the topic "My Hometown during the Third Reich." When, instead of chronicling the local folklore about freedom fighters and resistance to the Nazis, she begins to examine the town archives and to ask embarrassing questions, she is stonewalled. Up to this time the town has been hiding its culpability behind a convenient scapegoat—the mayor at the time, imprisoned by the Allies for wartime activities. Later in life, stung by her failure to complete the essay and to find the truth so securely hidden by the town's citizenry, the heroine becomes obsessed with digging into the town's archives and records, many of which are sealed. She uses the legal system and trickery to obtain access to archival records. In a broadly satirical manner, Verhoeven portrays the town's escalating attempts to stop the heroine with bureaucratic obstructions, telephone vituperation and threats, and the bombing of her house by masked neo-Nazis. When she refuses to be deterred, the town turns upon a new scapegoat for the crimes of the past, a professor, and honors the Nasty Girl for having exposed him. At the awards ceremony, when she realizes that the celebration is merely another way to end her prying and "close the books," she has a mental breakdown.

The film displays a confusing discontinuity here: it opens with the heroine standing, poised, above the town atop the town hall, calmly, almost gaily, giving background information on her hometown and beginning the narration, which is subsequently told in flashback; it ends with a freeze-frame of her fearfully hiding in the branches of a tree shrine outside of town. Because of this, the sequence of the narration is unclear. A change from the black-and-white of the flashback back into color may indicate a catching-up of time to the beginning frames, whereupon the narrative continues to the end. Or the change may simply indicate two different time sequences, a time switch within the flashback. Regardless of how the pessimistic tone of the closing frame is reconciled with the jubilant tone of the opening one, however, the use of black-and-white and color, which is fast becoming a cliché in movies about the past, is handled well. Scenes in black-and-white come to represent a time of innocence, of harmony with the rest of the town, before Sonja's discovery of the falsehood woven into the town's history.

In addition to the change in film stock color, Verhoeven provides numerous other distancing effects: the beginning zoom with the heroine, standing improbably but symbolically high over the town; her continuing explanations of events through voice-over narration; characters often speaking directly to the camera, breaking the narrative by relating their reactions to events. Moreover, although most sets are naturalistic, when the heroine is confronting historical truth the sets are stylized, often minimalist, with distracting angles and backed by huge photographs of appropriate interiors. (The fuzziness of the overenlarged photos give them a surprising depth.) One of the more effective uses of Brechtian distancing occurs in those scenes in which Verhoeven wants to expose the town's conspiratorial opposition to Sonja and her family. Twice in the film Sonja and other family members are sitting on a living room couch listening to an answering machine filled with threats. A film of a street scene of the town is projected behind them. The effect is of the couch moving along the street as if it were an open-air car and its occupants were being delivered to the nastiness of the town's inhabitants.

As in all film, distancing effects force temporary disengagements from the story and afford the viewer the opportunity for reflection upon the issues in the narrative. The issues here concern present-day Germany and its relationship to nazism. The town, described in the opening credits as a German "everytown," has buried its past and invented a lie about its resistance to Hitler. Then, after the lie is exposed, the town accepts its past but retreats behind another lie by passing its failure to actively resist Hitler and the Nazis onto one man, the professor. The stylized scenes dealing with historical truth are so different from the other naturalistic narrative scenes that they are, in a sense, indexed and put aside as part of a specific theme. Parentheses are put around them in this way, and they are lifted out of the narrative for special consideration and reflection.

In this film Verhoeven depicts the continuing failure of Germans to come to terms with the past. He implies that the legacy of the Third Reich still survives among the older townspeople with their guilt and complicity, and among the young with their brand of neo-nazism. Far from remembering, Verhoeven's Germans staunchly deny their past, establishing instead a distorted and false history, and punishing, even today, those who would have the truth.[19]

The Boat (1981). The captain (Jürgen Prochnow, in front) and the reporter (Herbert Grünemayer) look on as an Allied bombing raid sinks their U-boat. Courtesy WDR/Vogelmann and Inter Nationes.

chapter 3

▲▼▲

valorizing death

The classic war film valorizes war. It creates a world of positive values, which must be defended against enemies who would destroy it. Since defense sometimes entails great sacrifice, including death, the characters in these war narratives embody what are commonly known as the virtues of war: courage, loyalty, comradeship, and sacrifice. Those characters who die in battle are mourned as having died for their country. Death transfigures them, making them into heroes. In a traditional war film, death never seems to be in vain. These films offer spectators a viewing experience in which they can identify with the soldiers on the "good" side, mourn their death, and find meaning in their sacrifice. In short, war films reinforce a traditional reluctance to accept death in battle as an event without meaning.

The viewers' readiness to valorize death in battle has contributed to the dearth of completely antiwar films: classic strategies to produce identification with the fighting men and the tendency to find meaning in their sacrifice seem to preclude the presence of an unambiguous antiwar message. One of the few war films to contain an unequivocal antiwar statement is Lewis Milestone's *All Quiet on the Western Front* (1930), based on Erich Maria Remarque's best-selling and critically acclaimed novel of World War I. The film succeeds as a pacifist statement because it is void of the usual virtues of war: camaraderie is kept to a minimum; there is no eulogizing about the sacrifice of those who have died; and death in war is seen as the negation of beauty. This film leaves one with the realization that battle death, in this war, was for nought, that war as an institution is evil because it negates life. In the final scene the hero, dying in a trench, reaches toward a butterfly, but death prevents him from capturing it.

Few other films can claim to be unequivocally against war. More often they are like the German film *Morgenröte* (*Dawn*, 1933), which also deals with World War I. In *Dawn*, a submarine film, individual scenes emphasize comradeship among the sailors and their willingness to sacrifice for others. The film also uses the worry of the mothers of the men who are missing on the sub to increase the pathos of the situation. Such scenes counteract whatever antiwar sentiments might be found in the film. They divert the attention of viewers away from the negative features of war and help them focus on its positive features—sacrifice, courage, and bonding. The movie satisfies viewers' desire to find meaning in the senseless deaths of men in war.

Not surprisingly, *All Quiet on the Western Front* was despised by the Nazis, and they interrupted the film at several theaters, leading the government to ban any additional showings.[1] *Dawn*, in contrast, while also an antiwar film, was described by one national socialist reviewer as glorifying "the German military in a modest and touching way. No one can escape its effect" (Hembus and Bandmann, 77).

German film directors face a conundrum when making a war movie from the perspective of the Germans. The elements of the genre that bring viewers into the film and create a meaningful experience—sympathetic characters, a positive system of values, a righteous cause—require that historical reality be circumvented. That is, directors have to separate the characters from the government those characters are defending. They also must give the characters values different from those of the Nazi state. Finally, directors must create a situation in which nazism either does not exist or exists only in an ahistorical form. Yet if the films are meant to help viewers come to terms with the past, then the past must be presented as honestly as possible.

The Desert Fox

▲▼▲

Over the years filmmakers have made a number of films intended to re-create the experience of serving in the German military during the Third Reich. Some directors have focused on the virtues of war, excluding questions about whom or what was being served by those virtues. Others have focused, like Milestone, on war as the negation of life. From the first of the German battle films, Paul May's trilogy *08/15*, parts 1–3 (1954–55), to one of the latest, Nico Hofmann's *Der Krieg meines Vaters* (*My Father's War*, 1984), directors have distinguished between those who were fighting and those who were waging the war. They have spotlighted the virtues of battle, sometimes to portray them in a positive light (May's films), and sometimes to suggest that they are hollow (Hofmann's film).

An American film, Henry Hathaway's *The Desert Fox* (1951), is a precursor to the German films that look at World War II from a German perspective. Its approach is one that films such as *08/15*, *Rommel ruft Kairo* (*Rommel Calling Cairo*, 1958), and *Der Arzt von Stalingrad* (*The Doctor of Stalingrad*, 1958) consciously or unconsciously copied. Hathaway's film predates German efforts by several years. It was released by Twentieth Century-Fox in 1951 and stars James Mason and Jessica Tandy. The movie purports to be a chronicle of the last years of Rommel's career and appears to be an attempt to "set the record straight" concerning the manner in which Rommel died. According to the official Nazi version of Rommel's death, he died of battle wounds. According to the film, Rommel was torn between military duty and moral conscience. He could either continue to support Hitler, thereby fulfilling his military oath, or join a plot against Hitler and redeem his character. In the film Rommel commits suicide when the Nazis, having discovered his treason, threaten to harm his family if he does not comply with their demands that he kill himself and save the Reich political embarrassment.

Whether *The Desert Fox* serves history with this melodramatic fiction is not of concern here. We discuss this film, made in the Hollywood tradition, because of its themes and the strategies it uses to tell about the war from the perspective of a German officer. Many of these reappear in German films about the military: a dichotomy between good German soldiers and bad Nazi leaders; the hero dying not to serve the Nazi cause but to serve his conscience; lack of references to the concentration camps or to any of the other atrocities committed by the Nazis; death given a meaningful context; inclusion of a historical discourse that allows identification with the hero but makes it clear that he is nonetheless German and therefore technically the enemy. All of these themes and strategies from the American movie are taken over unchanged by German films on the war, with the exception of the last theme. In *The Desert Fox* the character of Rommel, even if sympathetic to viewers, is portrayed as an enemy. In the war films made by the Germans, Rommel and his counterparts become enlightened soldiers who fight the system from within.

Using classic narrative strategies to make its hero appealing and thus enhance audience identification with him, the film characterizes Rommel, the great military strategist, as a loving family man and a commander troubled by orders that needlessly endanger his men. At the same time he is characterized as a true patriot and supporter of his country. Even when he disagrees with orders, he believes they have to be followed. When he is called a coward by the Führer, he excuses the insult as an instance of poorly chosen words. Before his act of defiance he has a final showdown with Hitler. In this way the film firmly establishes that Rommel's decision to support a plot against Hitler is not an act of treason but one of patriotism. It will save Germany from a madman, who has turned for advice to his astrologer rather than to his generals. The narrative, by getting viewers to identify with Rommel, helps them understand the dilemma that must have confronted Germans in the military when faced with choosing between blind obedience and opposition.

Since the film is an American production, it never lets viewers forget entirely that the man with whom they are meant to identify is technically the enemy. Hathaway presents the narrative as a search for the truth about Rommel's death. The story is told by a British officer, who comments on his own discoveries in the case and who also comments on pseudodocumentary footage depicting the Allies landing at Normandy and other military successes. Although these inserts are intended to accent the urgency of the situation faced by the Germans and to help explain Rommel's position and eventual decision, they also help distance viewers from Rommel by reminding them about the war. The documentary quality of the inserts has another effect: it convinces viewers of the authenticity of what they are watching. As a result, Rommel's meetings with other conspirators and confrontations with Hitler seem less like fictionalized encounters and more like reenactments. Although the inserts may dispel identification with the fictional character, they do create an awareness of the historical character that the fictional one represents and suggest that the real Rommel had the qualities of the character portrayed in the film.

Films whose narratives depict a gulf between the Nazi leadership and the hero soldiers raise the problem of how to reconcile the narrative and historical discourses. How, for example, is it possible to show soldiers defending a value system that the conventions of heroic fiction say they must resist? For another, does portraying the hero-soldiers of the narratives opposing their leaders absolve them from responsibility? If these were films about an invented war during an invented time, these questions would be irrelevant. But since these are films about the Third Reich and about responsibility for what occurred under the Nazis, the questions must be addressed. As was discussed earlier, even a film as well intentioned as *The Murderers Are among Us* separates its hero and heroine from what occurred during the war. The film depicts an us-them polarity that excuses the "good Germans"—the non-Nazis, hence the hero and heroine of the narrative—from responsibility for acts that the "bad German"—the Nazi, of course, the villain of the film—committed. In war films, all military personnel, whether officers or not, have as their primary function the defense of their government. Therefore everyone in these films could be held accountable for what the government is doing. Moreover, a soldier who does not support his government could be viewed as guilty of treason. Thus, the dilemma that directors faced in making the war films described in this chapter was how to create sympathy for military men who served nazism and, at the same time, be true to history and show who carried responsibility for the war. The former goal was necessary if the fictional narratives were to be successful. The latter was necessary if the films were going to help viewers come to terms with the past.

Most German films about World War II follow the example of *The Desert Fox*: the films enable viewers to identify with a German military man (the hero) by giving him positive traits and separating him from the Nazi regime; they use historical discourse both to distance viewers from the hero and to create the illusion of documentary truth, thus bringing about identification on another level; they set up a dichotomy between the Nazi leaders in Berlin and the Germans who actually had to fight the war; they portray the problem with nazism as one that revolved around bad military orders emanating from Berlin; and they ignore the entire political, historical constellation that surrounded nazism and that made the winning of World War II by the Allies so important—that is, they ignore the murder of Jews and of political dissidents in concentration camps, the systematic dismantling of the constitutional state, and the ruination of Germany. Hitler is bad or evil within these films solely because he insists on total obedience to his edicts and because he believes that the soldierly virtue of fighting to the death is absolute and inviolate. Opposing Hitler is necessary because he is a bad militarist, not because of the system he commands. Indeed, in these films there is apparently nothing disturbing or immoral about national socialism as practiced in Germany from 1933 to 1945. To be sure, not all German war films conform to the paradigm of *The Desert Fox*. East German films are more forthcoming about who bears responsibility for nazism. But all of them copy the pattern to some extent, and even the films from East Germany create a history that is more myth than reality.

08/15

▲▼▲

In the 1950s a number of German war films following the patterns of *The Desert Fox* were released. The first German war films were part of a trilogy by Paul May, *08/15*, based on a novel by Hans Helmut Kirst. The first of the *08/15* films, part 1, was released in 1954 and was an instant success. It follows the men in a German boot camp up to the outbreak of war on 1 September 1939. Two more films in the trilogy followed in 1955. Part 2 depicts the exploits on the Russian front in 1942–43 of the men from the first film. Part 3 shows the remaining men staging a last stand in Germany shortly before the end of the war in 1945. In all three films, the character of Asch provides the viewers' point of entry into the narrative. In the course of the films he goes from private to lieutenant. Although he is an excellent soldier, he is continually questioning authority. Asch is an ideal character for viewers to identify with, for he is a courageous and dutiful soldier who nevertheless does not blindly follow fascist ideology. Herein lies one of the many problems of the *08/15* films: they create a hero who possesses all the classic virtues of war—bravery, honor, and patriotism—and lend him enough individual initiative to allow him to refuse the worst of his orders. On the one hand, as Anton Kaes writes, films like *08/15* "fueled nostalgic fantasies about adventures in exotic lands and the heroic life on the front" (17). Here, however, identification with a character like Asch serves less to satisfy a longing for adventure than a longing for exoneration from responsibility for what happened during the Third Reich, a tendency that Kaes also sees in the war films of the period. "They [the films] also distinguished between the honest soldier and the unreasonable, despicable regime, and thus succeeded in intensifying already prevalent apologist tendencies" (17).

Whereas this distinction between good soldier and bad government repeats itself in the films discussed in this chapter, it takes a particular twist in *08/15*: the ordinary soldier does not battle Hitler or his advisers but rather poor, cowardly, and even renegade field officers. The distinction is important, since the villains of *08/15* seem not so much to be following Nazi policy as their own ill-conceived whims. In part 1 Asch and his fellow privates lay a plan to expose the incompetence of the camp's officers. In part 2 Asch again undergoes a battle of wits with his immediate supervisor, a cowardly captain, whose policy of holding a position at all costs results in the death of one of the central characters. While he insists that the men stay and fight, the captain sneaks away from the battle.

At no time is evidence given that the captain's orders were anything but his own individual blunder. In part 3 Asch chases two renegade officers who are fleeing the line of battle in order to rescue state goods they have commandeered for their own gain after the war. In all three films, nazism, Hitler, and his advisers are left out of the picture. The fight seems to be between good soldiers and bad commanders at a level that not only exonerates the men but fails to implicate the regime.

Like other German war films, the *08/15* films totally ignore the subject of the Holocaust.[2] The *08/15* trilogy further distorts the historical picture by avoiding most Nazi iconography. There are few SS troops, and even fewer Gestapo agents. Nazi salutes, when given at all, are halfhearted. This avoidance of Nazi symbols precludes the development of the historical discourse usually found in Nazi-retro films. That is, there are no reminders in the film of the reality behind the fiction. It is not until the closing sequence of part 1, when documentary material—Hitler's speech on the day Germany attacked Poland, 1 September 1939—is brought in, that viewers even learn when this film is taking place.

Whatever distancing effect the film has on viewers enters by way of the comedy, which marginalizes the noncommissioned officers as vulgar, drunken clowns. A representative scene shows a shadow of the camp commander that fills the entire screen as he urinates in the camp courtyard. Another scene depicts a party of the officers at which they stand on tables, lower their pants, and pass gas. The humor is so broad that it serves to break the cinematic illusion, a service usually performed by the intrusion of historical memory. Unfortunately, without any history on which to reflect, this broken illusion causes viewers to reflect on the goodness of the men under these officers and to marvel that the German army became an efficient fighting machine.

The second and third films cannot avoid historical allusion since they take place, respectively, on the eastern front and in retreat. But they still avoid placing the history that they do offer in any perspective: the thousands of deaths on the eastern front, the total destruction of German cities because of the war on the home front, and the complete dissolution of German society as the war ended are all ignored. Instead, the last film closes with Asch and his comrade behind a prison gate as a German woman walks by with an American soldier. Asch's friend comments, "I don't think our type is wanted," and Asch suggests that they retire quietly into the background. His words are followed by a printed text, which offers the ubiquitous warning not to repeat history. "And so ends the darkest chapter in German history. Let's be on our guard that we never again have a dictatorship of the 08/15 mentality." Yet the almost six hours of film that precedes this warning depicts neither darkness nor despair nor a dictatorship that tried to destroy the democratic world.

Dogs, Do You Want to Live Forever?

▲▼▲

Later war films are more successful as warnings against repeating the past. They portray the darkness and despair of the Hitler years, focusing on the death and destruction that occurred on the battlefield. Their use of documentary or pseudodocumentary material helps lend veracity to screen events at the same time that it offers viewers a distance from which to reflect on the on-screen carnage. These films, however, also tend to gloss over the more negative aspects of the Third Reich in favor of presenting a division between the common soldiers and the high command. This division allows the films to avoid showing soldiers in any activity but defending themselves from a powerful enemy, thereby allowing viewers a safe identification with them. Frank Wisbar's *Hunde, wollt ihr ewig leben?* (*Dogs, Do You Want to Live Forever?*, 1958), for example, reflects contempt on the part of the fighting men, from draftees to career officers, for Hitler's war policies. Only one officer is shown to be a staunch defender of Hitler, and he is exposed as a coward. Other officers who support the Reich's policies do so not out of ideological conviction that Germans are the master race but out of misguided opportunism. At the same time soldiers engage in heroic fighting, display camaraderie, and are sincere about being good soldiers. The film thus draws a clear distinction between Nazi commanders in Berlin and the men on the front. The policies of the commanders are characterized as wrong, but the men nonetheless courageously and loyally follow their orders. The film never shows the ideology behind the orders, nor does it ever indicate that the men on the front believe in the ideology.

Dogs, Do You Want to Live Forever? combines a fictional narrative with documentary film footage reporting on the encirclement of the German Sixth Army by Russian troops outside Stalingrad and the German unit's almost total annihilation when the central command withheld aid that would have helped the army break through Russian lines. Viewers experience the narrative from the perspective of Lieutenant Wisse, a young, idealistic officer whose encounters on the front with his commanding officer, a coward, teach him that his idealism is misguided. Wisse shoots the commanding officer in the back as the latter tries to sneak away from a gun battle. Although ordinarily viewers might be expected to react to the shooting with dismay, to see it as an act of cowardice on Wisse's part, the scene develops in such a way that his act seems justified. Wisse is a good soldier who has been misused by his superior. Viewers, having identified with Wisse up to this point, understand the idealism that goes with being a "true" soldier, and yet they also accept the frustration that leads to the change of heart.

The film's documentary structure helps raise the narrative above the naive and revisionist subtext suggested by Wisse's quick conversion. In the initial sequence, before the fictional narrative begins, a scene of marching Nazi soldiers is juxtaposed with one of dead bodies in the snow-covered fields of the eastern front. As the screen fills with a banner proclaiming, "On to Victory with the Führer," the narrator remarks that a dead soldier does not care who won or lost the war. Such antiwar rhetoric soon disappears when the idealistic Captain Wisse appears and the narrative begins. The skepticism of the opening sequence, however, returns repeatedly in the course of the movie in the form of discussions among the officers on the front and propaganda broadcasts by Radio Moscow. Although the purpose of the discussions and broadcasts is to focus on how poorly the war is being waged by those in command, others are also implicated in the debacle occurring on-screen. In the final sequence of the movie an officer berates those who believe that only a few are guilty for what is happening: "Everyone is guilty who could have changed the situation but nonetheless went along and kept quiet because of their careers." The film cuts to Hitler, alone and filling the screen, as he stands in front of a window and hears that the Sixth Army is dead; he responds, "Enough pathos, put together a new army." The next scene shows the few remaining troops falling over in the snow. This scene is followed by a shot of a minister who hopes that "perhaps we will learn from this." A soldier near him responds, "And perhaps not."

Although the end of *Dogs, Do You Want to Live Forever?* is sentimental and naive, suggesting to viewers that a few words can help the world remember the mistakes of the past, critics of the film forget that the movie is intended to be neither a history lesson on the causes of the Third Reich nor a manual on how to prevent their recurrence. The film is a feature-length movie whose raison d'être is to offer spectators a film experience that can help them comprehend and reconcile how individuals acted in the Third Reich. Lieutenant Wisse's conversion to pacifism is not meant to exonerate him from his actions in the war. Neither is his early idealism and enthusiasm for the war intended to show he supported nazism. Rather, the film wants to show soldiers in a devastating battle situation and help viewers understand the troops' reasons for either continuing to fight or laying down arms. The film does not suggest that this is the way things ought to be, or even have to be, and does not pretend to show how people could have chosen differently, just that they might have been able to.

The Bridge

▲▼▲

From its initial release, Bernhard Wicki's *Die Brücke* (*The Bridge*, 1959), based on a novel by Manfred Gregor, has been considered by many critics and filmgoers "the classic anti-war film of the West German cinema."[3] The film was judged best film of the year (1959) by Berlin critics and won honors in other countries as well, including the Hollywood Press Association's Golden Globe (Ott, 258). In 1959 German critics were ecstatic about the film. The critic for the *Süddeutsche Zeitung*, for example, wrote that the film "was one of the most hard hitting, relentless, bitterest antiwar films that ever was projected on the screen." Klaus Hebecker, a Hamburg critic, wrote that "to make more antiwar films is pointless. *The Bridge* cannot be matched." And *Die Welt* wrote that the "film was one of the best German films in the past 25 years."[4] More recently, critics have tended to be less effusive in their praise for the film, and some place it in the same category as more conventional war movies.

The Bridge is about seven 16-year-old boys who are drafted into the Nazi army in April 1945, a few weeks before the end of the war. Originally slated to be sent into combat, but having received next to no training, they are instead given the assignment of defending a bridge that is set to be destroyed by their own troops the next day. The boys never learn that the bridge has no strategic value and that they are therefore not actually expected to fight. Eventually six of the young men die as they try to defend it.

The Bridge was not the first film to show boys in combat situations. In part 3 of *08/15* old men and young boys are drafted into the military. Here, too, the boys are told to defend a strategically questionable barrier into town. In spite of the potential tragedy in the situation, the comedic treatment in *08/15* is intended to show how desperate Hitler's army had become at the close of the war. Since there is no battle and consequently no one is injured or killed, the incident also casts favorable light upon the conquering American troops, a filmic nod to the troops that occupied Germany after the war. In *Kinder, Mütter, und ein General* (*Children, Mothers, and a General*, 1954), which starred Bernhard Wicki (Wicki was a well-known actor before directing *The Bridge*), a group of mothers go to

Stettin, the battlefront in March 1945, to bring their 14- and 15-year-old sons back. The film is replete with scenes of heroism that film critic Eckhardt Schmidt feels counteract the statement it makes against war (Hembus and Bandmann, 219).

In keeping with Wicki's stated intention to show that death is not heroic, *The Bridge* is void of humor and the glamour of battle: "In most westerns and war films, men die quietly and without pain. They are hit, fall over and are dead. . . . I wanted to show how one really died—not quickly and heroically, but suffering and screaming" (*Spiegel* 1959, 190). Indeed, his characters in *The Bridge* die in misery and pain, scenes made

The Bridge (1959). A young soldier prepares to avenge the death of his comrades. Courtesy Inter Nationes.

all the more unbearable to watch by the ages of the victims. The powerful imagery of pain and suffering notwithstanding, recent critics detect an element of sentimentality in the film that diffuses, or reverses, the film's antiwar sentiments. Kaes notes an ambivalence in the movie that "derives from Wicki's concentration on the fate of the German child-soldiers as victims, who are as innocent as they are apolitical" (17). Another critic questions whether the film's antiwar message is related to the nonstrategic nature of the bridge. "Had its defense been necessary," Hembus and Bandmann ask, "would the boys' deaths have had a purpose?" (Hembus and Bandmann, 191). The suggestion here is clearly that any portrayal of heroism, considering the cause that is being served, is misplaced.

Both the film's critics, who see the film as possibly affirming the virtues of war, and its defenders, who see *The Bridge* as strongly condemning war, overlook the role of the viewer in creating the film experience. On the one hand, the film is certainly ambivalent in its approach to war. The pathos accompanying some of the scenes bestows an element of heroism on the boys' deaths. As mentioned in chapter 1, the existential title the film was released under in South America, *And the Brave Die Lonely*, seems to glorify death in battle. Such a reading of the film is a distinct possibility, for audiences with limited or no knowledge of the history of the Third Reich would lack sufficient historical information on which to judge screen events. Aside from the fact that the boys are a bit young to be in training for battle, there is nothing in the film to suggest that they are being misused for an evil cause; their presence at the bridge is an unintentional, if tragic, mistake. Wicki intended the film as an antiwar statement: "I am against war. Everyone's against war. In *The Bridge* I wanted to show how these boys, who were children like thousands of others, were led by their false education to be capable of the worst horrors" (Hembus and Bandmann, 189). It is doubtful, however, that the film would be understood as antiwar by any viewers not receptive to an antiwar reading.

On the other hand, that the film generally does function as an antiwar statement suggests that most spectators are predisposed to finding that message. The message is conveyed because of the tension created by the interplay between the movie's classic war film structure and the spectators' knowledge of history. The first pulls viewers into the movie and its illusionary world, and the second reminds them of the cause the boys serve. Audiences easily identify with the young characters of *The Bridge*; they are the stock group of war heroes from any war movie, only younger. Their youth, moreover, increases identification with them, for it adds to their appeal. The boy-soldiers are endowed with innocence and future promise that causes viewers to invest more emotion in their survival than they normally would watching a war movie. But the situation in which the youths are engaged is of a questionable nature, not strategically but morally. The audience with a knowledge of history recognizes this, even if the film does not spell out the evils of nazism behind the boys' mission. Indeed, one could speculate that had Wicki included explicit political information about the boys' war efforts being rooted in the evils of nazism, such informational excess would have distanced viewers from the screen and thwarted identification with the youths, upon which the film's effect depends. Spectators familiar with the historical situation see the negative side to the positive traits—bravery, loyalty, patriotism, and sacrifice—that the boys possess. These viewers alternate between identifying with the youths' innocence, potential, and virtue and condemning, or at least rejecting, their service to the Nazi regime. While it is true that the film spotlights the "manly" virtues of war, the film is also a cinematic experience that leads to condemnation of those virtues.

Night Fell on Gotenhafen

▲▼▲

The praise with which *The Bridge* was greeted at the time of its release may have been due in part to the uncritical nature of some of the other West German war movies released in the late 1950s: for example, *The Doctor of Stalingrad*, directed by Geza von Radvany; *Haie und kleine Fische* (*Sharks and Small Fish*, 1957) and *Nacht fiel über Gotenhafen* (*Night Fell on Gotenhafen*, 1959), directed by Frank Wisbar; and *Rommel Calling Cairo*, directed by Wolfgang Schleif. These films tend either to emphasize the adventure to be had in the military or to reflect the cold war rhetoric of the 1950s. *Rommel Calling Cairo*, for example, is a classic adventure film. Its theme is espionage, its setting exotic Cairo. The film tells the story of a successful attempt to smuggle a secret agent and a radio engineer into Cairo during the 1942 battle for Tobruk. Even though the mission eventually is unsuccessful, its failure never reflects poorly on those who planned it and carried it out. The only negative portrayal in the film is of an English officer who unwittingly gives information to the agent. Without irony, the narrative allows him to save his honor by committing suicide. The same escape is allowed the German radioman, who kills himself just before he is to be captured. The film seems to be attempting to show that Germany's campaign in North Africa was a military exercise to help free the Egyptians from the British. Given that the movie was released just two years after the 1956 Suez crisis and the driving out of the British from Egypt, the film's agenda is questionable.

In contrast to Schleif's film, Frank Wisbar's *Night Fell on Gotenhafen*, released the following year, is clear about the misery, deprivation, and destruction caused by World War II. The narrative is based on a real incident near the close of the war, in which a ship with German women and children refugees on board was sunk by a Soviet air attack. Given the depiction of Soviet soldiers, one has to ask if this movie was made, in part at least, to justify the cold war rather than to come to terms with the Second World War. In a particularly emotional scene shortly before the bombing of the ship, an innocent, aristocratic woman, with whom viewers have identified, is shot and killed by advancing Soviet troops. Although the film predates the *Historikerstreit* (historians' conflict) by a quarter of a century, one can recognize in it a seed of the revisionists' argument that the German war effort in the East was caused partly by a desire to protect Germany from communism. As revisionist as the sentiments of *Night Fell on Gotenhafen* might be, it nonetheless engages viewers in a dialogue with history.

The narrative of Wisbar's movie is tightly structured and its characters sympathetic. None of the main characters is a Nazi or possesses any negative traits. In all these respects the film is an uncritical look at the past. Yet the film's historical discourse repeatedly interrupts the narrative and reminds viewers about the death and suffering caused by the war and Nazi Germany. At times these historical interruptions are sentimental. Early in the film, for example, the screen fills with Iron Crosses that slowly dissolve into crosses on mass graves. But even the sentimentality works to break the cinematic illusion and focus attention on history. Other scenes show deprivations caused by war, deaths of civilians and mass migrations from the East as the war ends. The refugees from the East, however, seem to be routed by the Russians without cause.

Night Fell on Gotenhafen contains one of the earliest film references to the roundup of Jews by the Nazis. A party is interrupted, and a Jew who has been hiding in the apartment is dragged off as one of the characters remarks, "We heroes stood here and let this happen." Of course, such momentary references to Nazi policy do not in themselves create a critical examination of history. For some viewers, the comment may be simply salve for an aching conscience. Nonetheless, the character's rebuke is clearly directed at the "heroes" in the audience as well as those on the screen. The admonition relates the fictional discourse of the film to the historical discourse; as viewers are reminded of the past and of where actions like those of the film characters eventually led, they may suddenly recognize that the deprivations, the deaths, and the need to come to terms with them have been self-inflicted.

I Was Nineteen

▲▼▲

War films made by directors of the former German Democratic Republic (GDR) are both more critical of Germany's past and yet equally as revisionist as films by Western directors. The hero of Konrad Wolf's *Ich war neunzehn* (*I Was Nineteen*, 1967) is a German-born Soviet soldier who has been raised in Russia—like Wolf himself—and now finds himself in the area around Berlin in the final days of the war. The film is episodic, depicting stages in the youth's reconciliation with his German heritage. He has been made provisional commander of a small town, Zwickau. As he struggles to establish a local government there, he is also called on to interpret in politically heightened situations: with German officers who have secured Spandau Prison and refuse to surrender; with an unrepentant German intellectual who philosophizes about the nature of power; at a May Day party at which Russians and German resistance fighters are present. Each episode has its own inner tension, and each helps the young German-Russian come to terms with his German nationality. In the first scene he reads from a diary in which he announces that he is 19 and has come to Germany with Soviet troops. The scene is reprised at the end, only this time he includes the phrase, "I am German and I was 19." The hero represents those Germans who have had to overcome the past and forge a new German identity. He can also be seen as representing the fathers of the second generation of 19-year-olds in the audience, who must continue what their parents started.

Wolf's films have been well received by critics in both the East and the West. Indeed, they seem to be valued more highly than their Western counterparts because of Wolf's perceived willingness to come to terms with the fascist past, an attitude that seems absent in Western films. *I Was Nineteen*, for example, broaches subjects avoided by the war films of Western directors: Nazi atrocities committed against the Soviets; concentration camp murders; the brutality of SS officers against German soldiers. In an evocative conversation, a Russian teacher asks a young German socialist what reply should be given to students who ask how the German language can speak both the names Goethe and Auschwitz. *I Was Nineteen* is of particular interest because of the way it presents its historical and narrative material. The film is a diary of the last weeks of the war kept by the movie's hero. The German towns, the negotiations, and the concentration camps are all seen through the eyes of the young soldier, who must undergo conversion to the realization of a new German identity. Identification is strong, and in spite of the episodic nature of the film and a structure that should provide distance from the movie, spectators are as involved in *I Was Nineteen* as in any melodramatic story. Involvement here, however, leads not to the film experience of identifying with the choices of individuals who, though not Nazis, were under the Nazi regime, but to identification with a German who must learn to love his country again.

Mama, I Am Alive

▲▼▲

Mama, ich lebe (*Mama, I Am Alive*, 1976) reflects the experimental style of *I Was Nineteen* in that it, too, relates its story through episodes that are united by an overarching historical discourse. Four German prisoners of war have decided for various reasons—revealed in flashback—to cooperate with the Soviets and train for a commando unit operating against German troops. Wolf's focus is again the gradual enlightenment of his young protagonists, who all have doubts that their decision to join the fight against Hitler and the Nazis is indeed correct. The film presents the political reawakening of the four soldiers as a ritualistic journey. On the train trip to a reeducation camp, they learn to understand the hostility and mistrust that they experience from the Soviet soldiers. At first locked in their compartments to prevent their escape, the Germans later share food and drink with their former enemies. From a freedom fighter who joins them along the way, they begin to understand the seriousness of the mission they face. It is also clear, however, that the freedom fighter's romanticism will not be enough to help them keep their resolve. Finally, at the camp itself they undergo reeducation, which culminates in a purification ceremony: sitting in a sauna, they switch their bodies as if cleansing themselves of their fascist past, a ritual reminiscent of a shower scene in *I Was Nineteen*. Later the four men undergo the first test of their resolve and fail. They refuse to fire on renegade German soldiers whom they encounter in the area of their camp because the soldiers are not attacking them but moving away. A few minutes later they find the body of a Russian comrade, who has been killed by the German renegades. At this point their political awakening is complete, and three of the Germans go on a mission in which they are killed. As the news is revealed to the fourth comrade, who stayed in camp, the scene, covered by a dense fog, is intercut with photos taken earlier of the four Germans.

In spite of its sentimental ending, *Mama, I Am Alive* functions much like *I Was Nineteen.* The film brings the viewer into the movie by means of sympathetic characters and produces not a cathartic film experience but a learning experience. Furthermore, each film uses certain techniques to produce both distance and identification. In *I Was Nineteen* diary entries written by the young German soldier serve this purpose. In *Mama, I Am Alive* a photo of the four men taken on their trip to training camp is used. The photo is viewed from various distances—sometimes showing all four men, sometimes only one or two, sometimes just their belts or boots, and so forth. In both films identification is needed if viewers are to learn the intended lessons (and both movies are unmistakably didactic), namely, that a radical break with Germany's fascist past is necessary if Germany is to survive. The learning transpires in classic cinema fashion: viewers are drawn into the films through clear-cut identification with exemplary characters who undergo a growth experience in the course of the narrative. And yet, equally important, the diary entries and photo inserts distance viewers from each film's characters by interrupting the narrative. Furthermore, the episodic nature of the films deprives the audience of an overarching story in which to get lost. Viewers are thus able to focus on the lessons to be learned.

Anton Kaes writes: "The films of the German Democratic Republic were profoundly concerned with the causes and effects of National Socialism, specifically with war, fascism, the persecution of Jews, and the resistance movement. These historical films . . . served as a warning aimed at preventing a renewed alliance of fascism, capitalism and war" (11). Although these issues are present in Wolf's films, his works deal with them only as they create a history for their intended East German audience. There is a definite agenda in his films.

Wolf, who died in 1982, was the son of Friedrich Wolf, a popular Communist playwright of the 1920s and 1930s. He migrated with his family to Russia after the Nazis took power and settled in East Germany after the war. His brother was Marcus Wolf, a former East German intelligence (*Stasi*) agent. Konrad Wolf's background was thus one that predisposed him to a worldview critical of fascism but apologetic about Soviet communism. Like films from the West, his movies divide Germans into two distinct camps: the bad Nazi, who is seen as an "other," and the good soldier, who defeats the "other." In the course of Wolf's films, however, the "other" is equated with the West and the "good soldier" with the East.

This polarity, which reflected the geopolitical situation as it existed in the two German states until the collapse of the GDR in 1989 and the subsequent unification of West and East Germany in 1990, creates a subtext for the films that exonerates East Germany from responsibility for the past. *I Was Nineteen* and *Mama, I Am Alive*, as well as Wolf's *Professer Mamlock* (1960–61) and *Lissy* (1957), manufacture a past for East Germany that explains its development as a socialist state built by a representative group of Hitler's victims—deserters, socialists, Communists, political dissidents, and sometimes Jews—who opposed fascist (Nazi) Germany. Even use of the term *fascism*, which the films use rather than *nazism*, serves a political agenda: it links the struggles of the past, when heroes opposed the fascists of the SS and Hitler's Third Reich, to the struggles of the present, when the descendents of these pioneers were opposing what the GDR referred to as the fascist West. The films fail to mention the collusion at the start of World War II between Hitler and Stalin to carve up Poland and the Baltic states. Absent also is any reference to the Western Allies and their sacrifices in defeating Hitler. Indeed, in *I Was Nineteen* the hero's words at the death of his friend, directed toward hidden Nazis, ring with stinging irony now that one can question the East's own brand of secret service system, as fashioned in the GDR: "We will catch you; we will find you; we will line you up. I won't forget you. . . . [I won't rest] until you have realized that it's over, once and for ever, it's over."

The Boat

▲▼▲

Wolfgang Petersen's *Das Boot* (*The Boat*, 1981) was a German film industry phenomenon. Its popularity in Germany and abroad was unprecedented. The theater version of the film earned $72 million, an unheard-of sum for a German movie.[5] Four years after the theater release, a five-hour version of the film shown on German television—Petersen shot the movie with the intention of cutting both the two-hour theatrical version and a longer version for television—received a rating of 50 percent, that is, half of the televisions in Germany were tuned to it.[6] The film's international success was also phenomenal. It played to packed commercial theaters in America—in both subtitled and dubbed prints—a rare feat for a German film. In England the five-hour version was received enthusiastically; the critic for the *Sunday Telegraph* wrote that the film made "all previous war films look wimpy, dumb and shrill" (Birkenmaier).

And yet the film was not without its critics, whose reactions ranged from asserting that the film glorified battle to characterizing it as an apologia for Germany's military. One critic, for example, wrote: "There's a suspicion of narrative whitewash at work, exonerating its characters from Nazihood. . . . [The men are] laborers victimized by unfair management practices."[7] Kaes, more sober in his tone, observes that the film reprises "the soldier as the hero pitted against criminal and crazy authority: this tried-and-true narrative war-film formula still works in Wolfgang Petersen's film *Das Boot* . . . and may account for its international success" (16). Such criticism has a degree of validity, for it is sometimes easy to forget the history behind the images and to ignore the cause that the men serve. At these times the film affects viewers as a typical war story does—glorifying the camaraderie of war and extolling the virtues of the common military man vis-à-vis the high command.[8]

That the film attracts audiences through conventional Hollywood strategies has been noted again and again by critics. Typical of the reviews are those by David Ansen, Jon Gartenberg, and Janet Maslin. According to Ansen, "This two-and-a-half-hour saga is filled with the tension, technological bravura and hard-bitten heroism typical of Hollywood movies."[9] Gartenberg says, "This film resembles the classic black and white war dramas in its depiction of the crew's struggle to survive."[10] Maslin writes, "Movies of this genre have been turned out by Hollywood plenty of times."[11] What the critics write is not entirely correct, however. While *The Boat* certainly employs the suspense strategies of a typical war movie, the German perspective from which the story is told is never entirely forgotten. There have been few movies, German or American, about the German military in which, on the one hand, the narrative is so well put together that the audience momentarily forgets which side the characters are fighting for, which cause they are serving, and yet, on the other hand, history is so pervasive that the illusion is continually broken. "Technical dazzle and skilled actors aside, the most basic question raised by *Das Boot* is: Can you forget what cause these men serve? I think not."[12]

The tension produced between the classic war story and the point of view from which the story is told (for Americans, the perspective of the enemy, the losing side; for Germans, that of the Nazis, also an enemy) creates the antiwar message in *The Boat* and may, more than the war story, account for the film's popularity. The war story of the film has elements of the classic horror or disaster story. In an essay on horror film, Douglas Fowler traces the tension created in horror films to three strategies essential to the genre: mystery, physical confinement, and a Cassandra situation.[13] In *The Boat* these three strategies are similarly employed to create tension. Almost as if considering the sensibilities of his international audience, Petersen seldom shows the submarine's enemy. Instead, the enemy remains a mystery presence lurking above the water. The ubiquitous periscope shots from Hollywood movies are absent. In one of the few periscope sightings shared with the audience, a British destroyer nears the submarine through a dense fog, like a sea monster attacking through the mist.

Physical confinement is as well developed as the mystery of the enemy. A submarine under water is obviously cut off from a wider world and avenues of escape. But here confinement is presented as more than the crew can endure, and their emotional breakdown is exploited to increase tension in viewers. The film uses a metaphor of entrapment akin to that used in such films as *The Poseidon Adventure* (1972) and *Alien* (1979) to draw viewers into this world of horror. The filmed set is extremely hemmed in, with aisle space so tight in places that two men have difficulty moving past each other. Supplies and produce (live chickens, fruit, etc.) are stacked and shoved into every inch of free space. Action is filmed from within a space, seldom from without, adding to the claustrophobic atmosphere. Petersen's direction offers no distancing moments to break the film's spellbinding suspense.

The third of Fowler's strategies for good horror films is also found in Petersen's film: namely, the Cassandra effect. The expression describes a situation of impending doom that no one listens to. In *The Boat* the audience knows, as does the captain, of the suicidal nature of the mission being undertaken. There is no possibility of averting disaster because there is no one to whom the orders can be appealed. (This is war, and the sub has received its orders from the high command.) Indeed, the high command functions as the "other," an impersonal and unchangeable force that even refuses to allow a war correspondent and the chief engineer to disembark when the sub docks in Spain. This scene more than any other suggests that Petersen's film, following the lead of Lothar-Günther Buchheim's novel, is intended to criticize the leaders of the war effort for sending the German military on a suicide mission. In this regard, critics are correct to suggest that *The Boat* creates a good German–bad Nazi polarity that tends to excuse the military for what occurred in World War II. They are also correct when they write that the film fails to come to terms with the past in that it never addresses questions of guilt and responsibility. Yet, as an antiwar film, the movie is successful.

Remarkably, the film achieves its antiwar flavor because of the point of view from which it is told. Audiences are made aware of the twist—at least, for foreign audiences the perspective is unusual—in the point of view of the narrative by the film's prologue, which announces that 75 percent of German submarine missions ended in annihilation for their crews, and then begins the story of such a mission. From the beginning there is a built-in tension between identifying with the ship's crew, as in any war movie, and realizing that the objects of identification are actually the enemy, that they serve a vile cause and that their fated defeat is justified. In this sense it is the historical subject matter of the film and the viewers' knowledge of history that create the experience of the film.

In his book on realism in film, Siegfried Kracauer concludes that since film cannot control historical subject matter, such material is unsuited for filmic treatment:

> Aside from their staginess, historical films have another characteristic difficult to bear with: they are finite; they obstruct the affinity of the medium for endlessness. As the reproduction of a bygone era, the world they show is an artificial creation radically shut off from the space-time continuum of the living, a closed cosmos which does not admit of extensions. Looking at such a film, the spectator is likely to suffer from claustrophobia. He realizes that his potential field of vision strictly coincides with the actual one and that, accordingly, he cannot by a hair's breadth transcend the confines of the latter. . . . Historical films preclude the notion of endlessness because the past they try to resurrect no longer exists. (78)

In *The Boat* this claustrophobia works for the film, however, not against it, adding a filmic tension to the conventional suspense. The presence of historical material suggesting that the world in the movie is closed and a mere reproduction of a bygone era increases the film's effectiveness by intensifying the claustrophobic feeling that the viewer experiences. The submarine's crew is trapped not only inside the boat but also in its closed historical situation. In addition to the sense of entrapment produced by the boat's confined quarters, the audience experiences the finite nature of the movie's historical material as entrapment. On the one hand, the audience shares the experience of the crew; on the other, the audience is reminded of the outcome of the historical moment and of the cause these men serve. Consequently, the viewer is trapped by fear that the men will all die. This amplifies the narrative experience and startles viewers with the recognition that they are hoping that these men, the historical enemy, will not perish.

Movies based on events whose consequences for the world were tumultuous enough to have become a part of memory are less "reproductions of a bygone era" than aids to the memory of the viewer in recalling that era. Far from no longer existing for spectators, a past as calamitous and tragic as the period of the Third Reich and World War II—whose effects are still influencing events 50 years later—continues to exist in their memories, either as actual experience or more likely as virtual experience gained from books, eyewitness accounts, films, and other fictional and factual sources. *The Boat* does not so much reproduce a past historical event that viewers can marvel at for its authenticity or bemoan its lack thereof, as it recalls an era for them and invites them to experience life on a U-boat in World War II. The cinematic illusion produced by any well-made classic film is "total, isolating, hallucinatory. The viewer forgets where or who he is" (Vogel, 9). Such is the experience of watching *The Boat*: the viewer forgets who the enemy is. The effect is only temporary, however; the viewers' historical knowledge and their recognition that the filmic world is one that history has condemned, indeed, one that viewers themselves condemn, break the illusion and bring about a reaction that differs from that to the ordinary war movie. Ultimately, then, this film does not glorify bravery, loyalty, and blind dedication but exposes the end to which the war virtues can lead. The characters of *The Boat* do not die for the fatherland, they die because of it—or more precisely, because of the virtues that brought them to follow Hitler unquestioningly.

Admittedly, such a reading requires that the audience know something about Nazi Germany. But the film helps out in this regard. Throughout the movie the viewers' historical awareness, whether brought into the theater or garnered from clues provided within the film, interacts with their engaged concern for the characters, producing a recognition of the futility and waste of this particular war and, by extension, of all war: the prologue announces that 30,000 of 40,000 men died on these U-boat missions; the drunken brawl at the beginning of the film points to a degree of cynicism among the heroes about the mission they are to undertake; when a British destroyer is sunk, the men of the U-boat cannot rescue the survivors, both because their quarters are too cramped and also because their orders forbid it. These scenes cause spectators to recognize the hollowness of this war and the emptiness of the values for which it is being fought. In the scene of the sinking ship, the interaction between character identification and historical awareness produces for American and other non-German audiences an additional, peculiar, and effective twist. Along with

The Boat (1981). An Allied bombing raid destroys the submarine base and the U-boat after the sub, having surviving many dangers during its mission, returns to port. Courtesy WDR/Vogelmann and Inter Nationes.

the characters, viewers experience triumph at the sinking of the enemy ship. They also experience the dismay and bitterness over the orders forbidding the U-boat crew to help the sailors from the doomed ship. But added to this scene is sharp dislocation, shock, and further dismay as viewers suddenly remember who the two combating forces are. In a sense, the American viewer becomes a traitor by investing approval and hope in the enemy of the Allied forces. The sudden change in perspective thrusts the viewer from the narrative with the realization of who is triumphing, where the orders originated, and who is dying. At the same time, after identifying with the characters, the enemy is no longer faceless. The viewer is free to recognize how empty and useless are all deaths in war.

Finally, the end of the film awakens viewers to the reality that the mission they have invested two hours in, that they expected would have a happy end because the film is modeled along Hollywood lines, is doomed and was doomed from the start. History tells that the Third Reich fell. To have the U-boat's crew be successful would be a lie about the larger history. The bombing of the sub's port, the death of the men, and the sinking of the sub serve to turn the movie around. In a sense, the end lets the audience off the hook for its support of so ignoble a cause as the Third Reich. The final conflagration turns the metaphor of the valor of men in war into a metaphor of the insanity of war by allowing the men to succeed only to fail, thus denying that there is any value behind the death and destruction on the screen. Unlike Hollywood films that ultimately affirm certain virtues, such as *The Desert Fox*, in which Rommel's suicide can be seen as an act of love to save his family, or Bernhard Wicki's *Morituri*, in which Marlon Brando's and Yul Brynner's acts can be seen as subscribing to a higher form of loyalty, patriotism, and bravery, *The Boat* denies any value to death in war. Nothing has been accomplished. The mission was not only without strategic meaning but it ended in the deaths of most of those involved.

One of the problems with *The Boat*, however, as with most war films—and the reason critics can find revisionist sentiments in its text—is that some aspects of war are viewed by society as positive; bravery, loyalty, patriotism, and sacrifice are accepted as virtues. When the film places these virtues in characters who are portrayed as sincere, it becomes difficult not to place value in their bravery, loyalty, and sacrifice. Death in the service of one's country is itself valorized: it is seen as necessary, meaningful, and transfiguring, regardless of the context into which it is set. The screen images in *The Boat* of young men dying thus transcend the meaninglessness of their deaths. The film sociologist I. C. Jarvie writes that "any influence a film may exert is at least a joint product of the intentions (and accomplishments) of the filmmaker and the predilections and interests of the moviegoer."[14] D. J. R. Bruckner, Seymour Chwast, and Steven Heller, the authors of *Art against War*, voice doubt that any film can be unequivocally against war: "Any film has thousands of images, so that one comes away with an impression that is one's own; it may reflect the intention of the director or the writer but . . . never . . . entirely. There is no art that is so dependent on the passions of its viewers at the moment."[15] It would seem therefore, that regardless of how critically the films of Petersen, Wicki, and Wisbar look at the Third Reich, their films will be read as critical of war only by those who choose to interpret death on the screen in this way. Others will be free to read the images of death and destruction more conservatively, as occasioned by virtues that society values because they preserve the society.

My Father's War

▲▼▲

In *Der Krieg meines Vaters* (*My Father's War*, 1984) Nico Hofmann created an antiwar film by frustrating the inclination of viewers to valorize death in war. This television movie eschews filmed images of combat and fallen comrades in favor of showing the consequences that deaths in war have on the home front. The film starts as the director, Nico Hofmann, reads a letter his father sent him in 1983 at the time Germans were debating the stationing of nuclear missiles in their country. In this letter, Hofmann's father quotes Marguerite Duras on memory: "Like you I have fought against forgetting. Like you I have forgotten. I have forced myself to kill the terrible, that which is the basis of memory, to no longer know or comprehend it, but I have forgotten. We must remember or else all will repeat itself." The narrative that follows these words illustrates the consequences if their warning is not heeded.

As in other films about Germany's past, *My Father's War* employs conventional narrative to bring viewers into the film and historical discourse to distance them from it. The narrative, which takes place during the start of the Russian campaign, is about a young man who, against the wishes of his mother, still supports the war, in spite of, or perhaps because of, having been dismissed from a paramilitary youth group. His mother is a socialist, as was his father, who has been killed in war. The film focuses on the tension that arises between mother and son because of her fear that he will be killed if he obeys his draft notice, and his fear that his mother's passive resistance to nazism will endanger her freedom and perhaps his. The narrative ends as the two say good-bye in a train station just before he leaves for military duty. Between the scene that opens the narrative—a shot of a radio tuned to the *Wunschkonzert*, a German propaganda program aimed at keeping spirits up—and the scene that closes the narrative—a shot of the young man looking at a series of war photos, which are the only visual documentation of death in war—the film deconstructs the typical war film, which often praises the virtues it is trying to condemn. *My Father's War* depicts the need of people affected by war to believe that war has a purpose, that men who die are dying for something. Even in *The Bridge* and *The Boat*, films in which the missions are strategically worthless, the men pursue the mission with a sense of bonding that transcends the orders and thus valorizes even a stupid cause.

The film's narrative and historical discourses speak directly to a human tendency to valorize loss. The narrative includes the death of four soldiers: the father of the protagonist, the son of a neighbor, the brother of a Hitler Youth member, and the son of a doctor. At one point in the film the mother tries to persuade the doctor to declare her son unfit for military service. He refuses and as part of his response tells her of the pride he has for his fallen son. The woman's skepticism of the doctor's reaction to death is supported by the mise-en-scène: as the doctor speaks of his pride he looks at a picture of his son, reminding the father of a time when the young man was still alive; the picture is not standing on a desktop but lying flat in its frame in a drawer, where it can be viewed whenever the doctor pulls out his desk drawer, as if he were pulling out a body in a morgue. The death of the neighbor's son is dealt with in the same symbolic fashion. The neighbor, in trying to console a member of the Hitler Youth for the loss of his brother, reads a eulogy extolling the virtues of dying for the fatherland. The eulogy, however, is interrupted by a knock at the door. The neighbor's son is being returned home on a stretcher, minus a leg lost on the front. In subsequent scenes the neighbor eagerly questions his son about action on the front, but the son refuses to answer. Finally, realizing perhaps where his own patriotic fervor has taken his son, the neighbor shoots his son and himself in front of a swastika and a map of the war campaign, across which is written the word *breakthrough.*

The hollowness of these deaths is echoed by the radio broadcasts that provide the backdrop to these and other scenes. At times the Wunschkonzert program plays nostalgic songs of love. At other times the announcer tells of the birth of yet another baby for the fatherland, narrates the exploits of victorious battles, or lists the names of men who have died bravely. Hofmann uses radio broadcasts in the background of his film to comment on the Nazi government's propaganda efforts to sentimentalize the war for those at home, to prepare them for the death of their relatives. The Wunschkonzert, Hofmann is suggesting, is the government's way of giving death in war meaning by showing how death is connected to the home front, to the continuation of society. To prevent the material from having a sentimental effect on spectators, none of the reported battles is ever given visualization, and no report is allowed to reach completion. Several times in the course of the narrative the mother gets up to turn off the radio, eliminating not only its influence on her as a listener within the narrative but its influence on viewers of the film.

The theme that permeates this film is the need to valorize death in war. The attempts of the neighbor, doctor, and Wunschkonzert listeners to come to terms with loss echo the conflict between the mother and son over the death of the father. Unhappy with her son's romantic view of war, the mother forces him to read a telegram from the war office describing his father's death as "brave." Afterwards she hands him a diary her husband kept on the battlefield, in which he describes the loneliness of war, the horror of seeing a comrade blown up in front of him, and the experience of holding the dying soldier in his arms. The scene is the aural equivalent of the final scene of death in *All Quiet on the Western Front*. In the images of both these films death is portrayed only as the negation of life. The father's sole presence in the film is in photos, which appear in the background of many of the scenes, serving to remind the mother and son, as well as the viewers, of his permanent absence.

As a statement against war, Hofmann's film succeeds where the others fail because he includes no battlefield images of the war. Although death is a major theme in the other films discussed in this chapter, they focus primarily on courage, camaraderie, and sacrifice—intrinsically positive qualities in the eyes of most viewers. When characters in these films die, viewers interpret their deaths as having a higher purpose. The deaths that occur in *My Father's War* take place off-camera. Moreover, the only bodies shown are those of the neighbor and his son, lying in front of a campaign map. Hofmann's demystification of war and death adds an extra dimension to the film. On the one hand, the absence of concrete scenes of battle allows the film to function, on an abstract level, as a statement against war in general. Without specific faces for viewers to attach their emotions to, feelings of grief become associated with loss of life in war. This general antiwar theme is continued by a series of photos at the end of the film that depict soldiers in various wars. Because these shots are not tied to a narrative, they involve viewers intellectually, reminding them of how wasteful and lonely all war is. On the other hand, the film's allusions to the Nazi period give its antiwar message specificity. The Wunschkonzert, Nazi hooligans, the patriotic neighbor, and the doctor locate this war in a specific period and offer the specific horrors of the Third Reich as a reason to avoid all future wars.

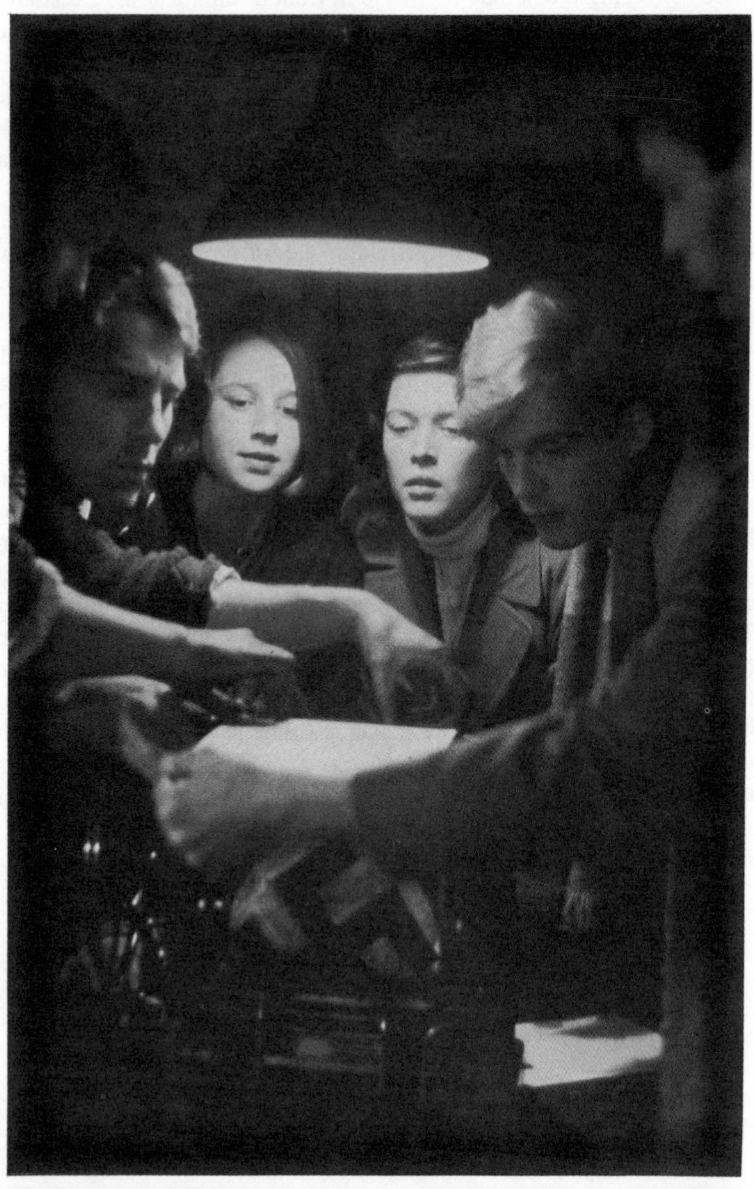

The White Rose (1982). Sophie Scholl (Lena Stolze, middle left) and her fellow conspirators print their newsletter, *Die weisse Rose*. Courtesy Filmverlag der Autoren and Inter Nationes.

chapter 4

▲▼▲

opposing hitler and the nazis

In *Casablanca* (1943) Ilsa, the character played by Ingrid Bergman, does not walk into just any gin mill, but into one populated by Nazis, anti-Nazis, and Rick (Humphrey Bogart), a man indifferent to both who has to learn to choose sides. The audience experiences the film through Rick's perspective, so that his education becomes that of the viewers as well. Although it would be fair to assume that in 1943 viewers would have been anti-Nazi, the film would certainly have strengthened that opinion. Michael Curtiz's classic film of resistance is of interest because the formula it uses is one followed to some degree by most films about opposition to Hitler: members of the resistance are portrayed as noble characters who have no self-doubts; they prize individual liberty highly yet are unselfish enough to recognize that personal sacrifice for the cause of freedom is a moral obligation; moreover, their goodness offers an absolute contrast to the Nazis' evil. Since the resistance fighters are always the point of entry for the audience, their experiences serve to educate the audience. The stark black/white polarity between evil and good seems appropriate in *Casablanca*. For one, the distinction between hero and villain is a staple of tendentious films. For another, portraying the Nazis as evil satisfied the expectations of the intended American audience, which would have rejected positive portrayals of the enemy. For postwar audiences the black/white polarity conforms to history's view of Nazi Germany.

The contrast between good and evil is present in non-Hollywood films about the resistance as well. On one side of the spectrum are the heroes (stand-ins for the spectators) opposed to nazism; on the other side are the Nazis, whose "otherness" saves viewers from finding points of identification with them. Describing this polarity in Roberto Rossellini's *Rome Open City*, for example, Arthur Knight states: "Underlying all is the determination to force the camera to the limits of realistic re-creation so that the audience not only sees but feels the terror and the courage of the Romans during the occupation years."[1] Of interest in Knight's remarks is his reference to the occupation years. To be sure, Italy could have been called an occupied country, particularly after Mussolini's fall, but the fascist element in Italy was indigenous and not totally an outside force: that is, even though the Nazis were occupiers, they had, at one time, been invited in. As Knight's description implies, however, Rossellini glosses over the indigenous quality of Italian fascism in order to concentrate on the resistance to Hitler, to emphasize that not all Italians had succumbed to the promises of fascism, that there were Italians with sufficient "courage" to fight the "terror" of the Nazis. In short, the film helped Italian viewers find an invigorated sense of self, and it helped foreign viewers restore the country's reputation after its 20-year acquiescence to Mussolini's iron-fisted rule. As in *Casablanca*, Nazis and fascists are portrayed as "others." The Italian resistance is a monolithic group of freedom fighters who are willing to undergo the worst possible tortures to rid their country of the Nazi plague, referred to in an emotional speech as "vermin."

In *La Notte di San Lorenzo* (*Night of the Shooting Stars*, 1982) Paolo and Vittorio Taviani look back with irony at war-torn Italy. Although their sympathies are clearly with Italy's resistance movement, fascists are more than the "Nazi vermin" of *Rome Open City*. Fascists come from the same villages as the freedom fighters and even from the same families. They do not seem evil as much as they seem misguided. In spite of their more human face and their indigenous origins, however, the fascists remain alienated from viewers. They remain an "other" controlled by the Nazis, who are capable of the worst atrocities—the exploding of a church where villagers have gone for sanctuary, and the close-range shooting of an unarmed woman. Just as such acts distance viewers from the fascists, acts of heroism attract them to the freedom fighters. The final bond between viewers and the resisters is made at an initiation ceremony in which the camera focuses close-up on each fighter as he takes on an assumed name. Scenes of this nature allow spectators to identify fully with the resistance, even as they recognize that fascism is not totally an outside force.

Portraying German resistance to nazism is more difficult than showing American or even Italian opposition. Since the United States was at war with the Third Reich, melodramatic heroics and strong contrasts between good and evil seem appropriate in a film like *Casablanca*. They also seem appropriate in *Rome Open City* and *Night of the Shooting Stars*, since a strong resistance movement opposed to Mussolini and the fascists existed in Italy and was at least partially successful in undermining the Nazis. Audiences are willing to accept the romanticizing of freedom fighters in these films. Audiences are not as generous toward a film about a German opposition movement; for while there was political resistance to Hitler within Germany, it was disorganized, without effect, and late in developing. To give such a weak movement the structure required to satisfy the demands of melodrama would be to grant it more importance than it had in reality. Any film that suggests there was organized opposition to Hitler is open to criticism that it is self-serving. Moreover, as a film about the past it is expected to portray history honestly. In a speech to the West German parliament on 10 November 1988, the fiftieth anniversary of the Kristallnacht pogrom, Philipp Jenninger, the parliament president, described Germany during the Third Reich as follows:

> The public for the most part remained passive, that was the attitude in regard to anti-Jewish actions and measures in the following years. Only a few joined in the rioting—but there was no rejection, no resistance worthy of mentioning. Reports speak of consternation and shame, of pity, yes, even disgust and horror. But only a very few were sympathetic, gave practical solidarity, assistance or help. All saw what happened, but the majority of them looked away and said nothing. [Even] the churches were silent.[2]

Given this historical picture, any depiction of an organized resistance would seem a distortion.

Nevertheless, there was resistance to nazism, however limited, within Germany. At one end of the spectrum were resisters who practiced so-called inner immigration. These people simply turned away from anything even remotely political and devoted themselves to a completely personal agenda. At the other end was the movement known as the Twentieth of July. The most organized of the resistance groups, it was composed mostly of Prussian Junkers (minor nobility) and military men around Col. Graf Claus Schenk von Stauffenberg. Between these two poles were individual resisters and small religious groups. The Red Chapel, for example, had one of its centers in Hermann Goering's Air Ministry; its members were alleged to have been in contact with the Soviets.[3] There were religiously inspired groups, such as the Kreisau Circle and the White Rose. There were also individual fanatics, like George Elser and Maurice Bavaud, who acted independently of any group in their plans to assassinate Hitler.[4] All these individuals and groups had disparate motives. Bavaud was supposedly a psychopath hoping to avenge a perceived wrong. The Junkers hoped to save Germany from the total destruction that they were sure would come with defeat (Rothfels, 72–81). The Scholl siblings, leaders of the White Rose, believed they were upholding the best principles of Christianity in their opposition. The Kreisau Circle was similarly motivated. Regardless of their motives, however, these individuals and groups attest that there was opposition to Hitler.[5] This opposition, while less organized than resistance in other countries, still contains as much potential for cinematic treatment as movements outside Germany. Unlike non-German movements, however, the German resistance requires more careful balancing of cinematic melodrama and historical fact.

Directors of films about the German resistance face an additional problem: in spite of the criminal acts committed by the Nazi regime, the Nazi state was representative of the German people, and actions against the government were construed as high treason. Thus a film narrative must justify the acts of sabotage, terrorism, and sedition committed by German characters who oppose their government. From almost any standpoint, it may seem unnecessary to justify the activities of those who resisted Hitler, to prove that their acts of treason were acts of true patriotism. Yet, as Balfour writes in *Withstanding Hitler in Germany*, a series of essays about individuals who opposed Hitler, there is one question that must be considered: "In what circumstances, if at all, does an individual have a right—or even a duty—to seek to overthrow by violence the government of his or her country?" (245). The films discussed in this chapter all address this question in some fashion: they depict the circumstances that move citizens to use illegal means to oppose their government; they dramatize the soul searching that individuals undergo before acting against their country; they make it clear that no other action is possible; and finally, they bring viewers to ask themselves if they would have acted in the same way.

The White Rose

▲▼▲

In 1942 a small group of college-age students in Munich began publishing a clandestine newsletter, *Die weisse Rose*, in which they criticized their government and hoped for its downfall. "Is it not a fact that today every decent German is ashamed of his government?" asks one issue. Another describes, in metaphysical terms what was happening in Germany at the time: "Everywhere and in all ages the demons have been waiting in darkness for the hour in which man would weaken, when of his own volition he would abandon his place in the order of things founded for him by God on freedom, surrender to the pressure of Evil, detach himself from the Powers of a higher order and so, having taken the first step voluntarily, be driven to the second and third and ever further with frenzied speed" (Rothfels, 13–14). The leaders of this group were Hans and Sophie Scholl, a brother and sister who had been enthusiastic members of the Hitler Youth. The strong religious values they had learned at home brought them to question the activities of the Nazi government, in particular its war policies. They were supported in their work by several close friends and a university professor. When caught, all were tried, convicted of treason, and executed within a period of five days. As late as 1982 their conviction was still in the records of the German judiciary. They were still officially traitors.

The story of the White Rose has been told twice on film—by Michael Verhoeven, whose most recent success is *The Nasty Girl*,[6] and by Percy Adlon, known in America for *Aus Rosenheim* (*Bagdad Cafe*, 1988) and *Rosalie Goes Shopping* (1990.) The two films are different in style and genre. Verhoeven's film, *Die weisse Rose* (*The White Rose*, 1982), is both a suspenseful thriller, complete with close calls and secret meetings, and an informative documentary drama. Adlon's movie, *Five Last Days*, is a character study and a dramatization of a diary. It lacks the suspense of Verhoeven's film but is equally informative about history. In place of suspense, the film offers insight into the motivations of its heroine and her cell mate. But the films share some commonalities: both portray the youthful heroine as an extraordinary person; the same actress, Lena Stolze, plays Sophie Scholl in both films; and the reactions of ordinary citizens to the events of the day play a part in both.

In Verhoeven's film Sophie Scholl comes to Munich to study at the university where her brother Hans is also a student. By chance she comes across evidence that her brother is secretly printing and distributing a newsletter critical of the Nazi regime. She eventually joins the young resisters and proves adept at getting the materials necessary for their enterprise. The movement starts to expand out of the Munich area into other cities; its young members grow less cautious under the mistaken belief that an overthrow of the government is imminent. Hans, Sophie, and one of their friends are captured, tried, and executed. An epilogue informs viewers that three other members of the group were also captured and executed and reminds viewers that the military putsch expected by the members of the White Rose was unsuccessful. The epilogue further reports on the status of the convictions in 1982, when the film was released.

The White Rose is an audience-pleasing thriller and an informative film. The melding of melodrama and documentary has not, however, pleased all movie critics, some of whom find that it trivializes history. H. G. Pflaum, for example, calls it *Genre-Kino*, or formula movie making.[7] Ruprecht Skasa-Weiss is more condemnatory, writing that the film leaves the viewer wondering "with whom he is dealing: whether Bonnie and Clyde, Baader and Meinhof [leaders of a radical political group of the 1970s] or Hans and Sophie Scholl."[8] There is some justification in the film for these criticisms, for Verhoeven chooses to focus on the successes of the resisters rather than on their failures and frustrations. Moreover, the activities of the young people increase in danger and complexity as their opposition movement grows. Tension and excitement reach their peak right before Hans and Sophie are captured outside a Munich University lecture hall. Verhoeven has structured the scene to presage the eventual triumph of antifascist forces over the Nazis. As the siblings are trapped, they scatter their pamphlets from a balcony of the huge foyer. These float down onto the students below like a refreshing snow shower. Thus even at the time of their ultimate defeat the student activists are triumphant. Skasa-Weiss reads the scene as "a last-ditch effort meant to awaken the people." But the newsletters have no effect on those receiving them. The scene points more to a victory in the future and to an acknowledgment that, in Verhoeven's words, "it's not true what my generation heard from their parents. It's not true that it wasn't possible to do anything against fascism."[9]

The elements that lend *The White Rose* the look of a conventional thriller create a feeling of optimism in spectators. The formulaic nature of the narrative invites viewers into the movie via the familiar signposts of the suspense genre: clearly defined heroes and villains, heroes who intentionally place themselves in danger, clandestine meetings, and close encounters. The exuberance and innocence of the young rebels make them sympathetic to the audience. After a successful mission to secure paper from a government office, Hans and Sophie Scholl ride their bikes through the streets of Munich defying the air raid siren's warning to seek shelter; for them the approaching enemy planes bring the defeat of Hitler and nazism closer to realization. From the opening scene, in which Sophie outwits a Gestapo agent who is trying to question her presence in Munich, until shortly before the Scholls' capture, the movie fulfills every expectation viewers have of the thriller genre. Following the formula for suspense films, the students outwit and defeat the enemy in all their missions impossible. Only the final mission ends in defeat. The arrest of the Scholls is a rude awakening for viewers. Once the cinematic illusion is broken, spectators are free to focus on the meaning of the group's activities. They realize that the movie is not a conventional thriller, that the activity of the Scholls is not typical melodrama that will play itself out in a happy end. The end of the movie engages viewers in a dialogue with history, provoking them to question the punishment of the Scholls and to ponder the nature of their resistance.

The announcement in the film's epilogue that the Scholls' convictions were still on the books created controversy. The German federal judiciary objected to the film's assertion that the judiciary supported the convictions of the members of the White Rose. Members of the judiciary claimed to have never passed judgment on the issue, since such matters were out of the federal court's purview. As a result of the epilogue's statement, the Goethe Institute (Germany's cultural office) refused to distribute the film abroad, a service that the institute otherwise provides German filmmakers. The movie also could not be viewed by most students because the *Landesbildstelle* (a state film approval board) had never approved it as suitable for children. Editors and judges weighed in with opinions about whether the federal judiciary officially had to lift the sentences or not. Most of the arguments, however, missed the epilogue's point, which was that no official German body had ever come forward and dismissed the charges of treason against the Scholls and their compatriots. In other words, the Scholls may have become heroes after the fact, a point the thriller facets of the film emphasize, but legally they were and continued to be considered traitors to their country, a point the epilogue stresses.

The docudrama elements of *The White Rose* illuminate the issue of treason. It must be noted that at no time does the narrative suggest that the actions of the members of the White Rose were treasonous. It is a given that their actions are morally justified; instead of defending the actions of the group, whose members are portrayed as cinematic heroes, the narrative shows simply how they acted and why. From the very first the film provides the audience, sometimes directly, sometimes indirectly, with historical background that comments on the motivations of Hans, Sophie, and their friends. For example, as Sophie moves into her apartment and meets the housekeeper, a familiar establishing scene in most films when a newcomer arrives in the city, she engages in a casual conversation about the war on the eastern front. For viewers, however, the conversation is not casual. An offhand remark by the landlady alerts viewers to the historical reality behind the narrative, reminding them of the thousands who were still to die in the East.

Allusions to the war on the eastern front become a primary means for engaging viewers in a dialogue with history: for instance, news of the atrocities occurring in Russia form the main theme of the clandestine newsletter distributed by the resistance group, and news of the defeat at Stalingrad, introduced into the narrative by a radio broadcast, is the catalyst for convincing the only nonstudent involved, the conservative Professor Huber, to join the group. Even during romantic interludes between Sophie and her fiancé, references to the Russian front remind viewers of the war. Although grounded in the fiction, such references to the war in the East cause viewers to question the war and to recognize the motivation for the students' actions.

For an ironic comment on who is the enemy and who the traitor, Verhoeven juxtaposes a Nazi poster admonishing workers in a munitions plant, "The enemy is listening in," with a shot of Sophie, now working in the munitions factory, as she witnesses an act of sabotage committed by a Polish prisoner. Sophie not only remains silent about the incident but later emulates the deed: she substitutes bread for the necessary wadding in the shells, even though the switch could cause misfires and the death of ordinary soldiers, her countrymen. The scene functions to remind viewers that Sophie's actions are no different from those of the foreign enemy and would, if uncovered, be punished harshly. Yet the sign asks viewers to think about who the real enemy is—those who work against the government, or the government itself.

On the day after the execution of the leaders of the White Rose movement, 3,000 students gathered at Munich University to condemn the Scholls' actions and to cheer the university porter who had turned them in.[10] This extraordinary turnout to actively cheer the death of three young people who followed an inner voice that told them their government was evil, a belief that is now widely held, never appears in the movie. Verhoeven ends his film with the execution. The director's inclusion of an epilogue reminding viewers that the convictions are still on the books leads viewers to ask, is treason an absolute concept that prevents any activity directed at overthrowing a government, regardless of the corrupt nature of that government? Assuming that the narrative of the film leads viewers to answer no, the epilogue leads them to ask whether they believe the students are guilty. The ending suggests a third question, too: would viewers have acted as the students did, knowing the consequences, or would they have been content to live with a corrupt regime, or perhaps even have condoned or supported the actions of the government?

The strength of Verhoeven's movie lies precisely in this last question. The film strongly suggests to viewers, whether they want to admit it or not, that they would not have stood with the rebels. In the majority of Nazi-retro films concerned with citizens going about their daily routine in spite of, or perhaps thanks to, the Nazis, there are times when spectators undergo an experience of identifying with "the wrong side." That is, viewers identify with men and women who have made the choice to support the Third Reich, either by working for the Nazis, by acquiescing to their demands, or by turning away and ignoring what is happening. The films give viewers the chance to be an ordinary citizen and yet be able to judge what these citizens are doing. Nazi-retro movies are a mirror in which spectators can see themselves. In *The White Rose* viewers sympathize with characters who have made the right choice, and yet the film never allows viewers to see themselves in the resisters. The Scholls and their friends are

The White Rose (1982). Sophie Scholl (Lena Stolze, left) sabotages shells in a munitions factory. The sign in back proclaims "The enemy is listening in." Courtesy Filmverlag der Autoren and Inter Nationes.

too dedicated and almost superhuman. Instead, spectators see themselves in the ordinary people around the Scholls. These characters represent a broad spectrum of the ordinary citizens found in other Nazi-retro films. In most such films, however, characters in whom viewers see themselves seldom give even passive support to the Nazis. They are mostly guilty of inner immigration or turning away from the events around them. In *The White Rose* the characters with whom viewers are brought to identify give passive, and sometimes active, support to the Third Reich.

In a pivotal scene Verhoeven reveals why the Scholls act as they do. Hans and his university comrades have been sent to the front as paramedics during semester break. After picking up wounded, Hans's troop transport is prevented by German soldiers from taking a shortcut through a restricted zone. Since the wounded require immediate treatment, the transport ignores the interdiction and drives through the field. There Hans witnesses the execution of scores of Russians, who fall into mass graves. This scene, which is constructed to increase identification with Hans Scholl, nonetheless distances viewers from him; it breaks the suspense of the fictional narrative and moves them to contemplate the historical meaning of the scene. Verhoeven cuts between the scene of mass murder and Hans's eyes as he watches the killings. Hans exchanges looks with an ordinary soldier, an acquaintance who is in the field as a guard. The soldier watches the killing and shrugs as if to ask: "What can I do? I am, after all, an innocent bystander only following instructions."

The mass murders, as presented here, are not just part of the fictionalized movie about youthful resisters. The scene is more brutal than any previous scene, and it is held on-screen for longer than is needed to satisfy the narrative. Because the scene does not follow the pattern of the rest of the movie, it breaks the suspense and interrupts identification with Hans. It does not call forth a simple emotional response—how could such a monstrous act be going on?—a response that would be consistent with the thriller aspects of the movie, but rather asks the viewer to contrast the reactions of the two young men, Hans and the soldier, to the act of horror. It is up to the viewer to decide which reaction might have been his or her own—to accept and turn away as does the soldier, or to risk death and commit acts against the state that might hasten the end of the war.

With this scene of mass murder in a Russian field, Verhoeven confronts viewers with an uncomfortable situation. Having identified with the political activities of the student resisters, spectators easily recognize and endorse the motivation of the White Rose revealed in this scene. On the other hand, spectators also recognize that the position of the ordinary soldier in the field presents a more typical response to governmental actions. The juxtaposition here of two responses to the Third Reich finds a parallel in scenes of civilian life. Whereas Sophie, the other students in the group, and Professor Huber respond by working against the Nazis, others respond like the janitor, who dismisses thanks for capturing the Scholls with a casual "I was only doing my duty."

Verhoeven's movie forces viewers to examine their own understanding of the responsibility each individual carries for the actions of the government. Viewers recognize that the Scholls and their friends commit acts against the Nazi regime out of strong religious convictions, that they oppose the government because it has overstepped the moral bounds that give it legitimacy. But viewers also recognize that the block warden, the postal clerks, and the janitor, all of whom inform on the Scholls, and the citizens who may not inform but who go along with the state nonetheless, also act out of loyalty, or what they perceive as loyalty, to their country. At a different historical moment, with another government, their actions would be considered legitimate. Because the fictional narrative leads viewers to side with the Scholls, the choice of the citizens who inform or passively support the Nazis is seen to result from opportunism and poor judgment. Yet the documentary drama suggests that the choice to go along with objectionable policies was not that unusual.

By melding fictional narrative and documentary drama, Verhoeven has created a disturbing and powerful film. The two narratives of *The White Rose* work together to prevent the vicarious thrill of identifying with the heroes and heroines (history continually interrupts the narrative to prevent this identification) and the pleasure of feeling morally superior that comes from historical hindsight (the suspense of the fictional narrative postpones the history lesson). Whenever spectators are brought into the movie through the eyes or ears of the heroic characters—listening to speeches, looking up when there is a knock at the door, watching as prisoners are murdered—these moments of witnessing history also take viewers out of the film and give them pause to reflect on historical reality. Although the fictional narrative may allow spectators to temporarily identify with the heroes and heroines, the historical drama makes it clear how exceptional these resisters were. It suggests to viewers that, rather than make the Scholls' choice, they might easily have made the choice of the townspeople and soldiers who represent ordinary people.

Five Last Days

▲▼▲

Percy Adlon's *Fünf letzte Tage* (*Five Last Days*, 1982) focuses on the religious faith that was the source of Sophie Scholl's strength in opposing the

Nazis. The narrative begins after the arrest of the group members. Except for an early scene in which Hans is interviewed, the movie is about Sophie's interrogation and her coming to terms with her political activities. The story is told from the perspective of Else Gebel, a woman with whom Sophie shares a cell during her imprisonment. From the first scene, in which she hears of the arrest of the students, until the final one, in which she prays for Sophie's soul, Else refuses to give up hope that Sophie may be spared execution. For her and for two other prisoners, Sophie represents the hope that nazism will not last forever. An actor who is being held for a minor political offense tells Sophie: "Even the others, the Gestapo are impressed by you. We are powerless. You are hope. The White Rose, in this time of being without hope, are our voices. The pamphlets, hope, hope, hope."

Percy Adlon is known for his films about women and their growth through contact with other individuals. His films are almost formulaic. In each, the central character's strengths and weaknesses are revealed in her contacts with others. In *Céleste* (1981) Adlon studies the isolation of Marcel Proust's housekeeper as she ministers to the writer during his last years. In *Zuckerbaby* (*Sugar Baby*, 1984) he reveals the beauty of the obese heroine as she realizes a love fantasy. In *Bagdad Cafe* the abandoned Jasmine's self-assurance surfaces as she confronts the bossy Brenda. The effect is similar in *Five Last Days*. Sophie Scholl's character unfolds against the background of the equally religious and stoic Else, who, unlike Sophie, believes that people have a duty to practice self-preservation.

Adlon became interested in the topic of the White Rose because of the relationship between these two women. He knew that Verhoeven was already at work making a film of the White Rose, and he was uninterested in treating the subject himself until he came across this line in a book by Hermann Vinke, *Das kurze Leben der Sophie Scholl*, 1980, translated into English in 1984 as *The Short Life of Sophie Scholl*: "There was another witness in those days between the 18th and the 22nd of February 1943, a witness who was moved by sympathy and empathy and who therefore was more involved and personal."[11] Adlon structures his film around Else. The audience becomes aware of the capture of the Scholls as their arrest is reported to her in the Gestapo headquarters where she works as an inmate office helper. From that moment, whatever viewers learn about Sophie comes from Else. Even in those scenes where Else could not have been present, Sophie relates the events to her: for example, a dream sequence and Sophie's interrogation by the Gestapo. The character of Else serves a double function: she gives veracity to the story, as hers is an eyewitness account; and she offers viewers an entry into the film, a perspective from which to relate to Sophie Scholl, whose saintly aura might otherwise be forbidding to them. Else, too, is noble, but her opinions are easy to share—indeed, viewers want to share them. Although she disbelieves completely and sincerely in the Nazi cause and is willing to fight against it, she does not forget that "God's first rule is self-preservation." Thus, although she is in the Gestapo jail, she works in the office processing other prisoners. In addition, her crime is not exceptional: she was helping her brother distribute antigovernment leaflets and got caught the first time she attempted to do so.

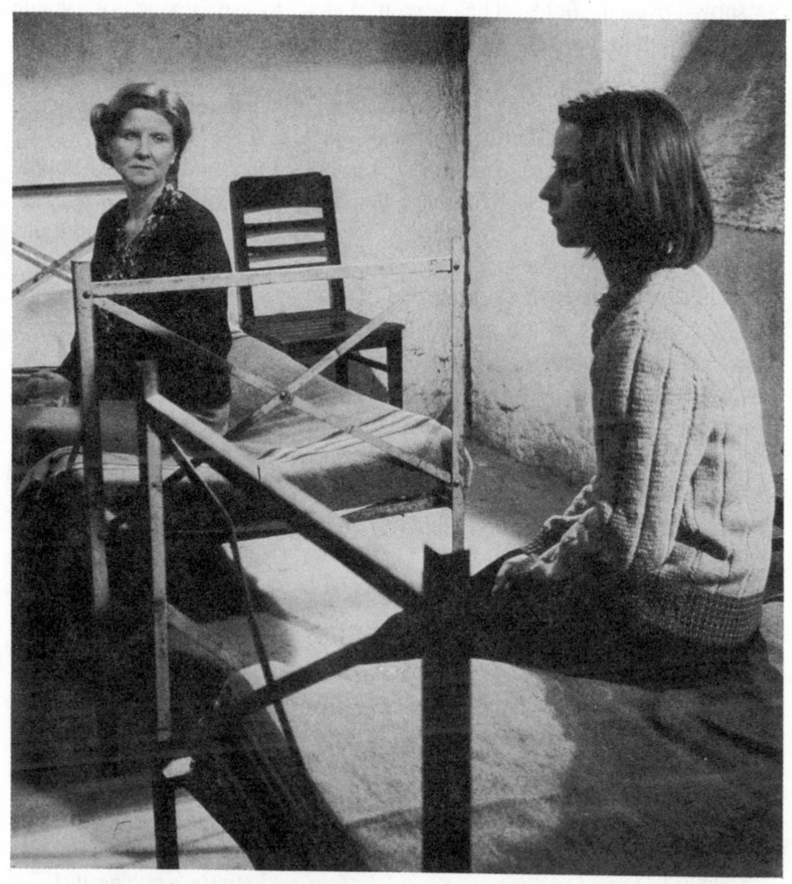

Five Last Days (1982). Else Gebel (Irm Hermann, left) and Sophie Scholl (Lena Stolze) talk in their cell. Courtesy Filmverlag der Autoren and Inter Nationes.

On one level, *Five Last Days* is a film of martyrdom. Reviewers have referred to the film as a hagiography, and to Sophie as Joan of Arc.[12] Sophie may not hear voices, but she is depicted as a saint. During her discussions with Else, in which the dialogue often turns to monologue, the camera captures Sophie's visage in close-ups; not only her words but even her facial expressions reveal her goodness. In one dialogue cum monologue, she compares herself to Moses. Opposition to Hitler and the Nazis is clearly a religious cause in her mind. To give in to the threats of the Gestapo and thereby save her life would be to betray her cause, even though the cause is already lost. During a conversation with Else, Sophie begins to narrate a dream in which she and her friends are running through a snow-covered field. The screen fades to an image of young people—Sophie, her brother, and their friends—frolicking in the snow as she describes her brother's proof of the existence of God: if there were no God to breathe fresh air into the atmosphere, all creatures would suffocate. As she relates her brother's philosophy, there is a shot of Hans exhaling into the air, his purifying breath driving away the clouds, just as Sophie believes the White Rose will chase the darkness from the German soul. The musical background—Schubert's "Death and the Maiden"—highlights Sophie's extraordinary character.

Those who criticize the portrayal of Sophie Scholl as a saint overlook the function it has in the movie. It places her actions beyond reproach. Viewers are directed away from the activities of the White Rose and toward the activities of the others in the movie—those who oppose Hitler in a modest way, and those who support him. It frees spectators to decide who the real traitors and patriots are. In one scene the camera focuses on the face of Sophie's Gestapo interrogator. This official delivers a long monologue about the achievements of the Third Reich, accented by the staccato sounds of the stenographer's typing. Punctuating his statements with appropriate, studied hand movements, he is an image of reasonableness as he tells Sophie that Hitler has

> eliminated joblessness, done away with the class system, shaken off the Jewish parasites. The Führer has won great victories and given the Aryan race new living space. There are good races and less valuable ones. The Führer may commit injustice if it furthers the good of the nation. We must obey him, regardless of what he commands, because he has the big picture in mind and we have only our selfish motives. . . . Do you and your pedantic morality want to return to the chaos of the Weimar Republic? Do you really want your defeatism to destroy everything that Germans have achieved through sacrifice since 1933? There is such a

> thing as German honor which even you must feel in your blood whether you want to or not. If you had thought about it, you would never have done this.

The camera is focused on the speaker throughout the monologue, which is delivered in a moderate tone lacking passion, as if even the speaker does not believe his words.

The monologue contains the seeds of its own deconstruction by any audience with a minimal grounding in history. Phrases like "Aryan race," "more living space," "Jewish parasites," and even the title Führer call forth a negative emotional response from viewers who know that these were code words to justify illegal expansion beyond German borders and genocide. Viewers who know the consequences of Hitler's policies—a ruined economy, a defeated country, bombed-out cities, millions of needless deaths—immediately recognize the hollow nature of the interrogator's words. They know who is destroying Germany. When the speaker suggests that the true patriot will follow Hitler even when Hitler breaks the law, Adlon cuts to a full shot of Sophie's face, which fills half the screen as she replies to her interlocutor's remarks, "You are mistaken." She admonishes him that his view of the world is wrong, not hers, and that she has a sense of guilt for Nazi crimes, which she begins to enumerate:

> . . . murder of Jews; kidnapping of Polish nobility to fill the bordellos of the SS; the men dying in barbed wire; innocent soldiers starving and freezing at Stalingrad; and the debasement of German women into baby machines. . . . I feel guilty because we can no longer read, write, speak, hear, and look at that which we find beautiful, worthy of knowing, and true. I feel guilty because I was too weak, too timid, and too apathetic to use my strength and all my thoughts against a murderous regime which despises humanity.

The camera cuts to the interlocutor, who responds, "Only what you do is aimed against the government and what I do is done for it." Again the camera cuts to Sophie, who proclaims, "You say that only to assuage your guilty conscience." And as if to grant her point, in subsequent scenes the interlocutor brings Sophie food in her cell and warns her she ought to write her parents since she is to be executed the next day. In a scene outside the narrative, the interrogator speaks to the audience and admits that none of the letters ever made it through the censors.

It would be difficult for viewers to relate to the extraordinary resistance practiced by Sophie Scholl. To help viewers understand her resistance, Adlon includes Else and two male prisoners, whose acts of opposition to the Nazis, while serious enough to lead to imprisonment, are ordinary enough not to intimidate viewers. Theirs was a more realistic reaction to totalitarianism. Although Else does not accept nazism ("The Nazis and the Christian faith do not go together") she embraces life ("One has a duty to stay alive"). Her transgression is to have distributed fliers for her Communist brother. One of the male prisoners insulted Hitler in a cabaret act; the other listened, and allowed neighbors to listen, to foreign broadcasts on his radio. Such individual acts of resistance were clearly not intended to defeat the Nazi system. But they allowed these individuals to keep the self-respect they might have lost by turning their backs on politics. The ordinariness of what they did helps viewers to identify with their acts of resistance. It also reminds viewers that there was an alternative between the martyrdom of Sophie and the criminal acceptance of the interrogator.

It Happened on the 20th of July

▲▼▲

The best-known German resistance movement was centered in a group of officers who, unsatisfied with the conduct of the war, plotted to kill Hitler. The leader of the movement, which has become known as the "Twentieth of July" because of the day in 1944 the assassination attempt took place, was Col. Graf Claus Schenk von Stauffenberg, chief of staff to the commander in chief of the home army. He had been wounded in the war and consigned to a desk job because of a paralyzed hand and a missing eye, over which he wore a patch. Stauffenberg headed a ring of officers who started plotting against Hitler in 1943. After several aborted attempts, Stauffenberg succeeded in placing a bomb next to Hitler during a meeting at an army camp on 20 July 1944. The meeting had been scheduled for a bunker but was moved to a building with windows, lessening the force of the explosion. Moreover, though Stauffenberg had placed the bomb near Hitler, before it exploded an aide moved the briefcase in which the explosives were located behind a pillar. As a result of the diminished force of the explosion and the protection afforded by the pillar, Hitler escaped with minor injuries. The officers behind the plot tried to keep Hitler's escape secret long enough to win over important elements in the army, but they were thwarted in this attempt and arrested. Several were summarily executed in the courtyard of the building where they were caught. In the ensuing months, thousands more were accused of treason and executed.

There has been controversy over the motivation of the officers involved in the plot. The main question has been whether the officers acted out of moral revulsion against nazism or whether they simply recognized that Germany had lost the war and wanted to negotiate better terms for their country. Less generous critics have suggested that the plot was inspired more by the Prussian military ethos than a strong sense of morality (Rothfels, 123). Doubts about the officers' motivation were spread immediately by the German ministry of propaganda, which characterized the rebels as "the small group of blue-blooded swine." Amazingly, an American broadcast by the Office of War Information used similar wording, characterizing the attempt as the act of a "small group of blue-blooded reactionaries."[13] More amazing were the commentaries in leading American newspapers. The *New York Times* referred to the attempt as reminiscent of "a gangster's lurid underworld" and noted that the plot was carried out "with a bomb, the typical weapon of the underworld." The *New York Herald Tribune* wrote that, "if Hitlerism has begun its last stand by destroying the militarist tradition it has been doing a large part of the Allies' work for them." In another editorial, the *Herald Tribune* commented: "American people as a whole will not feel sorry that the bomb spared Hitler for the liquidation of his Generals. Americans hold no brief for aristocrats as such and least of all for those given to the goosestep and, when it suits their purpose to collaboration with low-born, rabble-rousing corporals. Let the Generals kill the Corporal, or vice-versa, preferably both" (Rothfels, 154–55).

The attempted assassination of Hitler was first dramatized by G. W. Pabst in *Es geschah am 20. Juli* (*It Happened on the 20th of July*, 1955) (also released as *The Jackboot Mutiny*) and was recently the subject of an American television movie, "The Plot to Kill Hitler" (1990). Neither Pabst nor the director of the American film tries to come to terms with the controversy inherent in the material. Instead, both directors exploit the potential for suspense in the theme of assassination. Pabst's film together with a second on the Nazi era, *Der letzte Akt* (*The Last Ten Days*, 1955), may have been his personal apology for having returned to Germany in 1940 to direct two films for the Nazi-controlled UFA studios, *Komödianten* (*Comedians*, 1941) and *Paracelsus* (1943).

Pabst, who got his start in silent films during Germany's golden age (*Die freudenlose Gasse* [*Joyless Street*, 1925], *Die Büchse der Pandora* [*Pandora's Box*, 1929]) was adept at examining social and personal questions. Yet in *It Happened on the 20th of July* he avoids questioning the motives of the conspirators, focusing instead on the meticulous manner in which the coup was planned. His purpose is not merely examination of a historical event but dramatizing an act that was an attempt to rescue "what little honor Germans had left." In the closing scene Stauffenberg and several other conspirators are lined up in front of a firing squad and shot. Although this is an accurate re-creation of what occurred, the scene is staged to emphasize the martyrdom of the men involved. It is reminiscent of the closing scene in *Rome Open City*, when the priest, a member of the resistance, is shot. In both cases the directors film the executions to emphasize the nobility of the resistance, granting it greater importance than it perhaps had in history.

Indeed, Pabst's movie is structured around presenting the assassination attempt as a well-developed coup d'état in which all details had been worked out. Furthermore, the narrative suggests that even after the plot was discovered it would have been successful if Joseph Goebbels, the minister of propaganda, had not controlled the radio and thus been capable of assuring the public that Hitler was still in power. The American television film avoids exaggerating the strength of the coup attempt; it portrays the plot as less developed than Pabst's film makes it. Nonetheless, it too is structured around a polarity between good and evil. Thus, in both films the conspirators are noble, attractive, and committed to freedom; the enemy is an undifferentiated "other." Moreover, the close escapes, the phone calls, and the ominous shadows in Pabst's film focus attention only on the action of the assassination attempt itself and leave unexplored the moral implications of the act.

By focusing only on the rightness of the German officers' actions, Pabst's movie, perhaps inadvertently, contributes to rehabilitating the reputation of the German military at a time when rearmament was occurring in West Germany. Although it is doubtful that Pabst's intent was to give the military a clean slate from which to build a new image, the film produces such a subtext, as do several other films that appeared at the same time: *Canaris* (1954) by Alfred Weidenmann, a film about Gen. Wilhelm Canaris, who was executed near the close of the war for high treason; *Des Teufels General* (*The Devil's General*, 1955); Hollywood's *The Desert Fox* about Rommel, who was implicated indirectly in the Twentieth of July plot; and a number of others about the good officers in the military (although not necessarily about treason), such as *The Doctor of Stalingrad*, *Dogs, Do You Want to Live Forever?* and *08/15*.

In the end the question arises whether Pabst's decision to ignore the question of treason, which the officers must have reflected on before they acted, does not lessen the impact the film could have had on viewers. The film functions like other Nazi-retro films: the suspenseful narrative brings viewers into the film, and its historical subject matter periodically breaks the cinematic illusion. But the film itself offers viewers nothing to judge. That is, viewers are not able to reflect on the choices that the officers had to make before acting against their government, because the officers never reflect on them.

Stauffenberg and the other conspirators simply act out of the same military spirit that infuses any war movie. As a result, their plot to assassinate Hitler can be read as mere mutiny rather than the courageous act of high treason that it was. Pabst's conspirators do not so much resemble their historical counterparts as they reflect Hollywood's romantic image of rebels. Löwenstein has written that "a resistance movement against a modern, totalitarian state is nothing romantic. And each one must face the decision by himself, whether it is 'worth it'—whether the sacrifice of one's life under such conditions, horrible, mean, degrading, is not after all senseless . . . or whether it would be better to 'preserve' oneself, for a better, for the right moment" (37). In *It Happened on the 20th of July* the better moment is present from the beginning. Moreover, the loneliness of individuals who must decide on their own whether to risk their lives for a principle is lost in an action that grows like a mass conspiracy. The suspenseful nature of the movie does not preclude viewers thinking about the sacrifice the men are making, but it does make it more difficult.

Winterspelt

▲▼▲

In *Winterspelt* (1977) Eberhard Fechner focuses on a less dramatic form of treason than assassination. The movie, which takes place on the eve of the Battle of the Bulge, speculates on the reaction of American authorities to a hypothetical situation: what would have happened if a German officer, believing that an upcoming battle would bring senseless deaths and suffering, had tried to surrender his troops to the Americans? The narrative suggests that such an act would have been seen as an act of treason even by the Allies, and would have been turned down, though acceptance of the offer would have saved both German and Allied lives. The film ponders a question that historians have asked since the close of the war—namely, did the Allies' insistence on an unconditional surrender prolong the war and cost more lives? Fechner concludes that this is the case. His film portrays a military mind trained only for battle. To the American officers who must accept or reject the offer to surrender, the German officer's act is treason. Whatever merits the acceptance of surrender might have—it will hasten the defeat of the Nazis, it will save lives—are outweighed by the nature of the act: it is untrustworthy and moreover offends the military sensibility.

Fechner is best known in Germany for his documentaries and for the film *Tadellöser und Wolff* (*My Country, Right or Wrong*, 1975). His documentary style is very much in evidence in *Winterspelt*: he concentrates on dialogue rather than action. Although the movie takes place on the front line, there are no battles, only talk, which mostly centers on the topic of surrender and whether to do so would be considered treason. The officer is worried about his honor and thus takes elaborate measures to protect his reputation. Fechner had trouble initially in getting his film funded by the quasi-governmental film board because in the original screenplay the go-between in the negotiations between the American army and the German officer was a Communist. Fechner obliged the board and changed the character to an antifascist. Although the board presumably had political reasons for its objections,[14] the change also broadened the political impact of the film. Had the go-between remained a Communist, viewers could have understood and dismissed the officer's defection as ideologically motivated. With the change, viewers must come to terms with the moral correctness of the officer's decision to commit treason. In this they are aided by the officer's own reflection on whether it is morally better to follow his conscience and surrender, thereby saving thousands of lives, or to obey his military training and allow the deaths that he knows the battle will cause.

The Devil's General

▲▼▲

Helmut Käutner's *Des Teufels General* (*The Devil's General*, 1955) is adapted from Carl Zuckmayer's play of the same name. A major theme of Zuckmayer's play, which he began in 1941 and finished in 1946, is the nature of treason. In the drama, Oderbruch a subordinate of General Harras, who heads military aviation, sabotages planes and releases them for service on the front. Even though his orders cause the deaths of German pilots, Oderbruch continues to send the planes into battle in the hope that doing so will hasten the end of the war. Another theme of the play is that of the "other Germany," that is, those pockets of noncompliance with official Nazi propaganda that existed within the Third Reich. In the film, whose screenplay was co-scripted by Käutner and George Hurdalek in collaboration with Zuckmayer, the "other Germany" is the major focus and the theme of treason is made subordinate to it.

The Devil's General (1955). General Harras (Curd Jürgens, right) and chief engineer Oderburch (Karl John) in a defective plane shortly before it crashes. Courtesy ZDF and Inter Nationes.

Zuckmayer became interested in his subject after reading a newspaper notice that a supply major for the air force had died. The dramatist remembered his friendship with the major during his Berlin days, when his friend had warned him to leave Germany because "there is no more decency here." The friend would have to stay, though, because he knew no other life, but that one day the "devil will fetch us all" (Ott, 248). Out of this sketchy remembrance, Zuckmayer constructed a play, and later a screenplay, about General Harras, an officer who refuses to fly for a special SS air force. His cynical remarks get him in trouble with his superiors, but since he is otherwise above suspicion he is allowed to continue serving as he chooses. Eventually he undertakes an investigation into mysterious crashes of new military aircraft and discovers that his subordinate, and friend, has been sabotaging them. On a test flight he and his engineer, Oderbruch, are killed.

In the film the planes are ordered to the front over the wishes of Oderbruch. His sabotage is an attempt to keep the planes out of action, not to cause deaths in combat. Walther Schmieding points out that this change relieves the subordinate of responsibility for what occurs. The changes that Hurdalek and Käutner made from the original also shift emphasis to the general and his noble character. According to Schmieding, the film therefore becomes a vehicle to cleanse audience members of their guilt for the past.[15] Schmieding overlooks, however, that the film's contemporary audiences could hardly have forgotten Germany's role in the war by 1955, the year of the film's release. Besides, the play does not confront its audience with the question, "Where were you during the war?" Rather, it is a dramatization of an intentional and acknowledged act of treason.

Nonetheless, it is true that the film gives only a vague picture of nazism and tends to romanticize the past and the pockets of opposition to Hitler. In one scene a wife who has lost her husband in one of the sabotaged planes exclaims that she "never believed in the Nazis. My husband died for nothing." In another, Oderbruch proclaims, "Not only those who cause evil are evil but also those who stand for it." Such homilies probably were well received by audiences looking for diversion from what actually occurred in the past. Accordingly, even though the film shows indignation, it suggests that those who resisted somehow corrected for Nazi transgressions. This suggestion is heightened by the film's avoidance, for the most part, of depictions of Nazi crimes.

Brainwashed

▲▼▲

Films that treat the resistance in Austria face an intriguing problem: how to represent resistance in a country that was invaded and annexed like other countries, and yet also shared with Germany a cultural and historical heritage, bonds suggesting that it was an integral part of the Third Reich. Given the furor in recent years over the Nazi past of Austria's president, Kurt Waldheim, it is not an exaggeration to state that Austria was both a willing and a reluctant supporter of national socialism. The dilemma faced by directors is how to portray the resistance without at the same time turning the portrayal into an apologia for Austria's role in Nazi Germany. Furthermore, directors must decide whether to depict resistance as an internal movement against the government or as a fight against an outside aggressor. Two films produced almost 30 years apart—*Schachnovelle* (*Brainwashed*, 1960) and *Eine Minute Dunkel macht uns nicht blind* (*A Minute of Darkness Does Not Blind Us*, 1986)—approach the problem similarly. They portray Austria as the victim of German aggression and ignore the role that Austrians may have played in the national socialist policies of their country.

Gerd Oswald's *Brainwashed*, based on a novella by Stefan Zweig, is an example of a film that could have explored issues of guilt and responsibility among Austrians but went sadly awry. Film critic Karl Schumann wrote unkindly that the film proves, once again, how the German "problem" film has an "anti-Midas touch": "Whatever literary works it touches, it turns to chaff."[16] As harsh as these words are, they contain a grain of truth. Oswald, a Hollywood director and the son of the German emigré Siegfried Oswald, fashioned a conventional psychological thriller out of material that could have addressed the issue of Austrian acquiescence in the *Anschluss*, the annexation of Austria by Germany. Starring roles went to Curd Jürgens and Claire Bloom, both foreign actors who were well known to Hollywood. Jürgens plays an influential Austrian lawyer and patron of the arts who rescues artworks for the Austrian Catholic church by bringing them safely into hiding. He is captured by the Gestapo, sequestered, and brainwashed in the hope that he will turn over the art and support the Nazis, who feel a man of his stature could be of service to them in Vienna. Bloom plays a ballerina who sells out to the Nazis for career advancement but helps the lawyer escape once she realizes what her compliance with the Nazis means. This plot is placed within a frame that shows the lawyer, obviously ill, arriving at a ship that is to take him to freedom. On board, he confronts an arrogant Russian chess master by attempting to best him in a game of chess. The main story is told through a series of flashbacks suffered by the lawyer during the course of the game.

Striving to be topical by incorporating history, the main narrative offers typical signposts of the Third Reich: Nazi salutes, Gestapo sneers, and swastikas. In the frame the attempt to incorporate history consists of objections by some of the passengers, especially the arrogant Russian, to having refugees on board. The main narrative suggests that Austria had no choice but to accept the Anschluss, that individuals and institutions, such as the Church, proved powerless to resist it. And yet, no one in the film is treated kindly; all acquiesce too easily. The bellhop, raising his arm in the Nazi salute, has no reason to do so other than a desire to cooperate. Likewise, the ballet director, presenting Nazi art rather than his preferred works, is going along only for the sake of his career. The ballerina, until confronted by the lawyer's deteriorated condition and courage, is quite happy to benefit from the Nazi power brokers. Even the Church cowers before the Nazis, although there is little reason to do so. All go along, the film suggests, first out of fear, but also because eventually giving in is easier than resisting.

One bright spot occurs early in the inner narrative, as waltzing couples in a ballroom each pass before the camera, offering comments about the Anschluss. Couples are both pro and con, and the scene promises a film that might deal with the issue of the Anschluss itself. The director, however, abandons this theme and opts instead to develop the inner narrative of the film as a melodrama depicting the lawyer in isolation (the brainwashing) as he attempts to keep his sanity by memorizing the 150 greatest chess games in a book stolen from Gestapo headquarters. The attempt to break his resolve is underscored by discordant music, a faucet that drips louder the longer he is confined, and dramatic shadows thrown by the screen in the window of his cell. The window screen's shadow forms a chessboardlike grid on the ceiling upon which the lawyer plays his imaginary chess games. The melodrama in this middle segment places too much emphasis on the individual's struggle against an adversary, thereby losing the awareness of the enemy being the ideological system behind the conflict. The conflict is presented as solely between the lawyer and a Gestapo officer with a new method for making people talk. The suspense in the film stems not from the moral dilemma of resistance but from the question of whether the officer's new technique—new for him in that it is psychological rather than physical torture—will work. Consequently, even given the desire to reflect on history, no history is presented to the audience, at least not in the middle segment of the movie. Instead, this 1960 film reminds viewers as much about the brainwashing techniques of the cold war enemies as it does about the Nazis. Moreover, some linkage may be suggested between the nationality of the arrogant Russian chess champion, complaining about the presence of refugees aboard ship, and the subject of the main narrative.

A Minute of Darkness Does Not Blind Us

▲▼▲

Eine Minute dunkel macht uns nicht blind (*A Minute of Darkness Does Not Blind Us*, 1986), directed by Susanne Zanke, is based on the memoir of the real-life resister Grete Schütte Luhotzky, an Austrian active in the underground. In some ways, the film is much more engaging than *Brainwashed*: Zanke is not only interested in the suspense value of her subject matter but also concerned with questions of conscience. But *Minute of Darkness* never rises above being a film of rehabilitation for the Austrian character. The line between good and bad is precisely drawn, with the Austrian resisters on one side and the German Nazis on the other, an us-against-them scenario.

In spite of these problems, Zanke's film does grapple with the question of what options are available to those who disagree with a government in which their influence for change is limited or nonexistent.

Early in the movie, in a flashback, Grete and her husband discuss the necessity of leaving Austria so that they "will be able to hold our heads up after the war." They move to Istanbul, where Grete is drawn into the resistance movement. She returns to Austria to deliver a package but is captured and sent to prison when the movement is betrayed. Placed in pretrial isolation, she is finally tried and found guilty but is not sentenced to death as she had expected. The end of the war brings her release and her determination to pursue a career in architecture. This simple story provides Zanke with opportunities to focus on two themes: first, an examination of the relationships, following the Anschluss, between Austrians, the Nazis, and resisters; second, an exploration of a theme of equal importance to Zanke, namely, solidarity among women.

Zanke implies early in the film that, although Austrians are not actively fighting the Germans, they are opposed to the Nazis. Grete and the other women are befriended by an attendant in the paddy wagon taking them to prison and by a prison guard who sympathizes with their antigovernment activity. In a holding cell, Grete meets the inhabitants of a village whose residents have been arrested en masse for failure to cooperate with the Nazis. Grete's apparent ignorance of Nazi policy is a weakness in the film and would seem to be another means of exonerating the Austrians. Grete, who has had the advantage of not being in a country with a controlled Nazi press, has to be informed by an Austrian in prison of the use of the gas Zyklon B at Majdanek, the concentration camp. Furthermore, before her arrest she becomes ill upon discovering that a family of Jews to whom she was bringing a present has been taken away to a camp. She seems not to have known that such things were occurring.

The theme of women's solidarity occupies the film during the prison scenes that precede Grete's trial. Once in prison, Grete survives only because of the comradeship of the other women. Zanke builds the solidarity among the women through a series of scenes. As Grete enters the cell, she worriedly whispers "solitary confinement." She finds, however, that by moving a table to the window and standing on her toes she can see out and converse by sign language with the other women. Several other means of communication are developed by the community of women. They learn a system for communicating through the pipes by pounding. The language is taught during a session in which the women are all handcuffed in a classroom. They pound out a system of Morse code together. As the scene progresses, the pounding gets louder until it is clear that the resolve of these women, even in prison, will not abate. Following this scene, there is a cinematically effective and romantic scene of the women at their windows, shown only in silhouette, arms spread in Christ fashion, as one woman sings a lament. Solidarity is again the focus of a scene utilizing a peculiar means of communication. When the commodes in the cells are flushed at the same time, the empty pipes allow for momentary communication between cells. During one such session Grete, with her face next to the toilet, begins to sing the "Internationale," but here it does not so much signify solidarity among workers of the world as it does solidarity among women.

As Nazi-retro film, *Minute of Darkness* emphasizes a theme of solidarity among women during the Third Reich, a theme also found in *Peppermint Frieden* (*Peppermint Peace*, 1982) and *Deutschland, bleiche Mutter* (*Germany, Pale Mother*, 1979). In these three films war and Nazi ideology become male constructs. Zanke's film asks us to identify with the heroism of the characters, but their heroism has a distinctly feminine cast. As the women are let out of prison, for example, four of them lie in the grass and discuss the future. Grete wants to build humane homes for workers. The other women want to work with children or go into social work. It seems that politics will still be left to the men.

▲▼▲

The films of the resistance have one effect in common: they put the viewer at ease about history, suggesting that someone else carries the responsibility for what occurred under the Nazis. Directors are careful not to alienate viewers from the filmic world. The strategies they use to enhance the credibility of the narratives and to bring viewers into the film are varied: characters are portrayed as leading exemplary lives and "doing the right thing" as regards nazism. They are neither marginalized nor made into eccentrics, even though their efforts at resistance may be extraordinary.

The members of the White Rose, for example, are shown as otherwise normal students from good families, enjoying birthdays, watching good movies, and making love on picnic outings. The aristocrats of the Twentieth of July movement are good soldiers, good officers. Only in the American treatment of this movement is there a reference (in a comment by Stauffenberg's mother) to an officer coming from a different, a special, class of people. There is nothing in the characters that would make viewers reject them or question their actions. Even Jürgens's character in *Brainwashed* cannot alienate viewers because they are familiar with his bourgeois individualism from plays and other films. The characters in *Minute of Darkness* are decent to the core. They leave Austria rather than support the Nazis, and yet they also are willing to jeopardize their safety and comfort and work for Austria's deliverance. The officer in *Winterspelt* does not commit treason lightly but agonizes over his decision to surrender. In so doing he becomes someone with whom the audience can identify. In short, while the characters may be caught up in atypical situations, their lives are otherwise normal. Their normalcy may obscure the history behind their situations, suggesting perhaps that these heroes and heroines are engaged in a game, but it also offers spectators a position of comfort from which to think about the films. Some Nazi-retro films give audiences more to think about than others, but all ask viewers to answer the questions, "Where were you" and "what did you do, during the war?" Some invite a greater range of responses, however, than others.

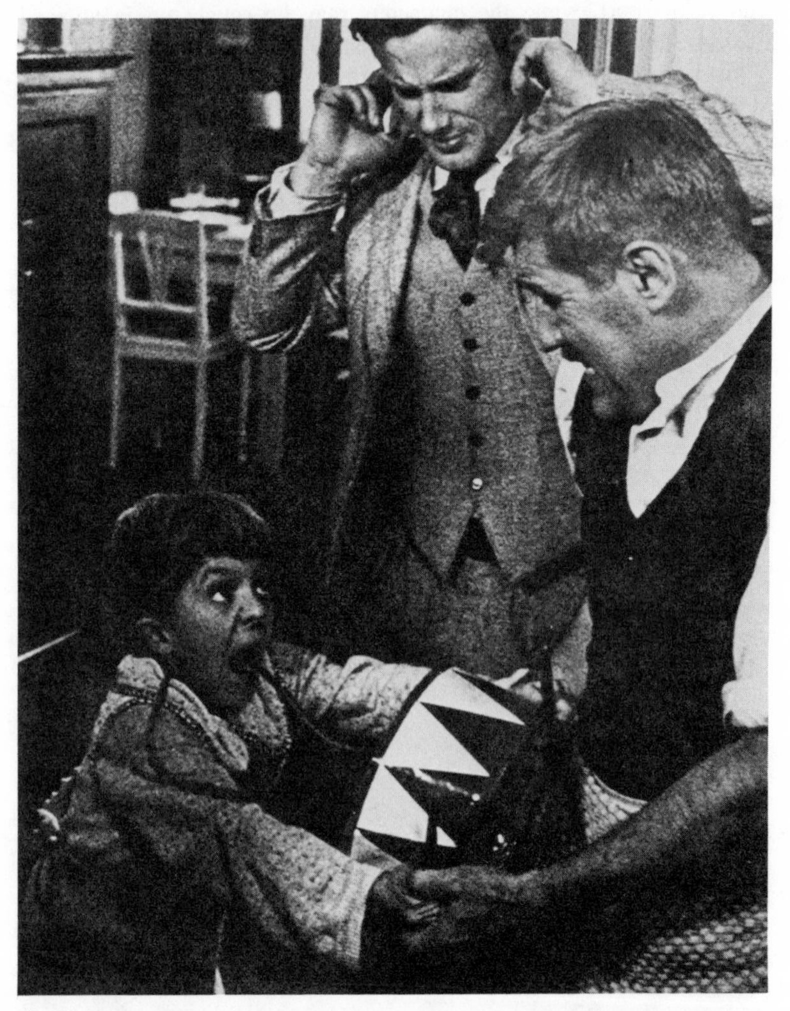

The Tin Drum (1979). Oskar's father, Alfred Matzerath (Mario Adorf, right), and a relative, Jan Bronski (Daniel Olbrychski), suffer Oskar's (David Bennent) piercing scream while trying to take his drum from him. Courtesy Inter Nationes.

chapter 5

▲▼▲

laughing at the "other"

When United Artists released Ernst Lubitsch's *To Be or Not to Be* (1942), the movie studio probably expected it to achieve the same success as Charlie Chaplin's lampoon of Hitler, *The Great Dictator* (1940). Lubitsch's film, however, was a failure. Although its lack of success can partially be attributed to the untimely death of the leading lady, Carole Lombard, the film's merriment in treating as dire a subject as nazism and persecution undoubtedly contributed to its downfall. Chaplin's film, after all, had been released before the United States entered the war against Germany. Moreover, its topic was a fictitious dictator in a fictitious land. By 1942 the United States was at war with Germany, the humorous adversary of *To Be or Not to Be*. William Paul notes that "the apparent split in *To Be or Not to Be* between comic characters and a realistic universe, the sense of consequentiality in the midst of all the flippancy," disturbed audiences and critics.[1] In short, moviegoers did not think that a dictator who had been funny before the United States entered the war against Germany was funny any longer. To laugh at death and destruction requires more distance than the changed circumstances allowed.

It may be difficult now, considering the portrayals of Nazis in American films and on American television, to believe that the Third Reich was ever considered an inappropriate subject for comedy. In films and on television the Nazi accent has come to signify either a complete incompetent or a monster so abhorrent that it deconstructs its own danger. Mel Brooks has contributed to this image of the Nazis as buffoons, first by lampooning them in *The Producers* (1968), and then in a remake of *To Be or Not to Be* (1984). In *Raiders of the Lost Ark* (1981) and its sequels, Steven Spielberg caricatures the Nazis as so absurdly evil that they cease to terrorize or be a threat. Although these films may initially frighten viewers, they know that nazism always destroys itself with its own excesses. Ironically, the Nazi caricature owes its lasting power to Peter Lorre, a political refugee from the Third Reich. Lorre played a child murderer in Fritz Lang's *M* and throughout his career traded on the persona he created in that film. His soft lisping voice and sinister look became his signature and was copied by cartoonists and comedians looking for an easy laugh.

On television the lampooning of nazism reached its zenith, or nadir, in the Colonel Klink character in the American show "Hogan's Heroes." Finally, in individual episodes of dramatic series as diverse as "Star Trek," "MacGyver," "The Twilight Zone," and "Mission Impossible," the Nazis have been reduced to a generic threat. They have become an inoffensive means to create humor and terror. The ultimate reduction of the history of the Third Reich into absurdity occurred in the 1983 American miniseries "V," which replaced persecuted Jews with persecuted scientists, transposed Nazi Germany to southern California, and metamorphosed Nazis into alien lizards from outer space. From these examples of trivialization it is clear that American popular culture not only looks upon Nazis as objects of derision and scorn—a status they do indeed deserve—but also reduces them to a nonthreatening "other." National socialism has been successfully banished to the margins of history.

In German popular culture, as might be expected, Nazis and nazism are taken more seriously. Of the over 100 German films and television movies that deal with the Nazi era, only a few are comedies, although many of the films contain humor as relief from the oppressive seriousness of their narratives. Thus a film like *The Marriage of Maria Braun*, which is primarily a melodrama, relying on the coincidences, moral ambiguities, and exaggerated emotions of that genre, has a sufficient number of comic elements to suggest a debt to screwball comedy. Barbara Hyams, for example, points to a similarity in style and pacing between the film's opening sequence, in which Maria and her fiancé are married amid collapsing buildings and falling bombs, and the opening of Howard Hawks's film *His Girl Friday* (1940).[2] In spite of the humor in *The Marriage of Maria Braun* and other films about the Third Reich, they remain primarily serious endeavors that include humor to provide comic relief or, as in Fassbinder's film, an additional means of distancing. Moreover, the humor focuses on the foibles and pratfalls of the non-Nazis in the films, making

The Marriage of Maria Braun. Maria (Hanna Schygulla), in the midst of a love affair, is surprised by the return of her husband, Hermann (Klaus Löwitsch). Courtesy Inter Nationes.

them more sympathetic. The Nazis are either a serious threat or an invisible "other," not the imbeciles portrayed by American films and television.

Although German films tend to treat the history of the Third Reich more seriously than American ones, there have been German comedies about national socialism, three of which—*Es muss nicht immer Kaviar sein* (*It Doesn't Always Have to Be Caviar*, 1961), *Aren't We Wonderful*, and *Die Blechtrommel* (*The Tin Drum*, 1979)—will be analyzed below. In these films the Nazis take on the same caricatured dimensions of Hollywood's portrayals: they are seen as buffoons, harmless dolts, or misguided shopkeepers. Furthermore, they are seen as inferior to their non-Nazi adversaries, and to the extent that viewers identify with the non-Nazis, they are seen as inferior also to the viewers. The extent of their inferiority is great enough that without a deeper understanding of history and national socialism, viewers could easily attribute Nazi successes to blind luck rather than developed and ruthlessly executed official policies.

Comedies in which national socialism provides the background illustrate one of the main principles of Henri Bergson's theory of humor: the focus of laughter must be directed outward. "However interested a dramatist may be in the comic features of human nature, he will hardly go, I imagine, to the extent of trying to discover his own. Besides he would not find them, for we are never ridiculous except in some point that remains hidden from our own consciousness. . . . To penetrate too far into the personality . . . would mean to endanger, and in the end to sacrifice all that was laughable in the effect."[3] Bergson's theory suggests that if humor in a Nazi-retro film, in which we are asked to laugh at Nazis and their supporters, is to succeed, it must place the characters being ridiculed in an inferior position to the audience. If not, the joke may be ruined as the audience realizes it is the butt of the joke and responds, "But that's not funny." In other words, the audience must not see itself in the Nazi representatives in a Nazi-retro film if the movie's comedy is to be effective. Fictional stand-ins for Hitler and his deputies must be caricatured sufficiently to preclude recognition of specific individual traits. To do so, however, is to marginalize the object of laughter, just as Hollywood has done. That is, to make Nazis laughable, filmmakers must first neutralize them to an insignificant force. To reduce their power in this way, however, distorts the role they played in history. Directors who wish to make comedies about the Nazis are faced with a dilemma: how do they remain true to history and yet make the audience laugh?

It is apparent that in a German film marginalization of Nazis and their supporters carries too much political significance to be acceptable. The director must therefore look for strategies to counteract the marginalization effect of comedy, a task that has not been altogether successfully accomplished in the movies under discussion. Perhaps this is why so few German comedies about Nazis are made: to serve the political requirements of the subject matter, the audience must somehow come to believe in the characters being parodied; but if reality enters into the caricatures, the humor of the film is lost. To preserve the humor, the characters must remain caricatures; but caricature tends to trivialize historical facts and perhaps even deny their historical reality. The more that historical characters are caricatured, the greater is the distance viewers feel from them; the greater this distance, the more likely that the joke will succeed because viewers will not feel that they are laughing at themselves. The greater the distance that viewers feel between themselves and the object of their laughter, however, the greater the likelihood that they will feel unaffected by the situations surrounding the caricatured characters. The result will be similar to the effect of "Hogan's Heroes," in which nazism has no political or historical meaning but exists only as a vehicle for humor. In this series, not only are Nazi villains eliminated as a threat to the non-Nazi characters—American prisoners of war—but they are eliminated as a threat to the viewers. These caricatures spare the sensibilities of viewers, who might otherwise see themselves in the villains if the characters were drawn more realistically. Admittedly, the possibility of recognition is remote in American films about the Nazis, but high in German films.

But in protecting the sensibilities of the audience by offering it only caricatures, film comedies about the Nazis trivialize their own political intent. By reducing the Nazis to absurd figures who are worthy only of scorn, a film comedy does signal its intent to fight their extremist views; as Jerry Palmer writes on the political intent of humor, "To mark something with the indelible seal of ridicule is intrinsically to indicate the will to oppose it."[4] But one has to ask: why waste energy opposing caricatures, particularly if the caricatures are feckless buffoons, as is often the case? In American films these caricatures have no purpose other than to marginalize the Nazis and turn them into the butt of the joke. American films make no effort to come to terms with history or to examine what Tony Pippolo refers to as the "twin themes of guilt and responsibility" in the Third Reich. Nonetheless, even portrayals like that of Colonel Klink in "Hogan's Heroes" can be criticized for presenting a distorted view of European history and sanitizing the horrors of existence for prisoners of war during World War II. Utilizing humor successfully in German films is even more difficult. The country is still trying to come to terms with guilt and responsibility for the past. It is probable, therefore, that German films will be held to a different standard, that what may be acceptable in American films on the Nazis will be unacceptable in German films, for reasons that will be explained in the following analyses.

It Doesn't Always Have to Be Caviar

▲▼▲

Geza von Radvanyi's *Es muss nicht immer Kaviar sein* (*It Doesn't Always Have to Be Caviar*, 1961), based on a novel of the same name by Mario Simmel, illustrates how easy it is to fail when making a comedy about the Third Reich. The film is a blend of spy movie and comedy, with the emphasis on comedy. The narrative tells of a French-born German who lives in England and accidentally becomes a triple agent while in Germany at the beginning of the war. His primary sympathies throughout remain with England. Like a James Bond character, he is adept at making love and making his adversaries look the perfect fools. In one tense situation, he takes time to have a gourmet meal with a Nazi colonel who is trying to discover the identity of the spy in their midst. During a close escape, he engages in a sexual interlude with one of the female spies, although time is limited. The comedy takes many forms in the film—slapstick, satire, parody, situational, and gags. For example, in one scene the hero stands in front of a portrait of Hitler in an identical pose as the Führer's. Or, as two of his colleagues are getting into a car, he tells one of them to be quiet because "the enemy is listening in"—a play on the sign warning about espionage, *Feind hört mit.*

The problem with *It Doesn't Always Have to Be Caviar* is that its comedy leads nowhere. The humor has laughter as its own end. When the hero duplicates the Führer's pose, for example, there is no justification in the movie for making such a comparison. The sight gag is funny, but unmotivated by the circumstances. The hero is a likable sort who has gotten himself into his current situation because of his easygoing nature. Viewers identify with him in the same way they identify with the hero in a romantic comedy whose distracted nature gets him into hilarious predicaments. He himself, however, is not a ridiculous figure, nor is he even remotely fascist in his politics or his behavior. Thus when the camera captures him in a position that is similar to Hitler's, viewers are distanced from the screen. But it is never apparent why alienation is being used at this particular point, or what equation the film is making between the hero and Hitler. There is nothing really to learn from contemplating the hero's predicament and how he got there. The fact is, he is in a mess but seems to be handling it well.

Films about the Third Reich need not, of course, display Germany's transgressions so openly and blatantly that viewers doubt the sincerity of the directors. One expects such films, however, not to ignore totally the film's historical referents. That is, even a comedy must acknowledge that its fictional world refers to a real time and a real place and, more important, must consider the seriousness of that time and place. Radvanyi forgets history in his comedy. The narrative would be just as effective set at any other time and involving any other constellation of countries. Set in the Third Reich, it becomes a travesty of history as it presents national socialism not as a cultural political force within the film but merely as a foil for laughter. There is no sociological grounding for the movement, no mention of ideology, and no political danger from the Nazis. In short, the film presents national socialism as an ahistorical phenomenon, similar to the way it appears in so many American films. And as an ahistorical phenomenon, it cannot refer beyond itself to the real historical moment, except perhaps to say that history was not as important as the history books report. If it does not refer beyond itself, however, then the film fails as a discourse on history and ends by trivializing its subject.

Aren't We Wonderful

▲▼▲

A similar fate almost befalls one of the most popular Nazi-retro films made in Germany, Kurt Hoffmann's *Wir Wunderkinder* (*Aren't We Wonderful*, 1958). This comedy, based on a novel of the same name by Hugo Hartung and a political cabaret developed from the book, received critical and public acclaim at its release.[5] It has remained popular over the years: in the United States it was a favorite offering of university German club film evenings until the early 1980s, when it was removed from general distribution. In Germany it is also popular among students and appears now and then on German television. The film has problems similar to those of *It Doesn't Always Have to Be Caviar* in that it also tends to trivialize the Third Reich. The film's characters are decidedly superficial, bordering on stereotypical. Its historical background is for the most part undelineated; the past is rendered as a series of well-worn clichés. The narrative reduces political conflict to comedic squabbles, ignoring the danger lying behind the conflict. Nonetheless, the film's overall structure raises it above a mere trivial portrayal of Hitler and the Nazis.

Aren't We Wonderful is a prepostmodern pastiche, that is, it speaks through several stylistic modes. In a true postmodern work, these styles would assault and confuse the senses, but here they are intended to soothe and enlighten the senses. Hoffmann's comedy borrows from cabaret skit, historical revue, romantic comedy, and melodrama. Its sight gags, verbal puns, misunderstandings, and caricatures elicit laughter in order to distance its audience from history. Yet its clichés, iconography, and allusions, unlike in Radvanyi's satire, invite comparison with their historical referents. Finally, its familiar narrative—boy meets girl, boy loses girl, boy marries girl—and its nonthreatening (in spite of the theme) atmosphere entice viewers into the movie's make-believe world. Comedy, history, and narrative offer viewers three perspectives on the past: the film's comedic discourse satirizes, parodies, makes absurd, and otherwise ridicules events and characters of the Third Reich; its historical discourse simplifies and makes representative these same events and characters; and its narrative discourse makes the events familiar in order to heighten the viewing experience. Problems do arise, however, from the subtexts that comedy, history, and narrative create for the viewer.

On the one hand, *Aren't We Wonderful* is structured like political cabaret: it has skits, whose situations viewers can easily identify; and it uses humor to limit viewers' emotional involvement in those skits. On the other hand, the movie is not entirely structured like cabaret. It uses the devices of narrative cinema to pique viewer curiosity about the characters, and the devices—plot, likable characters, easily identifiable enemies, tense situations, and happy resolution—in turn enable viewers to enter more easily into the movie and identify with the hero and heroine. This dual structure means that the members of the audience for *Aren't We Wonderful* are both attendants at a cabaret and spectators in a movie house. This structure provides them with a filmgoing experience that gives both distance from and involvement in the action on the screen, an experience that in turn prepares them to both accept a political message and ignore it in favor of entertainment.

As the opening credits appear, viewers hear the sounds of the audience's arrival, its own arrival, in the cabaret auditorium. Even though the "we" in the title suggests to viewers that they may be part of the satire in this cabaret, early scenes assure them that they will have sufficient distance from which to watch and experience the movie and laugh at its jokes; that is, like an audience at a cabaret, viewers will have positional superiority to events. The sequences that follow immediately after the credits establish the audience's moral and intellectual superiority as well. The camera in these early scenes traps Bruno Tiches, one of the film's villains, in a lie. As the narrative unfolds, it continues to trap him, increasing the difference between the self-image he wants to project and the real image that the camera exposes. When he claims to have changed—"my name is 'somebody else' "—the camera shows him to be the same old opportunist. When he insists he has come out against Hitler, the audience hears him admit that this happened only two years before, in 1956. In short, Bruno Tiches is portrayed as an inferior human richly deserving of the audience's scorn. The same belittling treatment is given to his friends and accomplices, the members of the Meisengeier family. Mrs. Meisengeier is a cinematic relative of Mother Courage. Although she lacks the wit and humanity of Bertolt Brecht's character—the title character of Brecht's 1941 play, which would have been familiar to German audiences—she shares her greed and willingness to use her children. As the owner of a bar in the heady atmosphere of Weimar Germany, she allows her daughters to work as bar girls, her eldest son to work as a gigolo, and her teenage boys to sell cigarettes and pornographic postcards. In a sequence that takes place during the Third Reich, she scolds her daughter, "A German woman doesn't smoke," all the while hiding a bottle of alcohol behind her back. Whenever the Meisengeiers appear, the camera captures their venality and monumental stupidity.

By reducing Tiches and the Meisengeiers to objects of derision the director allows his audience to feel superior to them. To not do so, as explained above, might ruin the comic effect of his jokes. Hoffmann keeps viewers at a distance from his villains by offering only caricatures of vices. As a result, the more these villainous characters are ridiculed, the greater is the distance viewers feel from them. And the greater this distance, the less likely it is that viewers will feel they are laughing at themselves; they are laughing at inferior beings who are not like them or their group. The laughter, in effect, marginalizes the villains and makes them easier to oppose. Indeed, the movie's portrayal so marginalizes Bruno and the Meisengeiers, and the Nazis whom they represent, that they cease to be a political danger. The hero, Hans Boeckel, reacts to them as if they were a fraternal organization playing a few pranks. He perceives Hitler and his followers as not worthy of serious consideration. Insofar as viewers identify with the hero, they may see the Nazis as he does—as parodies of ineffectualness. In one funny sight gag, the camera confirms Nazi fecklessness when it spotlights Hitler himself, or at least his boots, having a difficult time exiting from a revolving door.

Comedy, however, is only one of the discursive modes in *Aren't We Wonderful*. History is another, and its presentation contradicts the subtext created by the film's comedy. A cabaret skit offers a clear example of the danger that nazism represents in the narrative. Hans is attending a carnival celebration at which a student cabaret group is lampooning Hitler, in the same way that the cabaret singers who are part of the film's frame mock Bruno Tiches and the Meisengeiers. They sing of Hitler's origins as a painter, his overall incompetence, and conclude, "Adolf, you are a parody." Revenge for this ineffectual and therefore nonthreatening parody is taken, however, when a band of Nazi thugs, including Schally Meisengeier, breaks up the celebration by starting a brawl. The cabaret skit not only alerts viewers to the danger that the buffoon Schally poses for the film's hero but also refers them to Schally's historical referent, the Nazi thugs who disrupted social-cultural gatherings with which they disagreed. In this scene historical reality enters the movie, even if only for a brief time, and reminds viewers that the Nazis were not the harmless buffoons they see in the caricatures. The historical referents of the film point to a

Nazi party that was very much in control of the political situation and was a definite threat to democratic liberalism.

While the historical discourse in *Aren't We Wonderful* may give a truer picture of the dangers of nazism than the comedy does, correcting any impression the film gives that national socialism was a harmless political movement, it too falsifies the past by creating its own subtext. The only historical Nazi portrayed in the film is Hitler, whose appearance is brief and limited to a shot of his boots. The only Nazis in the fiction are Bruno Tiches, the Meisengeiers, and a few other thugs and goons, giving the impression that Hitler's power was based in the lowest class of Germans. History records, however, that Hitler's political base was broad and that his supporters came from all classes. According to the historian Gordon Craig, "The movement had a natural appeal to the lower middle class, which was the most vulnerable and the most resentful class in the country, but civil servants, teachers, members of the professions, and the Protestant clergy constituted a disproportionately high percentage of its membership" (11). Michael Balfour is more acerbic when he writes of the educated elite, "No natural scientists were prominent in the *Widerstand* [resistance]. . . . By 1938 there were 3,000 lawyers and 3,000 doctors in the SS" (13–14).

Aren't We Wonderful, for the most part, ignores the role that any but the underclass played in the Nazis' rise to power. For example, there is no indication of the support that Hitler received from academics. The only academic in the film, Vera's father, is an opponent of nazism. Also missing is any portrayal of the ease with which the media were able to switch to the Nazi banner, if they had not already done so before Hitler's chancellorship. With the exception of one opportunist, the entire staff of the newspaper where Hans works only reluctantly goes along, leaving one wondering if they all learned the Nazi salute merely to keep their jobs. The haute bourgeoisie, and even the petit bourgeoisie, the class that Craig says was most responsible for Hitler's success, are spared stigmatization with the Nazi label. With only insignificant exceptions, all of Hitler's support according to this movie came from the detritus of German society: the unemployed, the dissatisfied, prostitutes, and sociopaths. Furthermore, when the camera first focuses on the Meisengeiers, they are portrayed as wandering Gypsies. This portrayal is clearly meant to produce laughs and to suggest, as mentioned above, Mother Courage, and perhaps even Thomas Mann's "Gypsies in a green wagon."[6] It may be that allusions in the film to historical referents correct the picture, which comedy creates, of Nazis as ineffectual. Yet comedy also influences the picture of nazism that emerges from the film's historical information. And in cancelling out the subtext created by the comedy in the film, the historical referents create a second subtext that distorts the historical role Germans of all classes played in the Third Reich and that displaces Hitler's support to a group of outcasts.

The narrative level of *Aren't We Wonderful* creates its own subtext. Kurt Hoffmann's movie is both romantic comedy and old-fashioned melodrama. In keeping with both these film genres, its lead character is portrayed as both detached from reality and in conflict with it. As a romantic hero, Hans Boeckel is in a state of confused self-absorption, continually misjudging the situation around him. Even though this situation is dangerous, the focus of the genre excuses his lack of political awareness and assures the audience of a satisfactory resolution at film's end. In his role as a melodramatic hero, Hans Boeckel conforms to the expectations associated with the genre. He is a cardboard figure representing good going into battle against evil, and he acts, as does every hero in his situation, out of integrity, high moral character, and a sense of justice. Hans Boeckel, the hero, risks his life to help a Jewish friend escape the country (a theme that recurs in the majority of Nazi-retro films), refuses help from Nazi acquaintances to further his career, and jeopardizes his job after the war to combat nascent neonazism during Germany's postwar economic miracle.

It would seem that the narrative of *Aren't We Wonderful* offers still another subtext to direct viewers away from the historical truth. The world Hans inhabits is highly charged politically; yet, the political situation seems to present no real danger to him. Moreover, his choice to be apolitical and ignore what is happening carries no permanent consequences. The narrative portrays Hans as a drifter through history. As a student he laughs at the supercharged headlines of the newspapers he sells. Later, when advised by an opponent of nazism to read Hitler's *Mein Kampf* (1925–27), he replies, "That's not something people read." When asked by a Nazi thug if he has read the book, Hans Boeckel seems embarrassed and circumvents the issue. Finally, when he undertakes a positive political act and denounces Bruno Tiches as a Nazi, as film critic Hembus has pointed out, the war is over, and Hans is safe in his career (Hembus and Bandmann, 187). In short, integrity and morality are shown to be sufficient protection against the onslaught of nazism. While it is true that Hans Boeckel represents the pockets of decency and humanity that did exist inside Germany during the Third Reich, his survival suggests that his decision to do nothing against the indecency and inhumanity that prevailed was acceptable.

In light of what has been said above, it would seem that *Aren't We Wonderful* contains subtexts that trivialize and falsify history, absolving spectators from responsibility for what occurred during the Third Reich.

To the extent that this occurs, the movie would seem to be as much a failure at coming to terms with the Third Reich as *It Doesn't Always Have to Be Caviar*. For anyone who is not familiar with the events of the Third Reich, the comedic elements in the film suggest that the Nazis were benign fools, too inept and stupid to constitute a threat to democratic institutions. The film's historical references imply that only Germany's underclass supported Hitler and the Nazis. Finally, the narrative sets up a polarity between good and evil in which good, of necessity, triumphs, suggesting that its victory was without suffering and sacrifice. While these three subtexts may contradict each other, they also free spectators from thinking about questions of guilt and responsibility for what occurred in the past. *Aren't We Wonderful*, however, is not meant for audiences that have no knowledge of history, nor, for that matter, for audiences that want to avoid questions about the past. The film is intended for liberal, democratic viewers, such as would attend the cabaret that comments on the movie's narrative.

As mentioned earlier, entry into the film is through a cabaret, and like the audience of the cabaret, moviegoers are ready to be critical of what they see, including perhaps being critical of themselves. Moreover, viewers identify with Hans Boeckel. He is liberal, decent, and educated, traits that most people attending a political cabaret would ascribe to themselves and their friends. Viewers join the hero on his apolitical journey through the history of Germany in the first half of the twentieth century. Yet identification is never complete. The frame of the cabaret distances the audience from the hero and the narrative and causes viewers to ask, how could a man this astute and decent so misjudge the Nazis and fail to try to curb their power? The movie provides clear answers: Hans Boeckel may be intelligent and decent, but he is also naive, distracted, and uninterested in politics. He mistakes ideological goons for harmless buffoons. He is a German everyman who hides from the threat of reality by denying the threat and retreating into himself, mistaking inner immigration for political resistance. When viewers lose themselves in the narrative and identify with Hans Boeckel, they make the same mistakes that he does: they deny reality, just as he does, choosing to perceive the Nazis as bumbling idiots. Fortunately, their position in the theater allows viewers to recognize their error. They reflect on Hans Boeckel's misjudgment of nazism and come to judge his inadequate responses to it. The film brings viewers to question their own laughter at nazism and their acceptance of cliché in place of the particular. In the end they may even recognize that they are ready to reject the truth in favor of distortion because it is simply more pleasant for them to do so.

The Tin Drum

▲▼▲

Volker Schlöndorff's *Die Blechtrommel* (*The Tin Drum*, 1979), based on the best-selling novel by Günter Grass, was received well by critics and the public, both in Germany and abroad. In spite of its absurd imagery and irreverent view of history, it is generally not seen as a trivialization of its topic: the German middle class during the Third Reich. Although some critics object to the film's obscure symbolism, most praise its faithfulness to Grass's novel, its portrayal of nazism and the Third Reich, and its aesthetic merits. One American critic wrote, "Volker Schlöndorff's adaptation of *The Tin Drum* did more to reestablish the prestige of the German film than any single work produced since 1945" (Ott, 288).

The popular and critical success of *The Tin Drum* is not surprising if one considers the source and the director. Günter Grass's novel had been an international best-seller from the time of its publication in 1959. Although others had proposed to film the work before Schlöndorff did so, the prevailing thought had been that this was one of those novels that could not be filmed, especially considering that Grass did not, at first, want it filmed.[7] There are several reasons it was thought that the novel could not be transferred to the screen. The main character—the narrator, Oskar Matzerath—who is one of the most memorable figures in postwar literature, is a child-man who willed himself to stop growing at the age of three and whom most of the book's readers take to be a dwarf, in spite of Grass's insistence that Oskar is a normal boy. In addition to the casting problem, the epic proportions of the novel make it formidable for anyone wanting to film it. The narrative requires 500 pages to cover half a century. Oskar, now in a mental institution, tells the story in a series of nonchronological flashbacks. Moreover, the narrative perspective is inconsistent: sequences, sometimes even sentences, that start in the first-person voice shift into the third-person in the telling. Finally, the book's vulgar, bawdy imagery is daunting. Whoever has read *The Tin Drum* cannot forget the scenes of absurdity in the Danzig Polish Post Office, the black mass celebrated by Oskar and his gang, the young housekeeper Maria's savoring of the baking powder fizzing in Oskar's hand and in her navel, and a dead horse's head from whose every orifice eels crawl out and are then cooked for the evening supper. Any director who could master the problems presented by *The Tin Drum* would have a success.

Volker Schlöndorff, however, is not just any director. Born in 1939, he had the expertise to turn Grass's novel into a film blockbuster. He had already had experience in transferring novels to the screen: Robert Musil's *Der junge Törless* (*The Young Törless*, 1966), Heinrich Kleist's *Michael*

Kohlhaas—der Rebell (*Michael Kohlhaas*, 1969), Bertolt Brecht's *Baal* (1969), and Heinrich Böll's *The Lost Honor of Katharina Blum*. Indeed, since *The Tin Drum* Schlöndorff has gone on to specialize in screen adaptations of literary blockbusters: Marcel Proust's *Swann in Love* (1984), Arthur Miller's *Death of a Salesman* (1985), Margaret Atwood's *The Handmaid's Tale* (1990), and Max Frisch's *Homo Faber* (*The Voyager*, 1991). About his preference for screen adaptations Schlöndorff has said: "A great part of my experience in life is reading. A filmmaker translates an experience into cinema. And I consider it legitimate to translate my reading experience into film to try to recall what moved me."[8]

To solve the formidable problems of making a manageable film narrative out of Grass's epic tale, Schlöndorff eliminated the frame and flashbacks but kept Oskar as an offscreen narrator as well as a principal in the on-screen story. He also ends the narrative in 1945 rather than continuing it into the years of the economic miracle, as Grass does. To capture the novel's changing perspective, he shifts the camera's point of view, sometimes showing scenes through Oskar's eyes, at other times putting Oskar in the center of the frame as the object of interest. As he explains: "It will not always work to stay in Oskar's skin. Just as he speaks sometimes in the first person and sometimes, alienatingly child-like, in the third, so must the film narrative at times be quite subjective and at times show his shock from outside."[9] At least one critic has voiced disapproval of this technique, writing, "The Oskar in the film now and again becomes the offscreen narrator and distances the viewer from the screen and yet at the same time, because of narrative perspective, forces him to adopt Oskar's position. The two don't belong together."[10]

Yet the two really do belong together, for they are Schlöndorff's way of enabling viewers to both identify with his characters and be distanced from them and the film. As has been discussed, alternating between capturing and distancing the viewer is important to any film, but particularly to Nazi-retro films. For a film like *The Tin Drum*, it is crucial. Imagine, for example, that Schlöndorff had decided to keep his audience at a critical distance at all times, not a difficult task considering the bizarre conceit he was transferring to the screen: a boy who willed himself to stop growing at the age of three, thereafter commenting on the tumultuous events around him by banging on a tin drum and letting out a glass-shattering scream. To alienate the audience and prevent viewers from identifying with characters and events, Schlöndorff could have cast a dwarf as Oskar and kept his camera at a distance. This would have enabled spectators to witness what the narrator was saying yet not take part in the narration. If the story had been told from the distanced perspective of one of the midgets in the movie's circus scene, for example, involvement in the narrative would have been thwarted; viewers would have been presented with a variation of Werner Herzog's *Auch Zwerge haben klein angefangen* (*Even Dwarfs Started Small*, 1970)—distanced from the screen at moments when they should be entering it.

But Schlöndorff does not want viewers to be permanently alienated from the screen: "My films are only good when I can identify with one person in such a way that I am given a foothold."[11] In *The Tin Drum* this "foothold," or entry, is supplied by Oskar, played by David Bennent, a 12-year-old boy acting in his first film. It is primarily through his eyes that viewers are invited into the movie. References to the size of Bennent's eyes run like a leitmotiv through Schlöndorff's diary on the making of the movie. They are, as Andrew Sarris writes, "a-once-in-a-lifetime movie marvel."[12]

The back and forth between subjective and objective perspectives in *The Tin Drum* parallels the shifting roles of Oskar and those around him. Oskar, his parents, and his neighbors are sometimes actively engaged in the world around them and sometimes passive bystanders. This has left some critics confused about how to interpret Oskar's character. Eleanor Ringel, writing in the *Atlanta Constitution*, asks, "Does he [Oskar] represent encroaching Nazism? . . . Or is he a symbol of the gullible German people being encroached upon?"[13] Another critic, Joy Gould Boyum, asks, "Just what in this blatantly unreal and suggestively symbolic context is the bizarre Oskar meant to embody? Is he intended as an artist-outsider? As parody *Übermensch*? And if he is either or both, what does it all add up to anyway? Are we meant to find the key to nazism in Oskar's willful rejection of maturity? Or in his corresponding refusal of responsibility?"[14]

The dual perspective that the movie offers to viewers renders these questions irrelevant. Nazism is too complex a subject to be reduced to a few symbolic characters, to a simplistic allegory of a drummer witnessing history from his diminutive perspective. Grass's novel did not so reduce nazism, and neither does the film. By casting a boy with whom viewers can identify, using camera strategy that helps them enter into the narrative, and at the same time providing narrative distance that takes them out of the film, Schlöndorff allows viewers to participate in the film's world as well as to observe it. In this way the movie experience that viewers have while watching *The Tin Drum* becomes a metaphor for the underlying theme of the movie: the participation in, while remaining aloof from, what went on during the Third Reich. By identifying with Oskar and his relatives and friends while remaining detached from them, spectators are doing what the characters do: joining in the circus atmosphere of national socialism while remaining distant from it. The objective and subjective perspectives correspond to a desire to be removed from the action while also involved in it. This idea is expressed by several of the characters, but in particular by the film's hero, Oskar. The following two examples illustrate this idea.

When he is 12, Oskar's parents take him to a circus, where he meets Bebra and his troupe of midgets. Bebra is, at one and the same time, the future victim who escapes victimization by taking command of his situation, and an opportunist who knows how to use the tide of nazism to boost his show business career. His bizarre appearance and stage act distance viewers from the movie. He is made up like the devil and, resembling Mephistopheles, tempts Oskar to join their troupe. Oskar, however, prefers "to be a member of the audience and let my little art flower in secret." During their dialogue the camera focuses on Bebra, compelling identification with what he says. "Our kind must never sit in the audience or the others will run us. The others are coming. They will occupy the fairgrounds. They will stage torchlight parades, build rostrums, fill the rostrums, and from those rostrums preach our destruction." With distance eliminated, his statements become part of the audience's experience, at least until Oskar's parents come to take him away. As his last remark Bebra repeats, "They are coming," and this time the camera pulls back, revealing the worried looks on the faces of Oskar's parents and breaking the bond with Bebra.

Bebra's admonishment to take part, although meant for Oskar, is followed up in a later scene in which Oskar's father, Matzerath, replaces a portrait of Beethoven with one of Hitler (a motif found in several Nazi-retro films) and proclaims to Jan Bronski, his cousin-in-law, "A man cannot stand aside. He must join in." During the next scene, of a Nazi rally at the fairgrounds, the perspective again shifts back to that of Oskar, who has crawled under the speaker's rostrum to watch the festivities. But he does more than watch. He taps out a waltz beat on his drum as the festivities go on and, with this simple action, throws everyone off beat until the band, the audience, and the Nazi officials are all waltzing around the field. Throughout this scene the camera switches repeatedly between Oskar's perspective below the disrupted event and an outside perspective from which viewers see Oskar taking an active role in the disruption. One is tempted to ask here, would it really have been that easy to throw a monkey wrench into the Nazi movement? Nevertheless, the scene is another illustration of Bebra's message—that to control history you have to take an active role in it. But what has the scene shown? It has shown one man, Oskar's father, "joining in," which is not the same as being in control. And it has shown a child becoming a part of, and even influencing, the activity while hiding in a safe corner from what is going on.

The switching between objective and subjective camera perspectives, between merely observing and being in control, leads to an ambivalence that pervades *The Tin Drum*. All the characters are caught in the predicament of choosing between having to act and being acted upon. With the exception of Bebra and eventually Oskar, they all choose to be acted upon. Matzerath joins the party although he had been apolitical earlier. Jan Bronski, by barging into the Danzig Polish Post Office at the wrong time, finds himself fighting the Nazis purely by chance, he would have preferred to stay neutral. Sigismund Markus has himself baptized, hoping thus to fit in; when he finally recognizes that fitting in, for him, is impossible, his only remaining choice is to carry out the suicide to which his aloofness and refusal to emigrate have condemned him. Agnes, Oskar's mother, unable to choose between Jan, the foreign, irrational non-German, and Matzerath, the traditional, middle-class German, also ultimately dies because of her indecision. Only Oskar is able to choose to act in a timely fashion. First, he joins the entertainers and stays in control of his situation. Then, when confronted by the Russians, he presses a Nazi pin into Matzerath's hand. Matzerath tries to get rid of the pin by swallowing it, but he chokes; in this way, Oskar ends his own link with nazism. He is then free to choose to start growing again.

Nazi iconography in *The Tin Drum* contributes to the ambivalence that is the primary mode of the movie. The parades, the uniforms, the speeches, and the symbols re-create a 1933–45 Nazi Germany that seems real. The lurid reds of Nazi banners, arms raised in the Nazi salute, and the words spoken by the Führer about the start of the war—"Since five this morning, we have been shooting back"—are familiar to viewers from memory, history books, and, most important, other films on the Nazis. Even though the icons are distorted and obviously being parodied, their reflection in the eyes of the child Oskar balances that distortion; viewers expect a child to see things in an exaggerated way, and thus the icons become real. For the audience, the film's world becomes a believable portrayal of the German middle class in Nazi Germany. The iconography mirrors and alludes to how that middle class was misled and brought about its own destruction through its own gullibility. In one of the more powerful scenes, Oskar relates, in the form of a Grimm's fairy tale, the story of a people who once believed in Santa Claus when Santa Claus was in reality the gas man. His narration precedes scenes of a burning synagogue and by the death of Oskar's Jewish friend Markus. These scenes are followed by a triumphal procession of Hitler into Danzig, with only Hitler's outstretched hand and arm visible, cutting diagonally across the screen from lower left to upper right, signifying the obscene rape of the Polish Corridor. Nearby, a parade bystander swoons at the thought of seeing the Führer. In these scenes the perspectives shift once again. At one moment, viewers see Oskar in the frame; next, they are listening to him narrate external events. The ambivalence mirrors the confusion of the people involved in the events being depicted. Everything in the film seems factual, that is, it seems that this is the way people acted. At the same time everything seems wrong; people should not have acted thus. As confidante of the narrator Oskar—whose role in this bizarre yet real world is to guide viewers through Nazi Germany as observer-participants—viewers experience the same ambivalence as the characters. They go along with the choices being made even as they see the destruction these choices bring.

The ambivalence of the camera perspective in *The Tin Drum* does not allow viewers to feel separate from the characters, who are shown to be responsible for nazism. Viewers take part in the Rabelaisian atmosphere of the carnival, which the film uses as a metaphor for the Third Reich. The shifts in camera perspective, from subjective to objective and back again, put viewers in the center of the movie: the subjective perspective allows them to participate in the festivities; the objective helps them judge. Unlike *It Doesn't Always Have to Be Caviar*, in which the object of laughter becomes a marginalized "other" for the merriment of the audience, thereby reinforcing in the audience a sense of superiority, *The Tin Drum* gives no such assurance. The film goes beyond the accomplishment of *Aren't We Wonderful* also. In Hoffmann's movie the Nazis still remain inferior to those laughing. *Aren't We Wonderful* does, however, help audiences recognize that they are laughing at, and thereby marginalizing, something that was and is dangerous. In *The Tin Drum* Schlöndorff alienates viewers from the narrative so that they also recognize how their laughter is marginalizing a threat. The threat, however, is from people similar to themselves. In spite of the quirks and idiosyncrasies of the characters (most viewers can hardly identify with a wish to stop growing), viewers identify with those characters, at least insofar as ambivalence toward life and its choices is concerned.

The difference between Radvanyi's *It Doesn't Always Have to Be Caviar*, Hoffmann's *Aren't We Wonderful*, and Schlöndorff's *The Tin Drum* in their probable effect on viewers can best be explained by comparing them to four non-German movies: Mel Brooks's and Ernst Lubitsch's *To Be or Not to Be*, Bob Fosse's *Cabaret*, and Federico Fellini's *Amarcord* (1973). Although the intent behind the *To Be or Not to Be* films is serious, they resemble *It Doesn't Always Have to Be Caviar* in their portrayal of the Nazis as inferior "others." To be sure, the Hollywood films of Brooks and Lubitsch have reason to present the Nazis as an "other": they are meant for American audiences, which, at least while watching Brooks's film, is predisposed to laugh at Nazis. Nonetheless, there is no doubt that the Nazis in these films are characterized as inferior to viewers and that, in turn, the viewers are made to feel a certain smugness at having endured their antics. Were it not for the hindsight of history, which lets spectators know why the Polish Jewish characters are so desperate to escape Warsaw, these films would hardly rise above the trivialization of the past of which Radvanyi's film is guilty.

In *Cabaret* and *Aren't We Wonderful* one can again see a positing of the Nazi as an entertaining "other." Both films also depict opposition to the "other," an unwillingness to take the threat of the Nazis seriously. The outdoor scene in *Cabaret*, in which the Nazi youth sings "Tomorrow Belongs to Me," serves, like the cabaret in *Aren't We Wonderful*, to remind viewers of the error in perceiving the Nazis as harmless. During the song, viewers are pulled into the movie through the manipulativeness of a sentimental folk song-like ballad. Just as the characters in the meadow are swept along, so too are audience members. Even though viewers with hindsight know where the power of such songs led, and even though they may feel a chill at the thought of the power behind the ballad, they nonetheless are invited to join in the love feast for a little while. Eventually viewers are jolted back to reality and a sense of history by the evilly laughing face of the Master of Ceremonies; they can then separate themselves once again from nazism. Viewers recognize the evil implicit in the false patriotism, but they are not meant to feel implicated in it.

Finally, in Fellini's *Amarcord* the audience is guided through a carnival atmosphere. At times a storyteller gives viewers the distance they need to judge the events on the screen. At other times the camera makes them a part of the movie by involving them in the nostalgic reminiscing of the adolescent hero. The effect is similar to the one that Schlöndorff achieves in *The Tin Drum*; indeed, the similarity in styles between the two films is striking. So too is the similarity of intent: to explain the appeal of fascism and the reasons for its rise without excusing the people who allowed it to gain control of their hearts and minds. In *Amarcord* and *The Tin Drum* the carnival trope is turned on its head. In a carnival, the participant is made to feel a part of a group that is carrying on a subversion of mainstream thinking (Stam, 93–94). In these movies viewers join a minor but indigenous political movement that turns humanistic values on their head. Once the anarchy succeeds, the formerly marginalized group gains power and becomes the new mainstream.

Angry Harvest (1984). Elisabeth Trissenaar with Armin Mueller-Stahl before entering her hiding place in the cellar. Courtesy Inter Nationes.

chapter 6

▲▼▲

the "final solution"

Nothing reflects the criminality of the Third Reich more clearly than Hitler's policy of genocide, euphemistically referred to by the Nazi government as the "Final Solution." The Holocaust, which occurred between 1933 and 1945, reduced Europe's Jewish population by one-third. Approximately 11 million people were murdered by the Nazis. The number of Jews killed is estimated at just under 6 million.[1] Considering these statistics, one may find it surprising that *Der Spiegel*, Germany's respected weekly, thought it appropriate to include the following question in an opinion poll that it commissioned the Bielefelder-Emnid Institute (similar to America's Gallup organization) to conduct on the hundredth anniversary of Hitler's birth: "Would you say that Hitler was one of the greatest German statesmen ever, if it were not for the war and the Nazi persecution of the Jews?" Such a question seems not only pointless but obscene. It assumes that the war and the Holocaust were not central to the national socialist agenda but can be wished away by a subjunctive clause. Such an assumption has been repudiated by history. As disturbing as the question itself, however, were the results: an astonishing 38 percent of respondents answered, "Yes, he would have been in this case." To be sure, the results varied by party affiliation and education level, but 22 percent of those with a gymnasium (college preparatory school) education answered affirmatively. Among respondents who claimed allegiance to Germany's ultraright party, the *Republikaner*, the figure was 67 percent. Even in the Green party, composed mostly of Germany's liberal and left-wing groups, 18 percent agreed with the statement.[2]

From the first of the Nazi-retro films, *The Murderers Are among Us*, to one of the latest, *Herbstmilch* (*Autumn Milk*, 1988), directors, like the *Spiegel* poll, have bracketed out consideration of the Holocaust and the persecution of the Jews. In many of the films discussed in this book the Holocaust is treated only peripherally, if at all. It is as if the directors, afraid of dissuading viewers from facing the past, have excluded the worst horrors of what occurred. Obviously, one cannot expect every film that tries to help viewers come to terms with Germany's history between 1933 and 1945 to focus on the genocidal policies of the Nazis. The Final Solution, however, was a cornerstone of the new world order Hitler was trying to create. Consequently, films about the Nazis, regardless of their themes—battlefront, adolescence, resistance—should at least acknowledge Hitler's war against the Jewish people. Regrettably, most of the films do not acknowledge it, even if some do not entirely conceal it.

Before the American miniseries "Holocaust" (1978) played to a wide audience on German television in 1979, German Nazi-retro films made only vague or obscure references to the systematic killing of Jews that occurred under Hitler's rule. Movies made prior to this watershed year depict isolated instances of anti-Semitism but do not place them in the context of a government policy. *The Murderers Are among Us*, whose title promises to expose those who murdered for the Nazis, focuses on an incident of mass murder in the theater of war rather than on the killings that went on in the camps. *The Murderers Are among Us* shows the execution of prisoners of war and civilians, as do *The White Rose*, *The Pedestrian*, and the Italian film *Night of the Shooting Stars*, among others. As horrifying and criminal as the mass executions in these movies are, they are carried out by individual soldiers as acts of revenge for the killing of Germans. They are thus given a reason, as unjustified as it may be. Moreover, the executions depicted are random events, not the carrying out of a systematic government policy.

References to the Holocaust in films prior to 1979 are veiled and oblique. The frankest acknowledgment appears early in the history of postwar film, in *The Murderers Are among Us*. The headline of a newspaper that had wrapped the lunch of the film's villain informs viewers "2,000,000 People Gassed." The appearance of the headline is so brief, however, that it might be overlooked. Moreover, it never specifies who was gassed. Toward the end of the film, during the flashback when the mystery of the mass executions is revealed, the hero crumples a star he had meant for a Christmas tree. Perhaps it is a Star of David, perhaps not. The scene goes by too quickly to even guess if this is a subliminal reference to the Holocaust or not. A more straightforward expression of Jewish persecution under the Nazis occurs in Kurt Maetzig's *Ehe im Schatten* (*Marriage in the Shadows*, 1947). Maetzig prefers to focus on a single case of persecution, however, rather than on the enormity of millions of Jews being murdered. The movie, modeled after a true incident, is about an Aryan actor who kills his wife, son, and himself rather than submit to Nazi demands that he divorce his Jewish wife. The film narrows the practice of anti-Semitism under the Nazis to the quandary of one individual who must decide between his work and his wife. Even though the story is faithful to the real-life incident, the fictionalization tends to make the actor and his wife into martyrs of Nazi persecution. That is, they are shown—or at least the actor is shown—as having a choice in their persecution and ultimate death. This tends to trivialize the deaths in the film. Maetzig later disapproved of the sentimentality in his film.

On the whole, early East German filmmakers have been less hesitant to refer to Nazi persecution of the Jews, even though they too avoid outright acknowledgment of the Holocaust. Moreover, the prime objective of their films seems to be to glorify the socialist worker. Only as a secondary theme are the films concerned with coming to terms with Jewish persecution under the Nazis. For example, in *Sansibar*, an East German production made by the West German Bernhard Wicki (*The Bridge*, *The Spider's Web*), the director depicts the danger that the Jewish heroine faces as she tries to flee to Sweden. She undertakes her flight after her mother commits suicide in order to give the daughter a better chance to escape. The heroine flees to a fishing village on the Baltic and is there befriended by a Communist who wishes to leave Germany because he has witnessed the brutal murder of a comrade by the Nazis; an ex-Communist whose wife is insane and who is, therefore, careful not to be conspicuous; a minister who is trying to save an Ernst Barlach sculpture from the Nazis; and a young man who dreams of sailing on the Mississippi. This unlikely group helps the woman escape to Sweden. Afterward the men all return to Germany to take up resistance against nazism. The message is clear: these men, who all have socialist affiliations, are clearly freedom fighters whose bravery and steadfastness in the face of fascism is meant to encourage contemporary East German viewers to continue to support the socialist state. A similar agenda is evident in Konrad Wolf's *Professor Mamlock*, a film in which the Nazis prevent a Jewish doctor from practicing medicine.

In 1959 Kurt Hoffmann made a timid foray, in *Aren't We Wonderful*, into the topic of anti-Semitism and Jewish persecution. Hoffmann's film marks a rather inauspicious beginning for films that acknowledge Nazi Germany's official policy of persecution. Although the hero's Jewish friend, Siegfried Stein, has to flee Germany, the film never shows him in danger. No reason is given for the urgency of his escape. Moreover, at the end of the war he returns to Germany as a conqueror but also as a benefactor, suggesting that his experience has been of positive benefit to him. The next films to refer to Jewish persecution appeared in the 1970s; the dilemma faced by Jews under the Third Reich remained a peripheral concern. Often the Jews are placed in danger as a way of emphasizing the liberal and humanitarian leanings of the German heroes and heroines. In *Die erste Polka* (*The First Polka*, 1978), for example, Montag, a Jewish figure who plays an important role in the novel on which this film is based, finds refuge in the heroine's summer cottage. Although his presence is necessary to bring about the denouement of the young hero's crisis, his role is so reduced that one wonders if he was left in the movie version only to make possible an allusion to anti-Semitism and to show that some Germans were philo-Semitic. The film *My Country, Right or Wrong* gives the same impression. The Jewish wife of a non-Jewish neighbor is shown kindness by the German heroine of the movie. The German woman allows her neighbor into an air raid shelter after the Jewish woman is excluded from the shelter in her own building. Except for the references that Montag makes to the Russian pogroms of his childhood, in neither of these movies is there any explanation of why Jews needed to be in hiding or of what awaited them if they were caught. Only in *Mädchenkrieg* (*Girls' War*, 1977), a film made around the same time, is there a reference to death in a concentration camp, when the mentally retarded son of the Jewish banker is sent off to such a camp. The banker himself seems to escape deportation to a camp by hiding out in a brothel frequented by Nazi officers.

Considering that early Nazi-retro films were made to help viewers understand events that occurred during the Second World War, it is not surprising that filmmakers avoided direct references to the existence of concentration camps. The films had other agendas. For example, films about soldiers on the front, such as *08/15*, *Dogs, Do You Want to Live Forever?*, and *The Doctor of Stalingrad*, attempt to reproduce the experience of soldiers on the front for soldiers in the audience, for their wives, and perhaps even for their children. The films try to explain what it was to be a soldier and to show that being a soldier was not the same as being part of the Nazi regime. Although it would certainly have been more honest to bring the Holocaust into such films, doing so would certainly have thwarted whatever rehabilitative or regenerative effect these war movies might have had on viewers. For the directors to have revealed the nature of the policies of the government the soldiers defended would have discredited the soldiers along with the government. Some members of the audience may have wanted to see the military discredited, but the majority surely preferred what they saw: soldiers displaying the soldierly virtues of loyalty, patriotism, bravery, sacrifice, and comradeship. For similar reasons, the rubble films made immediately after the war also avoided showing the true reality of what had occurred. In the East German film *Somewhere in Berlin*, for example, not only is there no mention of the Holocaust, but there are few reminders of how many people died in the war. The film depicts black marketeers as the enemies of the people and emphasizes how destructive defeatist attitudes can be. The final scene—which shows a convergence of youth from all over Berlin to help a man rebuild his workshop—is a textbook example of the East's socialist-realist aesthetic dogma: art should portray the power and the strength of the people. In films of this nature, reminders of the crimes that Hitler, the Nazis, and their supporters committed would have been unwelcome.

Other national cinemas displayed a similar reluctance to come to terms with the Holocaust. Filmmakers from non-German-speaking countries found thematic material in the Holocaust sooner than did German-language directors, but with few exceptions, even in non-German countries, the earliest films were not made before the 1950s and very few were made before the 1970s. In part, the absence of the Holocaust from feature films can be seen as a reluctance to exploit the suffering of those who perished under Hitler and the Nazis. Also a factor, however, must have been a desire to avoid confronting the most odious part of the past. For example, Alain Resnais's *Nuit et Brouillard* (*Night and Fog*, 1955), a French documentary on concentration camps, was greeted with a notable amount of resistance. The powerful images of Resnais's film evoke the horrors of the death camps. It was initially barred from being shown at the Cannes Film Festival in 1956 because a five-second shot depicted a gendarme in a French concentration camp in a clearly recognizable French uniform. Not until the shot was altered and the uniform covered up were the authorities satisfied that the movie would not harm the national reputation or, presumably, lay open to question the strength and resolve of the French resistance movement.[3] It was not until Marcel Ophuls's *Le Chagrin et la pitié* (*The Sorrow and the Pity*, 1970) that a French director again dealt with the subject of French collaboration with the Nazis.

In Italy, early postwar films were concerned more with coming to terms with Mussolini and the country's own internal struggles between Communists and fascists than with focusing on the plight of the Jews. Not until Vittorio De Sica's *Il Giardino dei Finzi-Contini* (*The Garden of the Finzi-Continis*, 1970) was there any notable attempt to deal with the Holocaust in an Italian feature film. Luchino Visconti's *La caduta degli dei* (*The Damned*, 1969), filmed a year earlier, focused more on the general question of the nature of evil in the Third Reich than on the genocide of the Jews.

One of the early exceptions to the silence surrounding Nazi crimes was Orson Welles's *The Stranger* (1946), an American film starring Edward G. Robinson, Loretta Young, and Orson Welles. This dark and claustrophobic film noir revolves around exposing and punishing a Nazi war criminal who has become a respected New England citizen. The film was unique both in its willingness to deal with the topic of Nazi criminality and in its warning that the murderers were entering American society. It was not until years later, however, that Hollywood films stated directly what Welles's film only intimated: Nazi war criminals were helped by the American government to enter the United States. This is the main theme of the American film *The House on Carroll Street* (1988). The presence of former Nazis in American society plays a part in other films as well, the most recent being Constantin Costa-Gavras's *The Music Box* (1989).

The first film to place the Holocaust at the center of its story was *The Diary of Anne Frank*, (1959), a Hollywood release based on the 1956 stage play by Frances Goodrich and Albert Hackett, which in turn had been based on the posthumously published memoirs of a young victim of the death camps. *The Diary of Anne Frank* introduces several themes, and ways to explore them, that are found in later films. It emphasizes the potential of its youthful heroine and laments the destruction of this potential by the Nazis. It focuses on the humanity of its Jewish characters. It places the indomitable spirit of its characters, especially that of Anne, against the background of a hopeless situation. It uses an ensemble of characters who each represent a possible reaction to the horror befalling them. Finally, the film introduces a tone of romanticism and even sentimentality that recurs in the films that would follow.[4] The protagonists in these films are generally depicted as naive and innocent. They display superhuman strength and perseverance. Their struggles are dramatized into major conflicts between good and evil. On the one hand, the romanticizing that these films engage in serves the fictional narrative. It enhances the cinematic illusion and makes it easy for viewers to enter the film, to identify with the characters. The degree to which the films romanticize also serves historical reality. The Jews did struggle against their persecution, even when powerless to prevent it. On the other hand, romanticizing shifts attention away from the crimes committed against individuals and emphasizes instead their resistance. This shift in focus distorts history as it transforms the victims of a criminal regime into political, religious, and racial martyrs. It suggests that the Jews died for a cause. But the Jews did not choose to die; they were murdered.

Eastern European directors turned to the Holocaust as early as the 1960s. Among the films from the East are the Polish release *Ambulance* (1962) and the Czechoslovakian film *Obchod na Korze* (*The Shop on Main Street*, 1965). In the latter, however, the focus is on the relationship between the old Jewish woman and the film's non-Jewish protagonist rather than on Jewish persecution. One of the earliest films to depict the systematic murder of Jews in concentration camps was the Czechoslovakian film *Transport from Paradise* (1962), directed by Zbynek Brynych. It was the first film, and remains one of the few films, to construct a fictionalized narrative of life in a concentration camp from documented reality. The fictionalized narrative of *Transport from Paradise* recreates the making of a documentary of the "model" camp Theresienstadt. Hitler had ordered the making of a documentary of this camp, to be entitled *The Führer Gives the Jews a City*. It was to be shown to the world as an example of how well the Germans were treating the Jews. Hitler's "documentary" created orderly streets, shops, a town square, and even a bank. It showed the Jewish inhabitants of this "town" enjoying both work and leisure activity. Brynych's film exposes the town as nothing more than a facade for a movie. Behind the stage sets, it shows the miserable conditions of the camp. It reveals that paradise is only as deep as a studio lot. *Transport from Paradise* emphasizes the art of propaganda, of selling an image to the rest of the world. It then deconstructs the image and shows how efficiency, orderliness, and system, which were the lynchpins of the camp, were used by Nazis in their attempts to demoralize and dehumanize the inmates before sending them off to other camps.

The Wannsee Conference

▲▼▲

Transport from Paradise was released in 1962. Not until the mid-1980s did a German filmmaker attempt to make a narrative film about Hitler's campaign to exterminate Europe's Jewish population. That film, Heinz Scheik's *Die Wannseekonferenz* (*The Wannsee Conference*, 1984), is a fictional account of a meeting that took place in February 1942 among high Nazi officials at a villa in the Berlin suburb of Wannsee. No other movie about the Holocaust, German or non-German, fictional or documentary, states as unequivocally that genocide against the Jews was a central policy of national socialism. The film reflects the views of the so-called intentionalists in the historians' debate that erupted among intentionalists and functionalists in Germany in the 1980s. In the view of the intentionalists, the Holocaust was the final outcome of a planned effort to eliminate Jews from Europe. Conversely, in the view of the functionalists, the Final Solution was more or less stumbled into because of circumstances, namely, the threat from the Soviet Union. In the mid-1980s, the debate shifted to the question of whether the Holocaust was a historically unique occurrence. In this debate the functionalists, or revisionists, in an attempt to relativize Nazi crimes against the Jews, pointed to the atrocities committed by Stalin in the Soviet Union. Although the film is not directly tied to any of the questions posed in the debates, the director of *The Wannsee Conference* certainly hopes to counter revisionist thinking. At one point in the movie someone asks Reinhard Heydrich, chief of security police and SS officer presiding over the conference, whether using transport trains to deport Jews to concentration camps will not interfere with the transport of troops to the war front. His answer is blunt and shocking. "It is not a question of priorities. The steps toward a Final Solution are as important as all other war efforts. . . . Whenever we fight the Jews, we're fighting for the Reich."

The dramatized dialogue between Heydrich and the other official is not based on a verbatim transcript of the conference. Indeed, none of the dialogue is verbatim since no word-for-word account of the proceedings exists. Dramatic dialogue is reconstructed from the minutes of the meeting and from speeches the historical counterparts of the characters made on other occasions. In short, the movie is fictional. The director's intent, however, was never to reproduce the exact words of the meeting. Given the unavailability of a transcript, that would have been impossible. Rather, according to *New York Times* critic Serge Schmemann, he wanted to "re-create as accurately as possible the language, the mood, the style of the men who gathered at Wannsee, to assign them words that they could really have used."[5] This decision, which succeeds in creating a highly dramatic and gripping narrative, also leaves the film open to the criticism that it falsifies history. Raul Hilberg, for one, writes in the *New York Times*: "Taken one by one, these are small alterations of facts, but viewed in the aggregate, the interspersed queries and replies, correct or incorrect, disturb and distort the rhythm of the conference itself."[6] Although one could ask what the correct rhythm of this conference was and how Hilberg knows this, his concerns are valid. There are no markers in the docudrama to tell viewers that some speeches have been invented and others rearranged. Moreover, there is no narrator to give viewers distance from the screen. It falls on viewers to distance themselves from the reenactment. Distancing is difficult at times since the drama is often so tense and gripping, the language such a perfect mimicry of Nazi cant, and the actors photographic copies of the original principals. In spite of its transparency, however, the film does not mislead. Embedded into the re-created dialogue are references to its fictional nature. Twice in the film, the director inserts explicit references to the nonexistence of a verbatim transcript of the meeting. At the beginning of the conference, for example, Heydrich informs the secretary not to make a verbatim account of the proceedings. At the conference's end, he tells Eichmann that in his report he should "be as clear as necessary and as vague as possible."

Hilberg refers to *The Wannsee Conference* as a "fascinating experiment." It certainly is that. With the exception of the offscreen voice that introduces the villa and the subject of the meeting, there is no narrator in the film to help viewers interpret the images on the screen. Indeed, as mentioned above, there is nothing in the film that distances viewers from the cinematic illusion with the exception of the subject itself. The characters are attractive, the setting is comfortable, the situations familiar. Only the topic is horrific. The film tricks viewers into listening to these men; they are ordinary, reasoned, and pleasant. Even the flirting between Heydrich and the secretary is calculated to enhance his "regular guy" image. Viewers find themselves in the room. Their glances move with the camera from character to character, coming to rest on whoever has the floor in the debate. The boardroom atmosphere, which is prevalent in the movie, further brings viewers into the film. The illusion is broken, however, whenever viewers reflect on the topic of discussion. And when broken, viewers recognize how central to nazism was the policy of genocide. They are shocked at the way in which racial hatred so permeated the everyday that extermination of a people could be discussed in the atmosphere of a board meeting. The message of *The Wannsee Conference* is blunt. Dr. Lange, commander of the security police in Latvia, for example, reports on exterminations in Riga and delights in reporting that Estonia is "free of Jews." He is an unabashed caricature of a Nazi officer. Although some critics have found his characterization overdrawn, his presence contributes to the overall experience of the movie. In the final scene Dr. Lange holds a stick above his dog and makes it jump. By freezing the frame when the dog is in the air, the director creates an effective metaphor for the everyday nature of the brutality of the Nazi regime.

Charlotte

▲▼▲

Given the systematic brutalization of the Jews by the Nazis, many directors have focused on attempts by Jews to escape persecution and death. A number of films tell stories about Jews before, during, and after escaping Nazi Germany. In films from *Charlotte* (1981) to *David* (1978), from *Regentropfen* (*Raindrops*, 1981), *38—Auch das war Wien* (*38—Vienna before the Fall*, 1986), and *An uns glaubt Gott nicht mehr* (*God Does Not Believe in Us Anymore*, 1982) to *Das Boot ist voll* (*The Boat Is Full*, 1980), *Bittere Ernte* (*Angry Harvest*, 1984), and *Hitlerjunge Salomon* (*Europa Europa*, 1991), filmmakers have created an array of characters, locales and life-styles. The mood of their films ranges from melancholic to euphoric, from acquiescent to defiant. The tone varies from depressing to uplifting and from resigned to angry. As different as these films may be, however, they are similar in one respect: they are all concerned with the political awakening of their politically naive protagonists. Consequently, they all offer the viewer an experience in consciousness raising. In *Charlotte*, for example, an intellectual and bourgeois family learns that its high cultural and intellectual standing does not make it immune to the policies of the Nazis. In *David* the family of a rabbi learns that there is no place of refuge for Jews in Germany. In *Raindrops* a family that defines itself as not only Jewish but German-Jewish finds that its long history in its town does not protect it. In *Europa Europa* the young Jewish protagonist increasingly recognizes the magnitude of his peril if his ethnicity is discovered. In these films and others about the Holocaust, the political awakening of the protagonists motivates the story. Through the gradual growth in consciousness of the characters, viewers gain insight into the economic, psychological, and physical violence that preceded the Holocaust and ended in the liberation or the death of the individuals involved.

Charlotte is a Dutch–West German co-production directed by Frans Weisz. It is based on the life of Charlotte Salomon, a young Jewish artist who lost her life in Auschwitz in 1943. The movie's imagery of light and dark, life and death, is complex, and its narrative structure, which includes flashbacks within flashbacks, is complicated. At times it is difficult to understand the film's story. The movie is about the title character's search for answers to questions about life, death, and love. The opening scene shows the red glow of a sunrise barely visible through a large window in Charlotte's bedroom. Slowly the sun rises higher, and the light fills the entire room, awakening the heroine to a new day. This opening juxtaposition of light and dark continues throughout the film. Scenes bathed in sunlight, mostly taking place in Willefranche sur Mer in the south of

France, alternate with scenes of darkness set in Nazi Germany. By the end of the film images of darkness will prevail over images of light. The metaphor of awakening to the light will come to symbolize both the potential of the young heroine and the destruction of her potential at the hands of the Nazis.

The tension produced by the juxtaposition of light and dark imagery in *Charlotte* reflects the struggle in the title character, who is striving against the melancholia that has afflicted members of her family—her mother, an uncle, and her grandmother have committed suicide owing to it. Her struggle, in turn, is but a reflection of the overall struggle in Germany at the time. Just as she must battle the family disease that threatens to take her life, so she, her family, and their Jewish friends must battle the irrational hatred of the Germans that threatens to destroy them. In one of the most complex and powerful sequences of the movie, Charlotte's father, Dr. Salomon, is at the university giving a lecture on the sanctity of life. Referring to the growing irrationality in the country, he consoles his students by reminding them never to forget that "the positive forces that we, as individuals, and as members of society, depend on . . . in the longer run . . . always triumph over the negative forces of disease, oppression, and destruction." As he talks, the camera moves to the left and looks down a dark hallway. As Dr. Salomon continues, the camera shows two uniformed Nazi officers slowly making their way toward him. His voice gives way to those of a choir. The film cuts to the choir and a conductor, in front of whom the silent figure of Mrs. Salomon slowly rises. Gradually the choir is drowned out by shouts from the street of "Jews get out, Jews get out." The chanting mocks the optimism of Dr. Salomon's lecture. It breaks the cinematic illusion that the sequence had been creating and leads viewers to reflect on how misplaced the earlier optimism is.

Other scenes and characters reflect the fascination with death and dark imagery of German romanticism. In one scene, for example, Charlotte sits with her mentor, Daberlohn, in a rowboat as it glides across a lake. The screen is completely dark except for a ribbon of light that divides the screen. Daberlohn, trying to encourage Charlotte to continue her artistic work, advises: "If we dare not look death in the face, our work will never have any validity. Think of Orpheus. He had to descend to the underworld, the kingdom of the dead, to find Eurydice, and she was none other than his own soul." As lightning flashes, and to Charlotte's remark that she loves the storm he replies, "Thunder and lightning have been the greatest forces for cleansing the world." Romantic sentiments of this sort pervade the entire movie and reflect its theme: that life and death, light and darkness, rationality and irrationality, are intertwined in ways that cannot be fathomed. Such rhapsodizing about the romantic, underscored by the musical track, shifts the balance of the movie's polarities in favor of darkness and even suggests that fate has a hand in what is occurring. When at the end of the film Charlotte walks against the light toward the water, having earlier declared she found joy in life, it is unclear whether Charlotte has truly found life or whether she is willingly placing herself in a position where she will be captured by the Nazis. The viewer is left wondering whether Charlotte has succumbed to the family disease and is committing suicide.

Romanticism is also apparent in the way the film presents history. A radio announcer proclaims that Germany is rising. The screen fills with a torchlight parade and focuses on the marching boots. There is a cut to a class photo session. As the camera shows the girls posed for the photo, an offscreen voice intones the names of girls who are to be excluded from the photo. One by one, the young, clearly Jewish girls leave the center of the frame and stand on the side. Once again, light and dark are juxtaposed in word and image, and dark is victorious. Furthermore, the scene builds in such a way as to suggest that the victory of the forces of dark was preordained. Indeed, a comparison of Dr. Salomon's lecture about the forces of light always winning with what happens in the film and in history, gives rise to a note of fatalism. The nightmare of the Third Reich becomes a trial visited on the Jewish victims.

On the other hand, the movie provides viewers with the opportunity to see through the romanticism. The strangeness of the visuals and the elegiac tone of the acting have the effect of alienating spectators from the narrative. Pushed out of the illusion, the viewer is free to judge the characters' actions, to recognize that their political aloofness is a mistake. For example, in the scene of Dr. Salomon's lecture, the abrupt entrance of the Nazi officers into the arena of enlightened reason suggests that reason was not a viable force against Hitler. Beauty is similarly ineffective against the onslaught of barbarism. As beautiful as the choir's song is, it cannot drown out a chorus of "Jews get out." These scenes suggest that sometimes the idealism of philosophy and the beauty of art, if they are to survive, must give way to practical action.

David

▲▼▲

David (1978), directed by Peter Lilienthal, also makes a statement about practical action. The movie could not be more different from *Charlotte* in style and tone, nor in the cinematic experience it gives viewers. Based on the novel *David: Story of a Survivor* by Joel König, which in turn was based on the author's diaries, the film is totally without pretense. The use of a hand-held camera and natural sound in some scenes lends the film the look of cinema verité. Although the script is tighter than *Charlotte*'s allowing for less spontaneity than in other Lilienthal films, the style is, nonetheless, less controlled than that of Weisz's film. At times it seems that scenes were developed as they were being shot. The lack of pretense in style is reflected in the lack of pretense in the story—told in linear fashion without flashbacks or narration—and in the characters: a rabbi, his wife, and their three children, the youngest of whom is David. Not all critics have been pleased with the film's unpretentiousness. For example, Janet Maslin writes that "Mr. Lilienthal's tendency is toward understatement, and there are times when he carries it too far. Certain key aspects of the story are ill-explained."[7] In Judith Christ's opinion, "its pedestrian pacing, confused scripting, and unremarkable performances make it a minor addition to the film literature of the Holocaust."[8] On the other hand, the understatedness pleases some critics. Carlos Clarens writes, "Just when you thought you'd seen and heard it all about the Holocaust, along comes Peter Lilienthal's *David*, possibly the most lucid film account yet of that dark and haunting age. . . . There are no predictable melodramatics."[9]

The story tells of an adolescent Jewish boy who, between 1933 and 1943, witnesses persecution, is persecuted himself, sees his parents and his older brother taken to a concentration camp, and finally escapes to Israel. Lilienthal has said that he deliberately wanted the camera to know no more than David, from whose perspective the film is told. Since viewers identify with David, they might be expected to be as much in the dark about the meaning of particular events as the boy. But viewers have the advantage of historical hindsight, and so this is never the case. When the film begins, David is beat up by a group of boys in Hitler Youth uniforms. He is at a loss as to why he is being beaten, but viewers can call on their knowledge of history to understand what is occurring. Later he is at a celebration of Purim when a group of Nazis pass by the synagogue chanting, "Jews get out," which his father, hoping to allay the fears of those present, interprets as "Youth, come out." The time then moves forward to 1938, and David is moving in with his brother in Berlin. The owner of the apartment is a man who has changed his name from Cohn to Conn so as not to announce to the world that "a Jew lives here." The boy is again confused since his father has told him he must be proud of being a Jew. The audience recognizes the irony when Mr. Conn is the first character captured and tortured by the Nazis.

David (1978). David (Mario Fischel) changes quarters, keeping one step ahead of the secret police. Courtesy Inter Nationes.

David is indeed an underplayed and underdirected movie. At times it is like watching a documentary or even a home movie. At other times the film is suspenseful and offers the same melodramatic twists as more conventional films; by the end of the film the scenes are quite suspenseful. Viewers become as concerned about David's well-being during his flight from the Nazis as they do for characters in more classically melodramatic fare, such as *The Diary of Anne Frank* or "Holocaust." The result is that viewers have a classic movie experience—identifying with David and his family, becoming concerned about their welfare—yet they also have an "art house" cinema experience, being distanced from the characters and contemplating the story. The cinema verité style gives the film the look of Italian neorealism; the story resembles the "found story" that is the ideal of those films. As a result, viewers accept David's experience as his experience, not that of someone trying to convince them that he had this experience.

The viewers' cinematic experience while watching *David* is enhanced, but also manipulated, by the director's reluctance to let them know more than the characters know and by the viewers' knowledge, nonetheless, of what could happen to the characters. Along with David, viewers experience the fear of being hunted, but unlike him, they recognize the true extent of the danger he is in. Thus, even though the film lets viewers see the world only from David's perspective, they are not a captive of this perspective. Nothing in the film lets viewers outside of the film's world, but viewers can nonetheless contemplate the larger picture. They think of the concentration camp and possible death that await the hero should he be captured. The outside knowledge that brings viewers to reflect on the larger picture, however, also puts them back in the movie: their concern for the hero is increased by their knowledge of what could happen to him. In this way the movie manipulates viewers. It leads them to see only the answers David himself finds, or more accurately, stumbles upon because of his indomitable nature. Just when his ordeal seems darkest, a deus ex machina appears in the form of a boss with a conscience. Concerned about what is happening to the Jews, he helps David escape. This manipulation of emotions, more than the film's murkiness, may be what disturbs the critics. For the film truly has a Hollywood ending. The sound of a train, which in most Nazi-retro films is an aural icon of the period, signifying transport to the death camps, here is transformed into the sound of freedom. In the ensuing sequence, David is on a boat. The scene of him sailing toward shore is interspersed with newsreel shots of boats landing in what will become Israel and Jewish settlers welcoming others to the promised land. Like "Holocaust" and *Europa Europa*, *David* ends with reference to the future Jewish State of Israel.

Europa Europa

▲▼▲

The story of Agnieszka Holland's latest film, *Hitlerjunge Salomon* (*Europa Europa*, 1991), based on the implausible but presumably true autobiography of Salomon Perel, is told with considerable humor. The film's hero, Solly (also Solek), born in Germany of Polish-Jewish parents, is sent away from his family for safety. Through a series of improbable misadventures and close escapes he spends the war years first in a communist orphanage in Poland; then pretending to be German, traveling with the German army as a German-Russian translator; and finally attending an elite training school for Hitler Youth. Like Peter Lilienthal's *David*, Holland's film is concerned with the attempts of a Jewish teenager to escape Nazi persecution, and like *David*, the film has a happy ending. Solly, however, unlike David, never physically goes into hiding; instead, he hides in the open by concealing his identity as a Jew and becomes part of the system trying to destroy him.

This difference allows Holland to focus on issues other than flight from the Nazis. Whereas both Frans Weisz's *Charlotte* and Lilienthal's *David* concentrate on escape, *Europa Europa* examines through its hero, Solly, questions about national identity relevant to European unification. Holland asks, "What is a man in the twentieth century? Does our fate depend on us, on our choice of actions, or are we playthings of history, swept along in an absurd existence? Where is that fragile line between different cultures, different religions, different national or personal identities?"[10] In a humorous scene a professor at the school for Hitler Youth uses Solly as an example illustrating the Aryan physical characteristics. In another ironic scene near the end of the movie, the Russians who capture him disbelieve Solly's claim of Jewishness and hand him over to concentration camp inmates for execution. He is saved again from certain death only by a last-second recognition by his brother, an inmate at the camp. Upon learning from his brother of the fate of his family and others in the ghetto, Solly's response is that purportedly used by many Germans after the war "I didn't know. I thought . . . Madagascar. I didn't know."

A controversy occurred in spring 1992 when the German jury responsible for nominating films for the Academy Award refused to nominate *Europa Europa.* In response Holland accused members of the panel of being influenced by the film's historical theme: "They hate this subject, they really hate it."[11] In addition, members of Germany's film elite—among them, filmmakers Volker Schlöndorff, Michael Verhoeven, Wolfgang Petersen, and Margarethe von Trotta and actors Armin Mueller-Stahl, Senta Berger, and Hanna Schygulla—took out adds in trade publications asking that the U.S. jury redress the slight to the film by nominating it in as many categories as possible. The German jury's decision was based on two arguments. It felt the film was not a true German production, having been made with an international cast by a French-German partnership. Furthermore, jury members felt that the film's quality was not up to Hollywood's standards. One member referred to it as "trash." Another called it "embarrassing."[12] The film's co-producer, Arthur Brauner, countered the first argument by stating that the film was shot in German and had 13 German actors, including its main character. Moreover, 8 German writers contributed to the script.[13] The second argument seems to have been addressed by American critics when they awarded the film a Golden Globe. Nevertheless, German critics found the film "voyeuristic" and "unbelievable" (*Deutschland Nachrichten*, 7).

Holland makes the implausibility of Perel's story, however, work for the film, not against it. Rather than try to minimize the many coincidences necessary for Solly's story to end well, the director foregrounds his good fortune. Whenever the hero escapes another close call, Holland focuses on his face, which expresses the disbelief that viewers must be experiencing at his luck. Moreover, at the end of the film she has Isaak, Solly's brother, advise him: "Don't tell your story to anyone. Nobody will believe you." And to improve chances that the story will be accepted by viewers as true, Holland, in an epilogue, not only adds the now commonplace information about the fate of her hero after story's end but includes a cameo appearance of Salomon Perel, now 65, gazing out over a body of water in Israel.

Raindrops

▲▼▲

In *Regentropfen* (*Raindrops*, 1981) directors Michael Hoffmann and Harry Raymon likewise show the rise of anti-Semitism through the eyes of a Jewish boy, Benny Goldbach. Based on the reminiscences of Raymon, whose family emigrated from Germany when he was eight, the story tells about the awakening of Benny's mother and father to the dangers around them and about their decision to emigrate. It relates their journey from the Hunsrück region to Cologne and finally to Stuttgart, where they are denied a visa because of Mr. Goldbach's health. Filmed several years before Edgar Reitz's *Heimat* (1984), another Nazi-retro film set in the Hunsrück, *Raindrops* offers a view of Jewish life and anti-Semitism in a small German town, a reality Reitz's film fails to deal with.

Raindrops addresses the question many people have about why Jews stayed in Germany in spite of the rising instances of individual and institutional anti-Semitism. This question concerns many films about the Holocaust told from a Jewish character's perspective. In *Charlotte* the family's belief that it was protected by its social and cultural status prevented a more timely departure. In *David* the father's responsibility to the members of his temple keeps him and his family from leaving. In *Raindrops* the characters remain because they do not wish to leave Germany. The film makes it clear that Germany is home to the Goldbach family. Their decision to leave is not made lightly, for it is a decision to leave their home.

The Goldbachs recognize early that they are in danger from the Nazis. First a relative's store is burned. Then Mrs. Goldbach is reprimanded by the authorities for slapping an impudent Gentile in her store. Later Benny is scolded in school for not raising his hand in the Nazi salute. These insults escalate until finally the Goldbachs are banned from shopping in their town's stores and guards are posted in front of their own store so that Gentiles cannot buy from them. Gradually their circle of non-Jewish acquaintances, which the film implies was large, dwindles to none. Yet the Goldbachs have a hard time deciding to leave. Germany is their home. They exchange seder matzohs for Easter candies. They celebrate carnival. Benny has non-Jewish friends. The slap that Mrs. Goldbach gives the Gentile boy implies that she feels comfortable in German society. As she learns from this incident, however, "times have changed."

Viewers experience the indecision of the Goldbachs to leave Germany on two levels; the first is through Benny, the character whose perspective viewers adopt. The eight-year-old Benny becomes the eyes and ears through which they perceive what is happening to the Jews in Germany. Although the boy sees and hears about the fires, the store closings, the discrimination, he is too young to comprehend any of it. The adults keep the true danger from the children, not only to protect them but also to deny the true danger to themselves. On the way to the seder, Benny wants to know why he cannot take matzohs to a non-Jewish friend. His parents, rather than explain the precarious situation that the Jews are in, reply that they did not order enough. Likewise, at the seder no explanation is given to Benny for why the door has been locked, an act that in his mind will keep the angel from entering. Denial is also practiced when Benny comes home from school to find guards outside the family storefront. His parents scold him for being late, displacing their fears about the danger presented by the specific affront to the generalized fear that parents have when children are late.

On the second level, viewers experience the Goldbachs' troubles with knowledgeable eyes. As they watch Benny struggling to understand events and also watch his parents struggling just as hard to deny the importance of those events, viewers have the vantage point of history. They recognize the danger to the Goldbachs and sympathize with their attempts to hide from the truth. These two levels of perception allow viewers to experience the growing anti-Semitism around Benny, who barely comprehends it, while they also experience the fear of his parents, who deny the significance of the incidents of anti-Semitism.

Raindrops (1981). Benny and friend. Courtesy Inter Nationes.

The Goldbachs' denial of the true danger, however, does not derive simply from a fear for their own and their son's safety. It results also from a reluctance to make the choice of leaving Germany. The Goldbachs feel they are not only Jews but German-Jews. They obviously feel that they are assimilated into the culture. In a poignant scene at a graveyard, after their decision to leave has been made, the family stands beside the grave of Mrs. Goldbach's parents. The scene reminds viewers that the Goldbachs are not visitors or guests in Germany. They are residents as much as their non-Jewish neighbors. This is their homeland, too. The scene recalls the plaintive title of the German-French film critic Lotte Eisner's autobiography, *Ich hatte einst ein schönes Vaterland: Memoiren* (*I Once Had a Beautiful Fatherland*, (1984).[14]

The second half of the movie focuses on the difficulties the Goldbachs have in leaving Germany. Clearly, in 1935, the family had made a timely decision; as yet, Jews were being neither deported to concentration camps nor denied exit visas. Their difficulty getting out of Germany is due more to the reluctance of the rest of the world to accept them than to

Germany's desire to prevent their departure. Regardless of the cause, however, the confinement that the family endures is real. The film emphasizes their feeling of "captivity" through both mise-en-scène and camera work. For a while the Goldbachs must live in one of the Jewish houses of Cologne. (Many larger cities had houses that were set up to concentrate Jews in certain areas. This enabled authorities more easily to monitor the Jewish immigrants in the larger cities.) The boardinghouse, run by two eccentric sisters and filled with a mélange of characters, is too small for the number of people housed there. Scenes in the breakfast-dining room, in the parlor, and in private quarters show the residents crowded against each other. Movement in these scenes is restricted by other persons, tables, chairs, and walls. The Goldbach's one-room apartment becomes a metaphor for the imprisonment the characters feel. As his father practices his tailoring and his mother cuts fashion pictures from a newspaper, Benny has to play around them. The camera never cuts during the scene but follows the characters as they step around and over each other until they can no longer stand the confinement and explode in anger.

The scenes of confinement in Cologne prepare viewers to accept the hopelessness of the family's situation. After the Goldbachs travel to Stuttgart for the physical examinations required prior to being granted a visa, they must wait in a room at the American consulate, which is crowded with others hoping to emigrate. Those waiting discuss the rumors about the reluctance of the American authorities to grant visas. The tired looks on their faces indicate that many have been waiting a long while. Their worried expressions reveal a fear that they will be denied visas. The fears of the collective become actualized in the Goldbachs. The family is turned down because of scar tissue on Mr. Goldbach's lungs.

The treatment of restrictive U.S. immigration policies is especially condemning in *Raindrops*. Other films about the Holocaust also criticize the reluctance of the United States to accept Jewish immigrants. In these films, however, authorities are bombarded with applications in the eleventh hour. The question of whether exclusion takes place because of restrictive quotas or simply because of a lack of time to process everyone is sometimes obscured. In *Raindrops* the reason for nonacceptance is that the United States simply does not want the Goldbach family. That they cannot escape Nazi Germany is thereby shown to have been a result of not only procrastination on their own part but also the reluctance of the future Allied countries to accept Jewish emigrés.

Raindrops has a surprising lack of suspense for a film whose theme is flight from Nazi Germany: the directors avoid tension-packed scenes of escape. There are no anxious moments at borders and no furtive glances between characters at every knock at the door. As mentioned, 1935 was too early for such worries. The movie also avoids the moralizing about good and evil found in other films on the Holocaust. The strong effect that *Raindrops* eventually produces is due not to suspense or moralizing but to the humor in the film. The tragic potential of the situation that *Raindrops* depicts stands in strong contrast to the lighthearted manner in which the story unfolds. Instead of dwelling on the probable failure of the Goldbachs' plans (a possibility that is always in the back of viewers' minds), the film chooses to emphasize the lighter side of their ordeal. In the boardinghouse, a recital becomes a parody of a German soiree: one of the sisters sings an interminable aria as the camera shows the inhabitants crowded uncomfortably into the parlor. In another scene, as the parents sit in their restricted quarters, Mrs. Goldbach promises God that if He helps them escape she will cook only kosher. These moments are more than comic relief; they run throughout the movie and give it a humorous tone. The humor, however, contrasts with what viewers know is happening to the Goldbachs. It also contrasts with what they know happened to the Jews in reality.

The contrast between content and tone has a twofold effect. First, it makes the outcome of the film all that more heartbreaking and frightening. After receiving the news that they will not be allowed to emigrate, the family stands in a corridor as the camera pulls back. The scene resembles those in train stations. Finally, the screen goes black, and Mr. Goldbach is heard consoling his wife by holding out the possibility of escape through Cuba. His voice is drowned out by the sound of whistles, barking dogs, and eventually train wheels and doors. These undeniable sounds of deportation to the camps stand out all the more because viewers have been led by the light tone to expect a happy end. Second, the contrast between content and tone has allowed viewers to keep a critical distance from the narrative. It has encouraged viewers to focus on the *why* of the Goldbachs' situation more than the *what*. When the movie ends, viewers are disturbed by the coming tragedy, but they are also free to reflect on one of the reasons that the tragedy will occur. The Goldbachs are being kept in Germany not by their procrastination, nor by the Germans' reluctance to let them leave, but by the rest of the world, which refuses to take them in.

38—Vienna before the Fall

▲▼▲

Wolfgang Glück's film *38—Auch das war Wien* (*38—Vienna before the Fall*, 1986) followed closely upon the release of part 1 of Axel Corti's film trilogy, *Whereto and Back*, about Austrian Jews in the period 1933–45. Also appearing that year was Susanne Zanke's film about Austrian resistance, *A Minute of Darkness Does Not Blind Us*. Two years earlier the director collective of Karin Berger, Elisabeth Holzinger, Charlotte Podgornik, and Lisbeth N. Trallori had released another film about Austrian resistance, *Küchengespräche mit Rebellinnen* (*Kitchen Talks with Rebels*, 1984). These films came out at a time when the growing debate about Austria's position in the Third Reich was culminating in questions about the role that Kurt Waldheim, Austria's president at the time, had played in the persecution and killing of Jews in Yugoslavia. The German title of Glück's film is an allusion to the political significance of the debate: *38—Auch das war Wien* (38—This Too Was Vienna) alludes to a Vienna that was not part of the Anschluss. The film portrays a city that was more than marching boots and brownshirts awaiting a propitious moment to join Hitler's Germany. It reveals a subculture of the city in which Jews and non-Jews enjoyed each other's intellectual and social company. The ambience of this subculture, whose base was the theater, is described by one of the characters: "She from Prague, I from Budapest, here in Vienna, Jewish ferment. That for me is the concept of Austria." The allusion in the title to another Vienna calls attention to the Jewish character of the city's artistic and intellectual life, which the annexation into the Third Reich destroyed, and also points to the non-Jewish support for the Jews and to Austrian opposition to the Nazis. The English title, *38—Vienna before the Fall*, adds to these allusions a political dimension: Austria fell, that is, it was taken over by force and did not willingly accept union with Nazi Germany.

The film, however, is not an apologia for Austrian involvement in the Third Reich, even if it does cast a favorable light on Austrian citizens. Almost all of the Austrian non-Jews portrayed in the film, for example, are openly philo-Semitic. Even the Jewish hero's cleaning lady, perhaps reflecting her socialist leanings, is sympathetic to his troubles. Her son, who is a Nazi, is one of the few anti-Semitic characters in the film. All other anti-Semitic characters are encountered in Berlin, not in Vienna, creating the impression that anti-Jewish sentiment was imported into Vienna from the Reich. Even with this white-glove treatment of the Viennese, by the end of the film the impression is that the public willingly acquiesced in becoming part of the Third Reich, although it did so because of the worsening economy and not necessarily out of a love for nazism.

The non-Jewish heroine is reminiscent of Willie in Fassbinder's *Lili Marleen*: both women are artists who must choose between a Jewish lover and a career. The actress Carola Hell, however, is more talented than the songstress Willie. More important, she seems to have a moral center that the singer of the ballad "Lili Marleen" lacks. Carola Hell easily could advance her career by collaborating with the Nazis, and in the beginning she does appear on the German stage and in German films. She goes to Berlin to perform, against the wishes of Martin, her lover. Later, even after being harassed by the Gestapo for insulting Nazi officers and for making philo-Semitic remarks, she is willing to make a movie for a German company. In the end, however, she recognizes that she must give up her career and leave Austria in order to save Martin. Carola Hell's moral decision makes her a sympathetic character. Moreover, the melodrama of her decision to quit acting and flee the country with Martin creates an entertaining and suspenseful movie. History is a constant presence in *38—Vienna before the Fall*, however, constantly subverting the pleasure that the narrative might otherwise provide.

In few other films is the Nazi swastika so prevalent, reminding viewers of what is at stake in the couple's decision. The symbol adorns the uniforms of the officers who talk to Carola in Berlin and encircles the arms of those who arrest her. It flutters from banners that hang over the Viennese streets and appears on the arms of a truckload of Nazi hooligans who disrupt delivery of a liberal newspaper critical of the Anschluss. Likewise, when Martin is beaten and awakens the next day in his room, the first object seen in the shot is the swastika on the huge Nazi banner festooning his building, mocking his defiance. These icons of Nazi barbarism are a constant reminder that this formulaic plot structure about the dilemma of a woman choosing between career and lover is really about something else completely, something more urgent. The reds and blacks of the film, even in scenes without the swastika, impress on viewers the pervasive presence of nazism and make it clear that the choice here truly is between life and death. They remind the viewer that many who made the choice to go failed to escape. Thus, while the narrative suggests that a happy ending is possible—the characters are strong and recognize political reality—historical reminders tell viewers otherwise.

Publicity releases for *38—Vienna before the Fall* implied that the downfall of the principals can be traced to their aloofness from politics, "the fate of 'unpolitical people' in Vienna, in March 1938." That, however, is far from the case. The main characters are not unpolitical, at least not in the sense that they do not know what is occurring, or that they ignore it, or even that they do nothing against it. These are not weaklings who cringe before the tumultuous events driving their lives. Carola tells two SS officers in Berlin that she would like to perform *Nathan the Wise* for them, a play synonymous with philo-Semitism for Germans. When she rehearses

Schiller's eighteenth-century classic *Love and Intrigue*, she insists on bringing out political aspects of the freedom fighting in the play. Martin is likewise politically aware and no coward. He senses how dangerous the Nazi regime is and objects to Carola's having even innocent dealings with it. Although he is not, at first, planning to leave Austria, this decision is not a result of an unpolitical nature but of a romantic one. He has been a freedom fighter in Spain, and he believes that he could be one in Austria, too, if that were required. The choices made by Carola and Martin are not unpolitical or even apolitical; they are idealistic. The film brings viewers to an important insight about political resistance: it is not enough to be conscious of the political situation; one must also be able to interpret politics and recognize when to retreat to safety.

God Does Not Believe in Us Anymore

▲▼▲

Flight from Nazi persecution is also the theme of Axel Corti's *An uns glaubt Gott nicht mehr* (*God Does Not Believe in Us Anymore*, 1982), the first part of his trilogy *Whereto and Back.*[15] *God Does Not Believe in Us Anymore* follows the escape adventure of an Austrian Jew, 17-year-old Ferdinand "Ferry" Taubler, who, after the brutal murder of his father at the hands of Nazi thugs, decides to leave Vienna in the fall of 1938. Ferry is naive but matures quickly (this theme is also found in *David* and *Raindrops*) during his trek from Vienna to Prague to Paris, then to a French concentration camp in northern France, and finally to Marseilles in southern France. Along the way he meets Ghandi, a resistance fighter who has escaped from Dachau, and Helena, a half-Jewish woman, whose goal in life is to help Jews escape Hitler, and who takes a motherly interest in Ferry. He meets others also, among them, an actor who practices his English by reciting Shakespeare, and Kron, a Jewish hustler who survives by living off the troubles of the Jews, selling them visa extensions and forged papers. By the closing scene, Kron has gone crazy; Ghandi has been tortured to death; other Jews have committed suicide; the actor has been caught and will be deported to Africa; Helena is last seen running from the authorities; and Ferry, fleeing across a street, seems about to be hit by a car as the frame freezes. Escape was often impossible, even for those Jews who initially managed to flee Germany and Austria.

The film's origin as a movie produced for Austrian television contributed to the melodramatic nature of the narrative. The tale of Ferry and his friends unfolds as a classic escape movie. There are tense moments, romantic interludes, and dramatic conflicts. With each close call, the movie builds suspense, pulling the audience ever deeper into the adventure. Corti balances the story of Ferry's flight with a parallel narrative of the German army's march across Western Europe. The story of German successes is told through German newsreels, radio reports, and oral accounts (mostly rumors). These media are the sources of information, political and military, for Ferry and his friends, as well as historical sources for the movie audience.

The technique of showing history from the perspective of the Germans is effective in several ways. First, it functions perfectly as a Brechtian alienation device, breaking the illusion of the film's adventure. It forces the spectator to reflect on the historical aspects of the movie rather than only on the melodramatic ones. As much as the film's adventure narrative tries to build suspense and sustain the illusionary effect of classic cinema, spectators are never completely lost in the action. Instead they are alternately concerned with the fate of the characters—will they escape, how will they manage to get out of their predicaments, and so forth—and astounded by the ideological propaganda of the German newsreels. In one sequence, the German and Austrian characters are in a French concentration camp and are worried about the approach of German troops. They have been unable to convince the French to free them on the grounds that the Germans are the prisoners' enemy and not allies coming to free them, as the guards claim to believe. The scenes in the camp are juxtaposed with German newsreels. The narration speaks of "Germany's superior troops," who are "writing a new page of history, fighting for the life and freedom of the German nation." In this sequence, one is struck by the greater truth in the fictional story than in the real images of the newsreel. A later sequence, which also starts by showing the characters in prison, has a similar effect. The shots of the prisoners are juxtaposed with a newsreel account that is shockingly xenophobic. The narrator of the newsreel describes a glorious victory of the Germans over inferior peoples. The German victory march, he proclaims, has become the misery of the Negroes, the French, and the Asian hordes that were to be unleashed onto German culture as they had been in World War I. Again, one is struck by the contrast between the manipulated images of historical reality and those of the fictional narrative.

Second, history functions to bring viewers into the fictional narrative, for the archival film and radio inserts make concrete the fears and worries of the Jewish characters. Within the fictional narrative, the threat from the Germans is abstract; the emphasis is on showing how bureaucracy and corruption had to be overcome before safety was finally possible. Thus, the fictional narrative has the characters safely fleeing each country, only to be stopped by quotas, corrupt officials, and reluctant host countries. The protagonists are shown constantly on the move, fleeing the front edge of the approaching German forces and following rumors of a way out through first one country and then another, only to have each door shut before them. Each office is packed with increasingly frenzied throngs of refugees. In each place the characters are concerned not just with survival and staying unobtrusive but with accumulating enough money and black market goods to buy a visa extension or exit papers. The approaching threat of the Nazis is always just a rumor. "They are at such and such a place now." "They will never make it this far." Hitler is never referred to by name within the fictional narrative but only as "he." Thus, it is by way of the newsreels and the radio reports that the historical referents that are causing the rumors are brought into the movie, increasing the awareness of viewers of the broader context. This in turn makes the threat to the characters tangible and helps create suspense.

Finally, history increases the tension in the audience by blocking the avenues of escape that the characters believe are opening to them. As each succeeding newsreel informs viewers about the advancing army, the prospects of freedom for the protagonists become fewer. Spectators, having identified with the characters, want their flight from the Nazis to be successful. Yet history tells spectators to expect their attempt to fail. The relentless advance of the army introduced in the newsreels supports other images of blockage in the film. *God Does Not Believe in Us Anymore* uses motorized vehicles as an ironic symbol of imprisonment and entrapment. The camera frequently adopts the perspective of the protagonists, anticipating a need for a quick escape, as they look down streets and alleys. Parked and standing vehicles block their vision and their route of escape when flight becomes necessary. Except for the vehicles in the newsreel footage, vehicular movement is virtually nonexistent. When Ferry and Helena arrive in Marseilles, they are prevented from running any further not by the waterfront alone but by a ship—the very ship, in fact, that was to be their passage to freedom. The only cars and trucks shown in motion are the paddy wagons of the French whose arrival means capture and imprisonment for the protagonists. In the film's last sequence, Ferry is fleeing from a patrol; the last frame is frozen just as Ferry seems about to be struck by a vehicle—a jeep blurry with arrested speed, with two uniformed Germans just dimly visible within. The tanks and jeeps of the newsreel have finally caught up with him, as history and narrative merge in Ferry's death.

God Does Not Believe in Us Anymore is unrelenting in its portrayal of non-Jewish Austrians and French. Corti's narrative characterizes them as hypocrites and anti-Semites. Ferry's neighbors feign concern for the young man's welfare after the murder of his father. Yet they profit from his hardship. The landlady demands reimbursement for the windows broken by the hooligans who killed his father. The investigating police officer cheats him out of his mother's jewels and a gold cigarette case. The father's Nazi-appointed Aryan business partner denies that there is any money in the store with which to compensate Ferry for the father's half of the business. The three characters know that Ferry will need the money to emigrate, but their venality and anti-Semitism prevent them from showing compassion. The portrayal of the French is equally negative. Although Jews are allowed into France, they clearly are not welcomed. The non-Jewish French characters in the film are mercenary and corrupt. At the immigration office they are surly to the refugees and are willing to grant visas only against a payment of money, the amount of which continually goes up. When the French authorities hear of the German troops advancing onto their soil, they round up the Jews and place them in camps as enemies of France. To be sure, the internment of Jewish refugees reflects what occurred in history. Corti is, therefore, no more negative in his portrayal of the French than historical events allow. Nonetheless, the absence of non-Jewish characters friendly to the Jews and willing to help, for humanitarian reasons, places French anti-Semitism in a particularly strong light. The humanitarianism of other countries is likewise questioned. The attitude of U.S. authorities toward the plight of the Jews is summed up by one of the refugees, who laments that if he were Einstein or Thomas Mann the borders of America would be open to him.

The Boat Is Full

▲▼▲

Markus Imhoof, like Axel Corti, criticizes immigration policies that worked to keep Jews inside Germany and German-controlled countries. Imhoof's *Das Boot ist voll* (*The Boat Is Full*, 1980) tells about a small group of five Jewish refugees and one deserter from the German army who escape into Switzerland. The Jews were all sent back because of a Swiss policy that "all illegally entering foreigners were to be immediately deported." Although the law exempted deserters and political refugees, the Jewish refugees were sent back because of one stipulation: "Refugees fleeing purely for purposes of their race, Jews for example, do not qualify as political refugees . . . [and are] to be turned back without delay."[16]

The Boat Is Full exposes the hypocrisy of the Swiss government, which claimed to offer asylum to those forced to leave Germany during

World War II. That Switzerland's open border was not open to everyone becomes apparent if one contrasts the policy against Jewish refugees with a statement made by a representative of the Swiss foreign office in 1933 on the occasion of Switzerland's acceptance of Thomas Mann as a political exile: "Switzerland as a land of refuge for those hunted out of their country, that is our tradition. That is not only our thanks to the world for hundreds of years of peace but also out of recognition of the value that homeless refugees have always brought us" (Imhoof). Imhoof's film deflates this historical image by suggesting that the "land of refuge" was not open to all. Indeed, records reveal that as many as seven refugees were turned back daily from August 1942 to the end of the war.[17]

Symbols of closure open and end the film. As the narrative begins, a group of Swiss workers are quickly walling up a tunnel that leads from Germany into their country. At the film's close, the Jewish protagonists slowly walk across a long bridge back to Germany. Once on the other side, the crossing bar comes down, trapping them inside Germany and barring any hope of escape. At this point, the credits appear and inform the audience in which camps the various individuals died. The credits' effect is anticlimactic, the tunnel and the bar having already told viewers how these lives would end.

The message of *The Boat Is Full* was criticized by some in Switzerland. Extremists on the right threatened the director if he continued to allow showings of the film; the school board in Bern withdrew a recommendation to teachers that the film be used in classes; and a Swiss councilman complained that Imhoof was speaking at too many international film conferences (Imhoof). Although this reaction from the right suggests that *The Boat Is Full* is a calumny directed against the Swiss people, Imhoof's movie treats them quite fairly. Some of the characters are good; others are narrow-minded, their portrayals bordering on stereotype. All display either overt or latent anti-Semitic traits. Yet there is a small group willing to help the Jews, and many in the town seem genuinely disturbed when the refugees are taken away to the border. Moments of stupidity—one character believes that the Jews ate her cat, and another refers to them as a band of Gypsies (an epithet even worse than being called a Jew)—are balanced by acts of kindness, such as the willingness of the innkeeper and his wife to endanger themselves by hiding the Jews. Images of entrapment abound in the film. The locked doors, closed windows, and confined spaces remind one of *The Diary of Anne Frank.* When the Jewish refugees first appear, they are cowering in the corner of a barn. Even in larger rooms they are confined by frames, standing behind closed, sometimes locked doors or being filmed with the light of the window behind them, creating a feeling of no escape. The images of entrapment, however, apply equally to the Swiss residents in the movie. The innkeeper and his wife are trapped by their lower middle-class, village life-style, which does not allow them to understand fully the consequences of deportation. Other characters appear helpless in the face of the bureaucratic policy that forces the tragedy. For instance, a minister remarks, "Imagine if they all stayed. The heart is often stupid"; but then he offers advice on how the group might be able to stay.

The ambivalence in the townspeople, taken as a whole as well as in individual characters, is a strength of the film. The portrayal of a gray morality, as stated above, while lending balance, also suggests that the people would have done something if they had been able; unfortunately, their hands were tied, they had no other choice, as law-abiding citizens, but to acquiesce to the law. When the Jews are carted off to the border, the villagers stand around giving them food, remarking how terrible it is to deport them, especially the children. It occurs to no one that the town could have taken the children and the adults in. It occurs to no one that the system can bend a little. Viewers, of course, recognize the false choice being made by the townspeople. With the hindsight that history gives them, spectators can judge the error and cowardice in the actions of the Swiss. Thus, although the kind portrayal of the Swiss townspeople might mislead viewers, history helps them focus on the moral lapse that occurred when the Swiss did not condemn the policies of their government.

Angry Harvest

▲▼▲

Finding refuge among strangers is also the theme of *Bittere Ernte* (*Angry Harvest*, 1984), a German-language film directed by the Polish director Agnieszka Holland. The film tells the story of a Jewish woman and the Polish farmer who takes her in after she escapes from a transport that is taking her and her family to a concentration camp. During the escape she is separated from her husband and is also injured. The farmer treats her kindly at first, nurturing her back to health. Eventually his lust causes him to exploit her situation, and he begins to abuse her sexually. After a time he arranges another hiding place for the woman, who rather than continue to live in fear of discovery, commits suicide. To alleviate his feeling of guilt, the farmer gives money to the woman's husband, who appears after the woman's death, to enable him to migrate to America. From America, the husband and his new wife write, thanking the farmer for his kindness.

Holland has taken an uncomplicated narrative and fashioned a complex film about human relationships and victimization. Using these components, the director explores themes of faith, guilt, lust, gratitude, greed, and anti-Semitism. The woman longs for human warmth. Most members of her family have been killed by the Nazis; her husband was possibly killed in the escape attempt. She describes her present emotional state as "asleep inside." Her empty feeling begins to subside however, when the farmer helps her rediscover joy, even as she remains a virtual prisoner in his house. Her renewed interest in life is reflected in her smile, her lively conversation, a desire to dance, and the pleasure she has splashing in rain puddles on the rare occasions she is permitted outdoors. She refuses to see herself as a victim. The farmer likewise longs for human contact and exploits her physical and emotional vulnerability. As a former seminarian, he is awkward among people. Villagers mocked him when he was young and impoverished. Now that he is wealthy, he avenges past wrongs by exploiting others. His rape of the woman is simply the most extreme form of his readiness to exploit. Yet he is not evil. He is portrayed as truly confused about religion and morality. Furthermore, his sexual repression is so great that he wakes up at night in cold sweats, which drive him to masturbate. In his mind, the Jewish woman can save him from his sinful behavior by providing relief for his sexual desires.

History remains in the background in *Angry Harvest* in spite of the setting and the time. The film portrays victimization more generally than do other Holocaust films. While the Jewish woman is portrayed as a victim—of the Nazi regime, of anti-Semitic attitudes, of the man who is hiding her—she is not the only victim in the film. The Polish farmer is also portrayed as a victim—of his impoverished past, of his Polish heritage, of his repressed desires, and of his religious nature. Holland uses the Holocaust as an extreme situation in which to dramatize human situations that could occur at other times. Her decision to minimize its historical discourse gives the movie its complexity; it is also a major weakness. History, anti-Semitism, and the Holocaust become mere devices for keeping the woman imprisoned. By keeping history so firmly in the background, Holland cannot use it to understand and resolve the effects of this dreadful period. With so few historical referents, viewers are kept focused on the human rather than the political drama that is unfolding. They experience a great degree of identification with the characters, leading to a greater emotional impact when the woman dies and the man must face his responsibility for her death. But by emphasizing the human rather than the political drama, the film explains certain consequences as the result of forces peculiar to the individual: the man acts as he does because he was poor as a youth, he is sexually repressed, he is an ex-seminarian, he drinks too much, he is a naive peasant. The woman acts as she does because she is grateful, she is a victim, she is loved, she is lonely. The film suggests that the woman is a victim of the man's stunted emotional growth rather than of historical circumstances. It excuses the man's behavior as a product of his past, not the consequence of poor moral choices. When the woman commits suicide, the film suggests that she could not live, or did not want to live, without the situation that had victimized her. The man ends as an ironic tragic figure who never finds the redemption that he believed the war would bring.

One Day

▲▼▲

To date, no German narrative film has portrayed life in the death camps of the Third Reich. German movies about the Holocaust focus instead on Jewish life in Germany before deportation to the camps. Hollywood, on the other hand, has produced three successful television movies that depict life and death in the camps. "Holocaust" (1978), "Playing for Time" (1980), and "War and Remembrance" (1989) all dramatize arrival in the camps, selection of the victims, death in the "showers," and disposal of the bodies. Although accusations that these films exploit and trivialize human tragedy have validity, there also can be no denying that they give universal suffering a human face. Therein lies their value: for they bring viewers to think about where hatred and ignorance can lead. Egon Monk's television film *Ein Tag* (*One Day*, 1965) has a similar effect on viewers, although it takes place in an "ordinary camp" and focuses primarily on the non-Jewish inmates of the prison.

One Day alludes to the mistreatment and killing of Jews, but it is predominantly the story of political prisoners. The film follows a new group of arrivals at a concentration camp for a 24-hour period. The time is 1939, and the camp is within German borders. It houses principally Communists, other political prisoners, and criminals. Some Jews are present, but they are segregated from the rest, and the commandant of the camp is systematically trying to kill them off through overwork. The narrative is composed of a series of episodes linked by two overarching problems: the fear produced by the capriciousness of the SS controlling the camp, and how to prevent a group of healthy Jews from being killed through exhaustive labor, lack of access to regular rations, and lack of medical care. During the 24-hour period several Jews are saved by altering roll call lists, that is, substituting names of healthy Jews for prisoners who have died. The ruse works "for now," as one of the prisoners remarks.

Monk's film combines drama and history without any sentimentality. Unlike the Hollywood films on camp life, Monk keeps viewers at a distance from the characters. Strategies of distancing and alienation work to continually interrupt cinematic illusion. Although some characters receive more attention from the camera, are more attractive, and have problems on which the narrative concentrates, the structure of the film prevents viewers from getting involved in their problems. At least, involvement is never so great that the evil of the concentration camp itself is overlooked. The episodic structure of the film keeps viewers at a distance even in those situations that have a potential for suspense. By announcing, using Brechtian titles, what will occur before each episode, attention can be focused on the reality of the camps rather than on the fictional experiences of a few of the prisoners. Monk also diffuses the suspense that individual episodes might have, thereby thwarting any possibility of catharsis or resolution. Even though the film tells the story of these individuals, its true story is that of history. To this end, Monk intercuts several scenes from archival footage, for instance, scenes of Hitler receiving dignitaries, and a scene of Berlin theater life. The newsreel footage distances viewers from the drama, places events in the camp in a time frame, and provides background on how Germans outside the camp were experiencing the events of the day. In the final scene, which uses sound editing effectively, the narrative again leaves the camp setting. This time, however, the scene is part of the fiction, not material from the archives. From a camp scene at the end of the day, in which the prison guard barks orders at the inmates, Monk cuts to a scene in a local pub in which well-dressed businessmen and elegant elderly ladies sit, enjoying food and drink. In their midst is the main officer of the camp. The sound track continues to provide the sounds of the camp, not those of the pub. The contrast is enlightening, not only for its own horror but also for exposing the deafness of the people who tolerated what was occurring. Although *One Day* fails to deal with the Holocaust directly, it depicts clearly the atrocities that occurred. More significantly, the film implicates everyone, not just a group of sadistic guards.

The Yellow Star

▲▼▲

Although the focus of this book is feature-length narrative films, a few feature-length documentaries fall within its scope. Documentaries such as those by Eberhard Fechner and the two to be discussed here—Dieter Hildebrandt's *Der gelbe Stern* (*The Yellow Star*, 1980) and Katrin Seybold and Melanie Spitta's *Es ging Tag und Nacht, liebes Kind: Zigeuner (Sinti) in Auschwitz* (*It Went on Day and Night, Dear Child: Gypsies in Auschwitz*, 1981–82)—use strategies of narrative film. Like narrative films, these works use stories to help viewers reconcile the past and use conflict to underscore each individual's relationship to the past. And also like narrative film, they bring viewers to identify with the situations and personalities they depict in order to help viewers experience the past. Hildebrandt's *The Yellow Star* was released shortly after the American-made "Holocaust" played on German television and five years before Claude Lanzmann's French production *Shoah* (1985), one of the more powerful films made about the Holocaust. The film tells the chilling story of how the Jewish people were almost annihilated from Europe. Yet the story is never sentimental or trivial; it never individualizes the tragedy. In that sense, it offers another face to narrative films on the Holocaust, which usually present the fate of the Jews through the fate of a few individuals. *The Yellow Star* presents the fate of all Jews in Europe and thereby asks viewers to come to terms with the horrors of the almost total annihilation of a race rather than to empathize with the suffering of a few. Hildebrandt's film also serves as a historical complement to the feature films. Its archival footage gives veracity to the icons, allusions, characterizations, and personal outcomes found in the fictional works.

Although *The Yellow Star* is not entirely successful in explaining how a political movement could end in the mass murder of millions of people, it documents that the Final Solution was not, as the revisionists believe, a policy stumbled into by a nation losing a war. Hildebrandt mercilessly shows that the extermination of the Jews was not an act carried out in a vacuum by a group of 14 men in a country villa. It was, instead, an unrelenting campaign witnessed, tolerated, and sometimes actively supported by the public. Indeed, as the film intimates, the world witnessed the Holocaust as it was occurring, and if the film has a weakness, it is that it does not go deeply enough into the silence of the rest of the world at the sight of escalating violence against the Jews.

The Yellow Star tells the history of German persecution of the Jews from Hitler's takeover of the government until the end of the war. In the opening scene Goebbels's voice is heard offscreen as on-screen Nazi supporters burn books by Jewish authors on 10 May in Berlin's Opernplatz. Goebbels screams at his audience that Jewish intellectualism will be systematically destroyed. After his outburst, the narrator, speaking in a solemn but normal voice, cites Heinrich Heine's warning made a century before, that where books are burned, men will also be burned. The rest of the movie is divided into about 20 segments, each an escalating station on the path from burning books to burning people.

The Yellow Star takes as its leitmotiv the idea that even those Germans who did not prosecute the policies bear responsibility for what occurred—"We were witnesses if we were not the perpetrators." From the opening sequence of book burnings to the closing memorial for victims of Majdanek, the film presents evidence that the Final Solution policy was in place from the start. Its beginnings were in the public signs that warned Germans of "pickpockets and Jews," and in those that warned women of "Jewish rapists." Its continuation was in the propaganda films that idealized German (Nordic) facial features and caricatured Jewish ones. Its escalation was in the films that equated Jews with bacteria, in Hitler's speeches that called for the elimination of European Jewry, and in the words from the protocol of the Wannsee Conference, quoted in *The Yellow Star*: "Europe will be combed from West to East to find the Jews. These will be sent to the East to work. Many will die and after the war the rest will have to be dealt with because otherwise they will provide the seeds for a resurgence of Jews in Europe." These scenes are damning of any claim that the Final Solution was not an integral element in the policies of the Third Reich from the start. Furthermore, they are damning of a populace that claims it either did not know or could do nothing. Finally, they are damning of any attempts to separate the Holocaust from what occurred during the Third Reich.

The Yellow Star is not without problems. By creating such a strong identity between what the camera shows and the viewer, the film gives its visuals a quasi-fateful character. That is, the way the film builds momentum from beginning to end makes later events and the deaths in the gas chambers seem inevitable. Hildebrandt neglects to show that each new step toward the Final Solution followed a conscious decision to continue on the path. In other words, while the film helps viewers recognize that the Jews were persecuted, that the policy of persecution started with simple laws of exclusion and ended with a policy that denied their humanity, and that these policies were supported or at least tolerated by enough people to ensure their success, it never helps them see that support, or even silence, is part of a conscious choice. And as a conscious act, the opposite choice was also possible. That is, no one was forced to support or to tolerate the policies that led to the Final Solution. In a sense, the inevitability of the progression of visuals lets those involved off the hook.

It Went on Day and Night, Dear Child: Gypsies in Auschwitz

▲▼▲

In the films made about the Holocaust, the focus is generally on the millions of Jews who died under the genocidal policies of the Third Reich. While this is understandable, given the disproportionate suffering brought upon the Jewish population of Europe by the Nazis, this single focus limits the scope of death for which the Third Reich is responsible. Victims in the camps numbered about 11 million, and if all war dead, soldiers and civilians, are included, the total number of victims is estimated at over 35 million.[18] The war dead, particularly those killed in the East, are the topic of most of the films that focus on the war itself. In addition, East German directors have included the persecution of the Communists under Hitler in their films (*Sansibar*, *I Was Nineteen*, and *Professor Mamlock*, among others). Other groups, however, were also persecuted, among them, homosexuals (see Mel Brooks's *To Be or Not to Be*), the handicapped (treated in a new film, *Kalmenhofkinder* [*Children of Kalmenhof*, 1990]), and the Gypsies. Considering that the Gypsies are still discriminated against throughout Europe, including Germany, it is perhaps not surprising that they have been virtually excluded from films on the Holocaust. One film, *Aren't We Wonderful*, even lampoons Gypsies by showing a Gypsy family rising to a position of influence in the Nazi party. Katrin Seybold and Melanie Spitta's *Es ging Tag und Nacht, liebes Kind: Zigeuner (Sinti) in Auschwitz* (*It Went on Day and Night, Dear Child: Gypsies in Auschwitz*, 1981–82), a feature-length documentary on Nazi persecution of the Gypsies, is one attempt at correcting the oversight.

Seybold and Spitta structure their documentary into two parts, each calculated to produce a maximum of identification with the suffering of the Gypsies and also to give maximum background information on this neglected topic. In the first part of the film, Seybold interviews a Gypsy woman who lost most of her family in Auschwitz and who was herself an inmate there. Close-ups of the woman's face as she relates the suffering that occurred are, to be sure, manipulative. But her story is sufficiently gripping that a camera held at a distance would have involved viewers just as fully in her tale of persecution. The second part of the movie follows three generations of a Gypsy family as they tour Auschwitz. Two of the members, the uncle and a grandfather, had been inmates. The film follows the group around Auschwitz as the two men tell their stories of what occurred under the Nazis. Seybold and Spitta here combine present and past in scenes reminiscent of the Hungarian film, *Társasutazás* (*Package*

Tour, 1984), which follows a group of Hungarian Jews on a tour of Auschwitz, where they also had been imprisoned. In Seybold and Spitta's film, as the camera pans over the grounds of the camp, which looks harmless now, the words of the two men remind viewers of what once occurred here behind the barbed wire. As they tell their stories, the relationship of past to present is revealed. The tragedy that occurred back then is still present in the lives of the storytellers, in the lives of their families, in the lives of the Germans, and finally in the lives of the viewers. Here also Seybold and Spitta maximize sympathy for the Gypsies through close-ups, sympathetic faces, and tearful breakdowns. Considering, however, that disdain for the Gypsies is still tolerated, the directors' methods may be necessary to persuade viewers to listen to a story that they might otherwise ignore.

▲▼▲

Of course, all the films discussed in this chapter are manipulative insofar as they use classic cinema strategies to induce viewers to identify with the characters and their problems. The main criticism of a film like "Holocaust," for example, is that it not only trivializes the suffering of the Jews but also manipulates emotions. Perhaps, however, the only way to persuade spectators to recognize suffering on such a massive scale is to risk the danger of trivializing and sentimentalizing historical material. The facts of what occurred in the concentration camps of Nazi Germany are in the history books: 6 million Jews dead, another 5 million non-Jews dead. The films on the Holocaust are not meant to impress those figures on viewers. Rather, their goal is to make the suffering and the tragedy comprehensible by individualizing it, by personalizing it as story.

The results are uneven. Depending on how much viewers know about history, these films can distort the very truth that they mean to reveal. In *Wannsee Conference*, for example, the director portrays some of the participants in the meeting as "good guys" intent on preventing their colleagues from pursuing the goal of annihilating the Jews. In *Charlotte* and *David*, the flight of the Jews from persecution is personalized around attractive, young people. In the process, the problems the films are dealing with are sentimentalized and romanticized, although they are not thereby made any less tragic or any less truthful. The question to ask about *Charlotte* and *David* is whether they provide opportunity to generalize the fate of the heroine or hero to the whole of the tragedy that occurred. Or does the exceptional nature of their characters—rich, talented, brave, resolute—limit the tragedy in *Charlotte* to *her* tragedy or the triumph in *David* to *his* triumph? *David* offers an additional problem in that its hero is possessed of exceptional moral and psychological strength—David battling Goliath. Again, the question is whether the film's distancing strategies, which occur through the inserts of history, are effective enough to allow viewers to see how exceptional David is and to allow them to recognize that the Holocaust was a true tragedy in which the question of heroism was irrelevant. In this regard, Ferry in *God Does Not Believe in Us Anymore* provides a better role model since he is able, through his own naivete, to show that his fate is not unique, that it is one he shares with other Jews.

Girls' War (1977). Three sisters, Christine (Antonia Reininghaus, left), Sophie (Adelheid Ardnt), and Katharina (Katharina Hunter, right), in Prague before the outbreak of war. Courtesy Inter Nationes.

chapter 7

▲▼▲

the importance of remembering

We have been discussing narrative films set in the war years and the degree to which they provide a unique viewing experience to spectators who are familiar with the history of Germany in the twentieth century and who, in addition, share a belief that Hitler and the Nazis caused the world untold suffering. Whether the films deal with the war front, opportunists and other fellow travelers, the victims of the Holocaust, the men and women directly responsible for the murders, or the Germans who actively resisted the Nazis, they assume that their audience will have a good understanding of the suffering that occurred during the Third Reich. In this chapter we look at those films that are about ordinary citizens on the home front: the parents, children, and wives who played no direct part in national socialism other than living in Germany during the years 1933–45. Their primary concern was not supporting Hitler and his policies but coping with the hardship and suffering caused by the war and enduring their loss of freedom under the Third Reich. For viewers, these films create an experience akin to simultaneously having and analyzing a bad dream. While watching these films, viewers adopt several points of view that interact with one another. On the one hand, they identify with the camera and the main characters and interpret events as the characters interpret them; in other words, they share in the narrative. On the other hand, the historical setting never allows viewers to lose themselves completely in the dream. The strong opinions viewers have about the period prevent them from being taken in permanently and completely by the characters and the stories. As viewers watch, they are free to judge and interpret from a critical distance.

Identification with characters by movie audiences is, to be sure, not unique to Nazi-retro films. After all, the appeal of classic cinema is due partly to its transparency, which creates the illusion that what transpires on the screen is "real." Moreover, as we have emphasized earlier, Nazi-retro films use the formulaic characters and stories of genre cinema precisely because doing so aids the process of identification. The occasional interruption of that identification by the intrusion of extraneous material into this "real" world is also not unique. After all, the appeal of art house cinema is due partly to foregrounding, which frees viewers from the constraints of the narrative and allows them, in the words of Christian Metz, to hover, "like the psychoanalyst's listening, ready to catch on preferentially to some motif in the film, according to the force of that motif and according to my own fantasies as a spectator" (54).

Nazi-retro films offer a unique viewing experience not because of their poles of illusion and distancing—found to a degree in all feature films—but because of the way historical content functions to produce both effects. Historical background makes the world of the narrative familiar to the viewer. It is a code shared by director and viewer, and its presence on the screen and in the viewer's memory marks an entry point into the film. History provides the signs that Metz describes as "responsible for suggesting to the spectator the vector along which his permanent identification with his own look [gaze] should be extended temporarily inside the film" (54).

Conversely, historical markers point out the meaning of the events behind the narrative. Although the material of history is part of the narrative, its function does not stop with the telling of the story. Rather, as Kristin Thompson suggests, "the materiality of the image goes beyond the narrative structures of unity in film." Thompson points out that normally the materiality of a film goes unnoticed. At times, however, particularly if individual elements are not thoroughly motivated, "excess comes forward and must affect narrative meaning" (132). Although Thompson speaks primarily of stylistic elements—color, set design, and so forth—historical information can also supply excess that affects narrative meaning. History thus plays a dual role in Nazi-retro films. For one, it orients spectators to the screen world, facilitating thereby a place of entry into that world and causing their emotional involvement in the lives of the fictional characters. For another, it reminds viewers that what they are viewing is a fictionalized account of history. It gives them a crystal ball that lets them look into the future of the characters and their stories. Viewers can reflect *before* the results of the events take place. The distance for reflection that the crystal ball gives them allows viewers to judge the characters even while they are identifying with them.

Surely, creating a narrative about the role that ordinary citizens played during the Third Reich, or the role that citizens of any country play during times of historic upheaval, should be a humbling task for a filmmaker. Nonetheless, many have made such films. George Santayana's warning that "those who cannot remember the past are condemned to repeat it" has become a commonplace justification for the preoccupation of filmmakers (and of other artists) with Hitler, national socialism, and the Third Reich.[1] Directors seem intent on focusing on the past and thereby illuminating whatever lessons it may hold for the present. Rainer Werner Fassbinder's films, for example, are like morality plays in which the mistakes of the past are paraded in front of viewers to help them recognize what he views as the repressive (or fascist) tendencies in German society, a theme that runs through all of his movies. The fascist tendencies of pre-Nazi Germany provide the background for *Bolwieser* (1976–77), *Eine Reise ins Licht—Despair* (*Despair*, 1977), and *Berlin Alexanderplatz* (1983). *Lili Marleen* focuses directly on the Third Reich era; *The Marriage of Maria Braun*, *Lola* (1982), and *Die Sehnsucht der Veronika Voss* (*Veronika Voss*, 1982) show the lingering influence of fascism during the years of the economic miracle in postwar Germany. Even *Fontane Effi Briest* (*Effi Briest*, 1974), a film set in late nineteenth-century Germany, deals with fascist repression by suggesting that it was rooted in the suppressive and oppressive policies of the Wilhelmine period. *Veronika Voss* and *The Marriage of Maria Braun* are particularly concerned with remembering the past. These two films present metaphors of how memory functions to distort the past; that is, they do more than re-create the past with a vague hope that re-creation of former mistakes will help viewers avoid repeating them. *Veronika Voss* and *The Marriage of Maria Braun* also show that the way in which the past is remembered is important: not only must viewers remember the past but they must remember it honestly, for simply remembering the past is clearly not enough to prevent a recurrence of tragic events.

Veronika Voss

▲▼▲

In *Sehnsucht der Veronika Voss* (*Veronika Voss*, 1982), the last of Fassbinder's trilogy of films about social malaise during postwar Germany's economic miracle, the director pays homage to Billy Wilder's *Sunset Boulevard* (1950) and the screen magic of Hollywood, particularly as it was influenced by former directors of Germany's Universum-Film A.G. (UFA) studios. *Veronika Voss* is about a fading actress who has become addicted to drugs and whose addiction is being exploited by a mysterious doctor, a former Nazi. The narrative, which reaches melodramatic heights unusual even for Fassbinder, is a vehicle for the director to explore how film art creates illusion and how in turn illusion affects perception. *Veronika Voss* is a demonstration of the techniques of the old UFA-Hollywood masters—Douglas Sirk, Michael Curtiz, Josef von Sternberg, and Billy Wilder, among others. To be sure, these directors' techniques, from dramatic lighting, dark shadows, mirrors, and double exposures to mysterious women, plot twists, and musically punctuated moments, find their way into all of Fassbinder's films—but nowhere to such a degree as in *Veronika Voss*.

Fassbinder, however, is not interested in mere mimicry, tapping nostalgia, or reawakening old emotions. His purpose is not to re-create a memory of old illusions but rather to show the viewer how the illusions affect memory. To achieve his goal of exposing the mechanisms behind cinematic illusion, Fassbinder exaggerates his usual mannerisms until they burst the narrative world of *Veronika Voss*. He betrays his intention by overusing those tropes that represent visual obstruction: the viewer's clear perception of what occurs is blocked by doorways, windows, curtains, smoke, and rain. The heroine's face is often hidden by a veil, and she and other characters are viewed as reflections in mirrors and windows. Fassbinder not only emulates the old films but also emphasizes, through the self-conscious way in which he uses their techniques, that viewers should work to know what the visuals mean. That is, they must try to deconstruct the emotional tug of the fictional narrative and see behind it to some greater truth. In an interview about *Effi Briest*, Fassbinder commented, "I favor allowing the spectator himself to activate feelings about the characters when he is in the theater or watching television. However, the possibility of reflection must be incorporated into the structure of the thing. In other words, the staging of the film must produce distance and thus make reflection possible."[2]

Fassbinder wants viewers to think about how easily the past can be distorted. Moreover, he wishes them to recognize how willing they are to accept distortion if it will help them cope with unpleasant memories. To bring viewers to reflect on this situation, Fassbinder uses the techniques of the old masters but also employs a modern movie cliché—top-40 songs to create mood and to comment on screen action. One of these songs is Terry

Gilkyson, Rich Dehr, and Frank Miller's "Memories Are Made of This" (1955), which the director uses to suggest how powerful a hold the past has on the present. The lyrics further imply that memories are selective, being composed of bits and pieces of the past rather than the whole of history. Such selectivity is a way to control the past, to eliminate the memories that cause pain or are somehow unpleasant. Selecting what to focus on is also a way to handle the unpleasantness of the present. Veronika Voss, for example, drinks and takes drugs in order to hide her present situation. The same is true for her husband. Alcohol and morphine are but two narcotics used to alter perception, to disguise the truth; in his other films Fassbinder shows other addictions, other dependencies. In *Lola*, for example, he portrays the addictive nature of sex and wealth. In *The Marriage of Maria Braun* he depicts how the economic miracle makes people feel good about themselves and distracts their attention from the unresolved problems of the past.

In all three films the narcotic is supplied by a third party who is aware of the power it has to exploit human weakness. Looked at in this way, the leitmotiv of escaping into fantasy becomes a metaphor for what occurred in the Third Reich. Under Hitler, the mise-en-scène of the Nazi spectacle—as Hans Jürgen Syberberg so vividly presents it in his epic film *Hitler, ein Film aus Deutschland* (*Our Hitler: A Film from Germany*, 1977)—was its own narcotic, intended to appeal to the subconscious, to distract consciousness from reality, and thereby to alter perception. *Veronika Voss* serves as a reminder that movies not only help viewers recall the past but also distort the past by creating the memories that are to be remembered.

The Marriage of Maria Braun

▲▼▲

The way that the past is remembered is the theme of Fassbinder's greatest success, *Die Ehe der Maria Braun* (*The Marriage of Maria Braun*, 1978). The film, which some critics have compared with Michael Curtiz's *Mildred Pierce* (1945),[3] is essentially a melodramatic love story about a love that begins in Nazi Germany under siege and continues into the years of the *Wirtschaftswunder*, or economic miracle. As Fassbinder's movie opens, a poster of Hitler explodes upon the impact of a bomb. Amid the exploding debris, Maria and Hermann Braun, lying on the street outside the courthouse, sign their marriage papers. Hermann is sent to the Russian front, where he is reported as killed. Maria at first waits for his return, then takes up with a black American sergeant. When Hermann walks in on their lovemaking, Maria kills the American. Hermann confesses to the murder and is sent to prison. Maria next takes up with Oswald, a manufacturer, becomes his mistress, and rises to a position of considerable power within his company. Hermann is released from prison and leaves the country after making a secret deal with Oswald to do so. Upon the manufacturer's death, Hermann returns. Before he and Maria can enjoy the fortune that Oswald has left them, they are killed in an explosion caused by gas escaping from a stove that Maria has forgotten(?) to turn off. As the house explodes in the background, the screen shows a progression of portraits of German chancellors. Meanwhile, the radio announcer reports hysterically that the German soccer team has become world champion.

We have retold the story line of *The Marriage of Maria Braun* to emphasize the melodramatic nature of the film and to demonstrate how it intermixes history with melodrama. On one level, the film is a story about a neurotic obsession for a lost lover. On another level, however, as reviewers and critics have written, Maria's obsession with her marriage is a thinly disguised allegory of postwar Germany's relationship to its past: "Ethics not aesthetics, is Fassbinder's goal in grabbing our emotions while they're off-guard. . . . The world outside the frame of the film is what interests Fassbinder: metaphorically *Maria Braun* tells the story of postwar Germany: success at a price—a loss of emotions, a coldness now considered to be characteristic of Germans. . . . His characters are casualties of the economic rationalism that pervades our thinking: . . . we spiritually prostitute ourselves in the pursuit of a private materialism."[4] As apt as this interpretation might be, it is ultimately unsatisfying for two reasons. First, sex, exploitation, loneliness, and cruelty have become commonplace markers for social critics; always, they are equated with material success. Of course, given Germany's rapid economic recovery, which is depicted in this film, it is not surprising to find critics emphasizing a metaphor that equates German economic success with loss of soul. And once this equation is made, it is easy to conclude that the film's apocalyptic end is a Götterdämmerung brought about by too much too fast. The destructive explosion becomes a warning to viewers that they ought to reexamine their priorities in life. Secondly, to understand the film in this way, as an allegory or metaphor of the economic miracle, is to reduce the film to a melodrama with a message. Fassbinder's movie is more than this. Maria is part of the whole, a thread of the tapestry that is postwar Germany. She cannot be separated from the world she inhabits in the narrative and made to refer to some ethical principle. To construe Maria as allegory makes it difficult to reconcile the film's closing scenes with the rest of the movie. The final sequence becomes ethical reinforcement for the narrative, as

Noonan (44) implies, or facile politics, in the interpretation of other critics, or simply confusing, according to Vincent Canby.[5] None of these interpretations or solutions is completely satisfying.

The last three minutes of the film play an aesthetic-philosophical function, turning a narrative about obsessive love into a metaphor for the relationship of individuals to their past. As the final sequence begins, the time in the narrative is summer 1954. Even though the exact date is not given, the audience knows that it must be summer 1954 because a radio announcer is heard screaming enthusiastically that the Germans have just won the world soccer championship. Even if the viewer does not know this bit of esoterica (it would be unlikely for a German not to know it, but an American probably would not), the present of the movie is obviously somewhere in the mid-1950s, judging from fashions and Maria's age. The world of 1954, the time of the economic miracle, is linked in this sequence to the time of the Third Reich in two ways. First, the return of Hermann Braun after Oswald's death reminds viewers of the marriage that took place as bombs fell near the end of World War II. Second, the explosion that occurs reminds viewers of the opening of the film when a poster of Hitler was shown amid exploding bombs. The year 1954 is also linked with the future (the present day for the viewer) through a series of portraits. Starting with a negative exposure of Germany's first postwar chancellor, Konrad Adenauer, the screen shows the face of each succeeding chancellor—excluding that of Willi Brandt—in negative up to the portrait of Helmut Schmidt. Schmidt, the chancellor at the time the film was made, 1978, completes the series of faces. His portrait changes to a positive exposure as the audience's present is reached. Thus the narrative is extended into the present but also tied to the Third Reich at the end of World War II by the two dramatic explosions that open and close the film. It would be easy to conclude that Fassbinder is equating Schmidt with Hitler in this closing shot, as at least one critic has done (Rich, 86). Little in the movie, however, supports such a conclusion. Rather, it is likely that Fassbinder wished to show that past, present, and future are interdependent. The absence of Brandt's face from the portrait sequence lends support to this interpretation. Brandt left Germany during the war years. His role in what transpired during the period is therefore different from that of the other chancellors. Consequently, his photograph is left out.

The final three minutes are connected to the narrative not through Fassbinder's desire to equate politics present with politics past—he may indeed feel this to be true, but that is not how this sequence affects viewers—but through his desire to make it clear that the past is part of the present. In the melodramatic narrative that leads up to the final sequence,

Maria has devoted her entire life to her marriage to Hermann Braun, an earlier event of immense importance but short duration that she has allowed to dominate her thought and influence her actions. She apparently wants to forget the past when she throws Hermann's picture under some train wheels, but he comes back repeatedly to gain power over her, not physically but mentally, in the same way that memories keep recurring and haunting an individual's life. Maria herself actively keeps the memory alive by visiting Hermann in prison and working for his release. Her marriage becomes a metaphor for the past and the effect that it has on individuals: controlling them in proximity and from a distance, always entering the scene unexpectedly to wield power over those whose memory it is a part of. Maria's memories take on the semblance of a specter that haunts her at unexpected moments, as when, bewildered, she kills her black lover when her husband returns the first time. Upon his second return, his indifference to her during their reunion, which should be like a honeymoon, is disturbing enough to cause her to act absentmindedly and thus kill herself and Hermann.

By revealing the relationship of past, present, and future for individuals as well as nations, *The Marriage of Maria Braun* does not limit itself to being a simple statement that the past serves as a warning to the present. Rather, history is shown to be an indelible part of the lives of individuals and nations. The past is not something they can walk away from; nor are historical events something that simply by being remembered can be prevented from recurring or affecting our actions. Germany cannot forget the past (nor should it forget the past, if that were possible); but as that past recedes into history, how it is remembered is important. This point is emphasized by the year in which Fassbinder ends the narrative, 1954. Having won the soccer World Cup that year, Germany was embarking on a new era of confidence. The German self-confidence of 1954 paralleled the high self-confidence during the Third Reich. The question that the film poses is whether the past is to be remembered as an event of immense importance, but of only limited duration, or whether it is to be romanticized, as Maria romanticizes her marriage. Movies cannot prevent disaster by warning about the past.

Girls' War

▲▼▲

In Alf Brustellin and Bernhard Sinkel's *Mädchenkrieg* (*Girls' War*, 1977) historical sets and costumes identify the period as Prague between 1934 and 1946. Otherwise, history is only sketchily present, requiring viewers to fill in the gaps if the film's narrative is to supply any insight into the past. Hellmuth Kurasek, for example, writes in *Spiegel* that the war setting in the film provides "only a cinematic fire-glow that lights up the girls' faces."[6] Such criticism of the film's historical background, however, is misplaced. For that "fire-glow" makes it possible for viewers to enter into the world of the film's bourgeois characters—a father and his three adolescent daughters who have come to Prague for business opportunities. Although the war is left in the background, it is sufficiently present that viewers, whether they experienced the war firsthand or through relatives' stories, history books, or popular culture, can fill in what the background only outlines. Without depicting the Nazis and their atrocities, the film nonetheless re-creates a threatening environment. As a result, viewers understand the motivation behind the actions of the film's characters.

History in *Girls' War* is present in filmic clichés about the Third Reich. Karasek calls these the usual "tried and trusted collection of bordello and boots, cognac and Gestapo cynicism" and laments that they present nothing new about Nazi Germany (233). But the film is not meant as a history lesson about World War II and nazism any more than any narrative film is meant to be purely informational. The film's clichés allow viewers to orient themselves to the fictional world of the film and to more quickly identify with the protagonists as they struggle to survive in Nazi-occupied Prague. Spectators are familiar—or think they are—with the moral dilemmas the family faces because they are familiar with the stereotyped image of the Third Reich on film. Brustellin and Sinkel's use of clichés lets viewers anticipate the moral lessons of the movie: the making of choices in extreme situations.

The clichés of history that Karasek decries work together with the formulaic nature of the narrative to help spectators experience those moral lessons. The clichés put the moral decisions that the characters make into context. The formulaic narrative makes it easier for viewers to identify with the characters who make the decisions. For the situations the girls and their father face are those found often in classic melodrama: love triangles, opportunism, threats to the family, and heroic activism. These typical situations are familiar to viewers from countless films, and their familiarity makes viewers comfortable with the choices that the girls and their father make. For example, the father's decision to protect his family by agreeing to spy on his Jewish boss for the Nazis, although immoral, is understood by spectators who recognize that the family is threatened and who want the family to survive the war as much as does the father. Likewise, the decisions of one of the sisters to become a freedom fighter, of another to ignore the war by entering a convent, and of the third to suppl

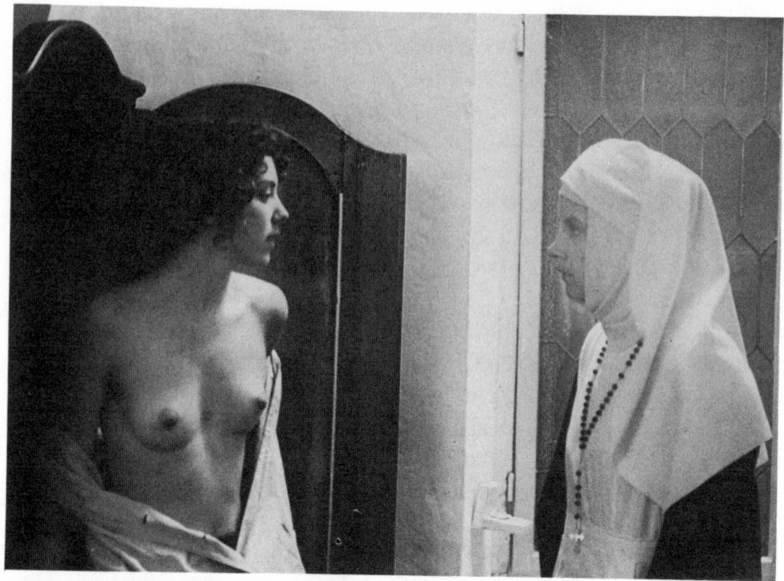

Girls' War (1977). Katharina, a freedom fighter (Katharina Hunter, left), and her sister Sophie (Adelheid Ardnt) meet in a convent where Sophie has fled the war and her personal problems. Courtesy Inter Nationes.

the Nazis with uniforms, reflect general reactions to the turmoil—namely, resistance, inner immigration, and opportunistic fellow-traveling. Regardless of whether viewers applaud or condemn these choices, they accept them as reasonable and motivated by the circumstances.

At the same time, however, viewers are free of the constraints of the narrative, unlike the characters in the film. Whenever the informational excess of the film breaks the filmic illusion and suspends the viewers' identification with the characters, viewers are free to judge the choices that the characters make. Excess manifests itself in a variety of ways: troops marching into the Sudetenland, swastika armbands, references to collaboration and resistance movements, and photographs of the girls in Prague. These bits of historical information break the cinematic illusion and remind viewers that there is a deeper significance to the events on the screen than the one present in the fictional narrative. That is, once the illusion is broken, viewers can recognize that the choices being made by the protagonists of *Girls' War* represent choices made by ordinary citizens in the actual historical situation, but that the majority of these choices were self-destructive since they were made in the service of a regime that committed acts of atrocities and acted against the best interests of its citizens. Thus, at the end of the film, although spectators may sympathize with the sisters as they are deported back to Germany, they can accept the outcome of the movie from history's point of view. Deportation of these women, regardless of the dislocation it causes in their lives, seems minor compared to the dislocation that their government caused.

The First Polka

▲▼▲

Klaus Emmerich's *Die erste Polka* (*The First Polka*, 1978) has a more seamless narrative than *Girls' War*, making it harder to pass judgment on its characters. The film has neither the narrative frame nor the metanarrative inserts that Brustellin and Sinkel's film has to break the cinematic illusion. Moreover, the situation of the youthful protagonists and their mother in *The First Polka* is less extreme and thus easier to identify with. The narrative unfolds without any interruption, producing more suspense, sentimentality, and pathos than in *Girls' War*. As a result, viewers seldom get outside the narrative long enough to be critical of the actions of the characters or even to see where mistakes are being made. The film takes place over a 24-hour period on the eve of World War II and ends with a radio speech by Hitler announcing Germany's attack on Poland. But the narrative centers not on Germany's preparations for this attack but rather on the problems of a fictional family, the Pionteks, living in Gleiwitz, a city with both German and Polish inhabitants and situated on the, at that time, German side of the German-Polish border. When the film ends, the son has run away after killing a Nazi soldier in self-defense; his sister is on her honeymoon, having recently married a German officer; and the mother and uncle have completed some real estate transactions that should, now that war has broken out, realize a profit.

Nothing in *The First Polka* breaks identification with the characters. Moreover, nothing in the film allows viewers to focus on the historical events occurring in the background. The attention of viewers is instead directed to the personal dilemmas of the characters. But even though the film does not foreground history for the viewers, the knowledge they have of historical events foregrounds the history for them. When the movie ends, viewers are well aware that the events in the background have unleashed a war on Europe whose aftershocks are just now dying down with the apparent collapse of communism in Central Europe. Furthermore, because the bonds of identification are so strong in the film, viewers want to know how the war affected the characters. The movie's open end encourages speculation. After all, the boys will have reached draft age before the war is over. There is a good possibility that the daughter could become a war widow. And most significantly, since Gleiwitz became a Polish town after the war, the lives of the adults will most likely be radically altered. The film leaves open whether the mother and uncle were punished for speculating in land and whether they were driven westward with so many other refugees after the war. Thus, while the narrative may not reach beyond itself, viewers can project a future for the world depicted in the film. Furthermore, the more complete their knowledge of World War II is, the more threatening will be the future that viewers project. As the film ends, the heroine is praying in front of a home altar as Hitler speaks on the radio. The scene is a poignant reminder to viewers who know the history that the invasion Hitler is speaking of is the start of a six-year nightmare with which Germany is still trying to come to terms.

The weakness of a film like *The First Polka*—at least as it deals with Germany's past—is that viewers can overlook or not even be able to see the meaning of its historical background. The characters go about their normal lives as if nothing of note were taking place around them. The dizzying events of their personal lives—the daughter's marriage, the adolescent rivalries of the cousins, the father's terminal illness—prevent everyone from seeing what is taking place on the periphery, the buildup of German troops in their town. Unfortunately, the degree to which the film focuses on these private problems also prevents viewers from seeing beyond the center to the periphery and recognizing the error the characters make when they ignore the political situation around them. The polka danced at the end of the movie, the son's "first polka," becomes a metaphor for the way the characters deal with their surroundings. Just as polka dancers focus on one spot to keep their balance in an otherwise dizzying situation, the characters in the movie concentrate on the immediate concerns of the day in the hope of not losing control. In this atmosphere of private problems, it is also difficult for viewers to focus on the history that is in the film. The son's first polka is followed by his initiation into the adult world of guilt when he kills an army sergeant. As the film ends and Hitler's voice is heard on the radio, viewers are more concerned with the fate of the young man—who is now running from the authorities, although no one saw his crime—than with the coming war. Only as the credits roll can one reflect on the possible political and historical effect of the war on this family and the way in which they have contributed to events. One can just as easily, however, choose not to reflect on the historical reasons for what has transpired and instead wonder at the vicissitudes of fate and the way it has affected this family.

The First Polka (1978). Family and guests listen to the radio for news of the impending war. Courtesy Inter Nationes.

Both *Girls' War* and *The First Polka* point up how easy it is for a filmmaker to create a past that does not seem all that undesirable. Even though it includes scenes of advancing Germans, *Girls' War*, for example, can mislead one into overlooking the ideology that was responsible for the events in the film. It is true that viewers can fill in the historical gaps, that they can remind themselves that the film's events take place during the Third Reich. It is also true that viewers can judge the choices that the characters make and reflect on the consequences these choices have in the private lives of the characters as well as in the larger historical picture. Nonetheless, *Girls' War* never comes to terms with nazism, never suggests that fascist ideology had taken control of the German spirit, and, moreover, never makes it clear that the ideology was detrimental to Germany, to its institutions, and to its citizens. Viewers can surmise this by what they see in the film, but they can ignore it as well. The same is true of *The First Polka.* In an attempt to focus on the hero's "coming of age" and the mother's concern for economic gain—at times she comes across like a middle-class Mother Courage who in the face of war can concentrate on raising money for the family's future—Emmerich loses sight of the Third Reich. Although Hitler has been in power six years at the time the narrative is taking place, the film hints at the negative aspects of the Third Reich only once: Montag, the film's only Jewish figure, hides in the Pionteks' summer house because of local persecution. Moreover, his problems seem more self-imposed than societally imposed. Even the German-staged attack on the radio station that Hitler used as an excuse to start the war seems within the rules of allowable political intrigue. After all, nations frequently engage in disinformation campaigns. The film suggests that Hitler's deception was like any other trick of the spy game. Historically, of course, it was of great importance; but in the narrative of the movie the attack is peripheral.

By relegating Nazi ideology to the periphery, the directors of *Girls' War* and *The First Polka* remove from view the immediate consequences of the Nazis' rise to power and create narrative worlds that are nonthreatening and therefore more conducive to identification. While identification may help viewers enter the screen world more easily and find pleasure in the movie, deemphasizing Nazi ideology also creates an illusion of normalcy, giving the impression that maybe life under the Nazis was not all that bad.

Autumn Milk

▲▼▲

Joseph Vilsmaier takes the depiction of normalcy during the Third Reich one step further. In his film *Herbstmilch* (*Autumn Milk*, 1988) the director portrays the harsh reality of peasant life in Bavaria during this time and brackets out the unpleasant aspects of nazism. Vilsmaier is clearly trying to create a history for the peasants that shows the struggle for existence on the land weighing more heavily on their minds than any political concerns. As sincere as his attempt is, and as valid as his insight may be, the movie distorts truth in its creation of "normal peasant life." This distortion is a result as much of the way Vilsmaier has chosen to tell his story as of his avoidance of the subject of the average citizen's responsibility for the past.

Autumn Milk is based on the memoir of Anna Wimschneider, who wrote about her life out of a need to tell her story. She describes in linear fashion, in simple and sometimes ungrammatical prose, the hard life she had as a peasant woman in Bavaria. Her story chronicles the sorrow but also the happiness that she experienced from childhood to old age. Her brief description of her life before the death of her mother is followed by longer descriptions of life as the elder of two girls and of having to take over as woman of the farm at age eight. She tells of her courtship with Albert, a neighboring farmer, and her problems with a cruel mother-in-law. These sections take the memoir through 1945 and are followed by an epilogue on life in postwar Germany, including the problems of inflation and refugee resettlement. She ends her story with the Wimschneider family's migration to town. Although references to the Nazis, Dachau, the Jews, and the war enter her narration, it is primarily a telling of the story of her life as a peasant woman; thus political history remains in the background while personal history takes the foreground. In spite of the secondary role assigned to political events, these events are presented as honestly and truthfully as one would expect a reminiscing narrator to remember them. Nonetheless, the overriding sentiment of her story is summed up in her closing sentence: "If I ever were to come into this world again, I would not again be born a peasant woman."[7]

Joseph Vilsmaier restructures the loose narrative of the memoir to create dramatic development. In an attempt to capture the book's first-person narration, he adds a beginning and closing frame of the elderly Anna Wimschneider looking back on her life. Between these frames he concentrates on the years from 1938 to 1945. Besides reflecting seven important years in Anna's life—during which occurred her courtship with Albert, their marriage, his induction into the war, and the birth of her first child—these were also the most important years in Nazi Germany. Thus, by limiting his narrative to these seven years, Vilsmaier moves the historical background of the memoir into a central position. At the same time this focus gives the film the dramatic impact most viewers hope to find in a narrative movie. Whereas historical references are plentiful in the memoir—indeed, it contains more historical information than the movie—their role there is subordinate to the tale of Anna's life as a peasant. In the film history is no longer subordinate. Rather, as reflected in the events that take place in the public sphere, it assumes a prominent role. In addition, interest in Anna's life as a peasant has been replaced by interest in her domestic problems. The film thus sets up two narrative spheres: the public sphere in which history unfolds, and the private sphere in which Anna's story is told. Although the two spheres cross, they never seem to touch each other.

Two climactic moments in the film show clearly how Anna interacts with the public sphere but remains separate from it. Following a sequence in which she is dragged through the dirt by an ox, Anna goes to town to get a male prisoner of war to help with the field work. After greeting a photographer with whom she trades on the black market, she enters the

Autumn Milk (1988). "If I ever were to come into this world again, I would not again be born a peasant woman." Anna (Dana Vavrova) plows a field on her farm. Courtesy Cine International and Inter Nationes.

office of the Nazi functionary and demands that he send her a worker. The camera emphasizes her superiority to this petty bureaucrat by giving her a privileged place in the frame's composition. She commands the center of the frame as she glowers at the official, a district leader. At another point she towers over him as he sits at his desk. He remains seated throughout the sequence and shares the frame with a secretary who stands behind him, the camera focusing on her disgust with his ineptitude and delight at his comeuppance. In a shot-countershot sequence, Anna is in the center of the screen with open space all around her. The district leader is also in the center of his shot but is hemmed in by the clutter on his desk and the wall behind. The dialogue likewise displays Anna's superiority to the district leader and underscores her feeling of standing apart from nazism. She glances around the room, sits down in the middle of it, and defiantly proclaims that she will not move even if she has to stay as long as the district leader's "Thousand Year Reich." She stands at his desk and announces he will be cursed for not working his land and instead exploiting it for the quick wealth in its trees. Then the camera, shooting from behind the dis-

trict leader, films Anna walking defiantly toward him. Scoffingly, she claims that the Nazi party will not touch her, that it needs mothers and peasants. In a final coup de grace, she proclaims that she will be around long after he has been hanged. This entire sequence emphasizes Anna's separateness from the district leader and his ideology. It is *his* Thousand Year Reich that she will outlast, and it is *his* hanging that she will get to see. It should be noted, however, that Anna's superiority is not based on a political or moral position. Rather, she feels that as a peasant she is invaluable to the Nazis and thus deserves help from the Reich. For this reason, even though Anna separates herself from the Reich, she still demands a prisoner of war to help on the farm. Even as she comes in contact with the public sphere and benefits from it, she still remains separate from it.

The second climactic moment comes immediately after this sequence. Anna receives a worker. Through a lyrical interlude in the snow, Vilsmaier indicates passage of time. One day Anna is accused by her mother-in-law of stealing food and trading it on the black market. She is forced to beg forgiveness from the other relatives who own the farm. As she pleads with Albert's uncles and aunt that she traded for her child so that he could have medicine and warm clothes, the camera shows the child, Anna, and the cruel face of the mother-in-law. Before the relatives can pass judgment on her actions, however, Albert returns from the war; as in a fairy tale, he banishes his mother from the house for having been so cruel to Anna. Anna's black market activity is forgotten now that Albert has returned. The war also seems forgotten in this scene. One of the uncles remarks, "The war isn't over, is it?" perhaps expecting that the war can end as easily as an evil mother-in-law can be banished. In any event, the only reminder of the war is a superficial wound that Albert has received.

For spectators who are not familiar with the history of Germany under national socialism, the film's historical discourse is without meaning. Although we have often mentioned the importance of knowledge about Nazi Germany for viewers of Nazi-retro films, the point bears repeating here. For viewers who know little or nothing about Nazi Germany, the icons of the Third Reich that abound in the film are reduced to simple narrative devices, adding color to a story of love and farming. If one does not know about the black market economy and the profiteering that went on among the peasants, Anna's cry that she did it for the baby stands unopposed. If one does not know that countless lives were lost on the eastern front, the irony of Albert's superficial wound in Italy is lost. If one is not familiar with Dachau and the extermination camps, references to it are mere generalized threats arising out of the repartee at a peasant supper. In other words, if one is not familiar with what occurred under the Nazis, then the film has no critical perspective and is an epic of peasant life, nothing more.

It is probable, however, that most viewers are familiar with nazism and that the icons the movie introduces are sufficiently recognizable to call forth the deprivations and horrors occurring in the years 1938–45 under Hitler and the Nazis. Furthermore, the film so foregrounds historical references that knowledgeable viewers cannot escape the associations these awaken in them. They will recognize the irony in Anna's reference to the Thousand Year Reich and in her mockery of the district leader when she threatens that he will be hanged. They will understand the allusions to a black market economy among the peasants, who were able to barter food for materials and services. They will nod knowingly at the enumeration of death notices of soldiers on the eastern front and cringe at the mention of Dachau and the thought of the inmates murdered there and at other camps. There is also the possibility, however, that even viewers who know about the past will choose to see a comforting version of history in *Autumn Milk*. For Vilsmaier seems to be offering them a revisionist view of the past. Nowhere in his movie does he show a direct relationship between what occurred during the Third Reich and the peasants of the narrative. No one, of course, can deny that peasants and average citizens lived in a private sphere and that this sphere had little, if any, influence on political decisions. Nonetheless, people in the private sphere, whether they lived in the city or on the land, acquiesced to the events around them. In Vilsmaier's movie, however, except for the district leader—who, as was pointed out above, is an outsider—every one in the film remains untouched by national socialism.

The distance between peasants and Nazis that Vilsmaier constructs creates a dangerous, although perhaps unintentional, subtext. To be sure, the movie is about the harsh life of being a peasant, not about politics in the Third Reich. Nonetheless, Vilsmaier has chosen to concentrate his film adaptation of Wimschneider's memoir on the years that were most important to the Hitler regime. One therefore expects that his film must be saying something about the relationship between peasant life and nazism. By foregrounding Nazi icons and showing their distinctness from the peasants, the film suggests that the Third Reich had little or no effect on rural Germany. Moreover, this subtext builds until it takes over and dissolves the film about coming to terms with the past into a film about the glories of the German countryside (what Germans would refer to as a *Heimatfilm*). For example, in the final sequence of the narrative, before the film returns to the frame, Albert, Anna, their child, and a prisoner of war are in their fields. A plane is heard overhead, and the camera follows Anna's glance upward to reveal a low-flying aircraft. Anna waves as if completely unaware that there is a war in progress and that the plane in the sky could be the enemy. Luckily, Albert remembers that Germany is at war and pulls Anna to the ground. The prisoner of war likewise pulls the child down and covers its body. The plane strafes the ground once and flies away. The four get up and walk home. The strafing has been a retarding moment to remind the audience of the war before the film's happy end. The scene changes to a peasant house, and a barefooted Albert leads a barefooted Anna into their peasant courtyard, where they dance slowly to the "Cuckoo's Waltz." The camera circles around them, establishing the mood of a true happy end. The camera cuts to relatives looking on from a window with tears of joy in their eyes. They represent the viewers who look on from the theater, wiping away a tear as they contemplate this lovely story. But what about the war? What about the Nazis? Indeed, what about how hard it is to be a peasant in Bavaria? None of that seems to be of consequence in the lives of these particular peasants. Although the film is based on the story of historical figures who lived during one of the most significant and devastating times of the twentieth century, it turns out it has not been about those figures or about that time at all. It has instead been about a märchen peasant-prince and his wife whose land comes under a vague but evil spell. Once the spell is broken, the framing device can return and the elder Anna Wimschneider can continue her walk. As she walks through the beautiful German countryside, an offscreen voice, presumably that of the old woman—who was played, by the way, by the real Anna Wimschneider—recites a recipe for Herbstmilch, a dish for the poor, for the elderly, and, one is tempted to add, for those who fondly remember the good old days.

Most disturbing about Vilsmaier's movie is that its style creates a veneer of objectivity that seduces spectators into believing that the world as depicted actually existed. His camera work is straightforward. There are no bizarre angles, no telling close-ups, no distorting lenses, and no grainy newsreels to interpret the past. The entire narrative is a flashback, and there are even flashbacks within that. But this framing, which should capture the first-person perspective of the memoir, thus showing that the images of beauty have been colored by the storyteller, has no effect since the camera tells the tale, not a narrator's voice. In the book the reader can compensate for Anna Wimschneider's perspective on events and experience her tale as a partial truth. It is one version, Anna's version, of what occurred. In spite of trying to capture this first-person perspective, Vilsmaier obscures the narrator in his film when he has his camera tell the story. Without a narrating voice, the film visuals become objective truth. The narrating camera and the objective camera lens are one, and together they try to convince spectators that the war years were as depicted: short, pretty, and with no lasting effect on anyone. By adopting so objective a style, Vilsmaier presents a past that fails to reveal the hidden reality behind the outer images of beauty. And these outer images show the past the way many viewers want to remember it: a private time ruled by the personal virtues of hard work, kindness, warmth, and cooperation.

Heimat

▲▼▲

A similar attempt to separate "History" from "history," motivated Edgar Reitz to make his epic *Heimat* (1984), in which nazism once again appears as an outside force.[8] When *Heimat* premiered in 1984, it was an event. Conceived of as a theatrical film, it nonetheless runs over 15 hours. Consequently, apart from marathon weekend showings at selected theaters in Germany and abroad, its primary medium of exposure has been television. Appearing weekly over 11 weeks, the series reportedly emptied streets as viewers stayed home to tune in the continuing saga of the Simon family of Hunsrück. Eventually 25 million viewers saw some part of the movie, a remarkable accomplishment for a film, in spite of its miniseries format, that was demanding in both its subject matter—a historical chronicle focusing extensively on the Third Reich era and the years leading up to the Nazis' rise to power—and its means of production—black-and-white scenes alternating with ones shot in sepia and others in full color. In spite of its broad popular appeal, the film also enjoyed critical success in Germany and abroad. Here, finally, was a movie about Germany in the twentieth century that put "large history" in its proper perspective and told instead the "small history" of ordinary German villagers.[9]

But by telling the "small history," the film raises the same reservations as Vilsmaier's *Autumn Milk*. Anton Kaes, in a thorough analysis of the film, summarizes both the positive and negative responses to it. He reports that, for the most part, critics in Germany, France, and Britain reacted favorably. It was not until the film premiered in New York that strong negative voices were heard. Kaes attributes the American reaction to the initial negative reception in the *New York Times*, the *New York Review of Books*, and the *Village Voice*: "Three influential American papers . . . had taken umbrage at the fact that *Heimat* had excluded important parts of the National Socialist past" (183). The issue at stake is immediately clear. Just as German critics have focused on the aesthetic quality of *Autumn Milk* and thereby all but ignored the fact that it presents a spotty picture of German history, critics have done the same with *Heimat*, focusing on the made-in-Germany quality of the movie rather than on the history that is being presented. For example, Henri de Bresson wrote in *Le Monde*: "Germany has suddenly found a soul and a home. As if Edgar Reitz suddenly liberated a longing in the hearts of Germans that wants to show itself publicly." On the other hand, Timothy Garton Ash wrote in the *New York Review of Books*, "Remember, remember, this is a film about what Germans remember. Some things they remember in full color. Some in sepia. Others they prefer to forget" (Kaes, 183–84).

As Kaes points out, Reitz brought on some of the criticism himself with his outspoken claim that his film was a response to Hollywood's treatment of Germany's past in the television series "Holocaust." The year "Holocaust" played in Germany, Reitz had just experienced the disastrous release of his movie *Der Schnieder aus Ulm* (*The Tailor from Ulm*, 1978). He had retired to the Isle of Sylt to think about his filmmaking career. The winter was bad, and he was thus housebound for days with nothing to do but watch television:

> So I was forced to watch "Holocaust" on TV, and was offended to see German history reduced to the level of fiction in an American film studio. And here I had just had the experience of seeing an idea reduced to artificial meaninglessness by the studio treatment I had been forced into in Prague. I saw how it was taken seriously and how the question of guilt in German history was being discussed up and down the line by all the great German intellectuals on the basis of this travesty. I watched the horrible crocodile-tears of our nation. . . . I saw how that kind of film created the untenable equation: love the good and hate the bad, avoiding inner conflict, inner truth.[10]

Reitz's rejection of "Holocaust" is clearly informed by three major impulses: his belief that Hollywood trivialized and thus falsified Germany's past; his dislike of melodramatic polarities that divide the world into pure good and pure evil, with no dramatic shadings possible; and finally, his feeling that the remorse and breast-beating the series was calling forth in Germany was insincere. His answer to the major flaws in "Holocaust" was to create a film that (1) avoids trivializing great historical moments essentially by avoiding them (his film focuses on private lives, not history, as will be explained later), (2) rejects Hollywood polarities of good guys-bad guys by concentrating only on characters for whom good and/or evil is not an overriding issue, and (3) elicits nostalgic response to what is portrayed by eschewing most of the unpleasant aspects of his subject. It is easy to understand why American critics were against his film. What is difficult to understand is its almost universal acceptance by European critics, since Reitz simply replaced American or Hollywood clichés with his own.

Reitz's style creates the illusion that his film is a window onto the past. The director explains that, as a teenager, "the view through the small projection-room window onto the screen was for me identical to the view of the world. . . . All dreams of the world come through this small window. And that's how I still see film today. The screen is a window, an opening into the world of poetry."[11] Reitz's window into a world of poetry awakens viewers' memories. His characters are quirky enough to help viewers fondly recall their own relatives, yet they are not so odd that they disrupt the viewers' ability to identify and sympathize with the inhabitants of Reitz's fictional town of Schabbach, in the Hunsrück district. Furthermore, the characters' situations are familiar from other films and thus allow easy recognition. Meanwhile, the film avoids showing the political world, where difficult choices that disrupt the comfort of living must sometimes be made. The seduction of the audience by the sympathetic characters and familiar situations is enhanced by the manner in which this epic tale is told. The story of the villagers of Schabbach unfolds at a leisurely pace: over 15 hours in playing time, and 60 years in screen time. At the end of the series viewers can feel that the people of Schabbach and Schabbach itself exist. Reportedly, some Germans were surprised to learn that the town is fictional. Familiarity with the characters is further enhanced by the "chronicler," whose passion is collecting photos of the villagers. Reitz uses this village oddball to give veracity to his tale. The folks of Schabbach exist as surely as one's own relatives do; there are, after all, so many photos of them.[12] Moreover, their family history reflects the history of families with whom viewers may be familiar, perhaps even their own. The Simons represent a German "everyfamily" as it makes its way through history. Its members start out as preindustrial peasants and end as affluent members of Germany's business community. In short, Reitz's film shows how the healthy values of village life helped a family make it through the war and how these same values are helping it prosper in present-day Germany. In this way, the film strikes chords of nostalgia and thankfulness at the same time: nostalgia for the good old days, and gratitude that the virtues learned in those good old days have allowed so much progress.

While Reitz did not like what Hollywood made of Germany's past, he also did not like the guilt it brought out in his countrymen. To counteract that effect, he created a past that produces not guilt but comfort. Instead of insincere tears of remorse, his history produces tears of joy; in place of characters who embody a good-evil dichotomy, he substitutes a populace removed from making decisions about good and evil, right and wrong. As mentioned earlier, this is history writ small, the history of the everyday made popular by oral historians. Kaes points out, "In a certain sense, *Heimat* resists the attempt to write *one* history of Germany and thereby to reduce the multiplicity of contradictory aspects of concrete experience to a linear causal story . . . there is no such thing as *the* history of Germany—there is only a web of innumerable everyday stories" (173). While this is true, the film also avoids the question of where these individual stories fit into the larger historical picture. Whether or not a linear history is valid, the truth is that Nazi Germany did exist, and it is also true that it existed with the support of its populace, the villagers of the Hunsrück region included. Yet in *Heimat*, history writ large enters only from the outside. The villagers remain uninvolved in the Third Reich.[13] At least for the most part nazism is an outside force. And as soon as it disappears, Germany can commence with pursuing its destiny into the Wirtschaftswunder and beyond.

On the one hand, it is difficult and perhaps unfair to fault Reitz and Vilsmaier for wanting to show a "normal" or "normalized" past. There is little if anything to be gained by wearing the past as a national hair shirt to convince others of one's remorse for the sins of the fathers. On the other hand, the past should not simply disappear into a foggy mist. Stanley Cavell writes that "[movies] become further fragments of what happens to me, further cards in the shuffle of my memory, with no telling what place in the future."[14] If this is so, then the scenes in *Heimat* and *Autumn Milk* could enter into and mix with the truth. The "memories" they produce in the viewer may mingle with and thereby change the historical record. Reitz has reduced the pictures of the past to a photo album. Just as there are no embarrassing photos in family albums, there is nothing "embarrassing" about Germany in *Heimat*. Except for Eduard, none of the main family members are Nazis, and he is led into the party by his opportunistic wife, Lucie, an outsider who after the war ingratiates herself with the Americans as quickly as she had with the Nazis. The only other Nazis are depicted as unsympathetic characters whom no one in the village likes. All of the characters who support nazism disappear once the war is over. That is, Reitz makes no attempt to deal with the moral questions after the war.

In *Heimat* and *Autumn Milk* two histories exist side by side: the history of the people, and the history of the politicians. Neither has an effect on the other. Because the films keep personal history and political history separate, they create a subtext that suggests there was a gulf between the people and nazism. While it may be true that many Germans were not Nazis and would not have supported their government had they known the full extent of Nazi policies, it is also true that they did support their government. Nazism was not an outside force that arrived uninvited.

Heimat and *Autumn Milk* point up a problem with making films about private lives during great political moments. On the one hand, to place these lives in the center of the historical moment gives them power, which they historically did not have. On the other, to remove them from the political sphere suggests that individuals are incapable of exercising moral judgments about the actions of their country. Such removal also suggests that citizens have no responsibility to exercise such judgments.

Heimat (1984). Lucie (Karin Rasenack), Eduard's wife, shedding her Nazi past, accepts a ride into Schabbach in an American jeep. Courtesy WDR/SFB/Edgar Reitz and Inter Nationes.

My Country, Right or Wrong

▲▼▲

Eberhard Fechner's *Tadellöser und Wolff* (*My Country, Right or Wrong*, 1975) likewise focuses on the lives of private citizens during the war. By using irony and by foregrounding the consequences of war, Fechner is able to avoid sentimentalizing the past. At the same time his characters are as appealing and his situations as familiar as those in *Heimat* or *Autumn Milk*. In spite of his emphasis on the destructive power of war, Fechner's main focus remains the private life of a middle-class family, separate but not removed from the realities of the Third Reich. His movie, in two parts, was made for German television. It is based on Walter Kempowski's autobiographical novel of the same name and displays the same gentle irony found in the book. Rolf Becker states in his review of the film that Kempowski's purpose was to "show the people what they did wrong but at the same time offer them a comforting pat on the head."[15] As in Vilsmaier's film, Fechner's narrative is placed within the frame of a flashback. Here also the author of a memoir is looking back on his adolescence. And like Reitz's film, Fechner's work makes use of old photos to set the stage of the story and involve viewers more deeply in it. Fechner's frame, however, ties Germany-present to Germany-past directly. The person reminiscing is not silent but comments on the past and its legacy for the present. Whereas the photos in *Heimat* are of people, calculated perhaps to involve viewers in the lives of the characters, the photos in *My Country, Right or Wrong* are of remembered landmarks and shows them both before and after their destruction in the war. By showing both the good and bad of the past, Fechner is able to make nostalgia work for him. While he may create fond memories of times past, he also shows how those times past were destroyed as a result of the policies of the Third Reich. Moreover, by showing that the narrator and his family never actively opposed Hitler and national socialism, he implicates them in the events that caused the destruction.

Fechner unites historical fact and narrative fiction from the opening sequence of the film. As the narrator introduces the locale and time, Rostock, a seaport on the Baltic coast, in 1938, he points to photos of the ruins of famous landmarks. He remarks that those were indeed "glorious times: the year the synagogues were burned and Austria was annexed." And as he introduces the characters in an idyllic domestic setting, the first words are those of the mother, who proclaims, "How beautiful things are." This interplay between reality as perceived in a bourgeois home and the reality of national and world politics becomes a theme of the movie. The domestic story alone is akin to a German "Life with Father" or "I Remember Mama." Fechner gently caricatures the Kempowski parents as an authoritarian and short-tempered but understanding and loving husband and father and a strong but slightly scatterbrained wife and mother. They approach the turmoil around them as if they are above the fray. Even though they recognize the political situation of their country, they feel distant from it. Through this characterization of the parents as people who are good but essentially unconcerned with politics, Fechner foregrounds the error in their thinking. His satire reveals that even though the parents feel unaffected by the political sphere and believe themselves not responsible for what occurs, they are indeed affected by nazism and bear some responsibility for its consequences. The Kempowski family comes into direct contact with the war and Nazi policies frequently throughout the film: Their son-in-law, a Dane, is arrested for making a slanderous remark. Mr. Kempowski is called up for duty. The family inherits a shipping company that was bankrupt but, thanks to the war, is now realizing a profit. In spite of these contacts, they feel apart from what is going on. Mrs. Kempowski constantly reminds the family that they are doing well, not just to reassure herself, or out of superstition, but because she at first truly feels unaffected by the war. To be sure, the family goes along with everything that is happening because of its conservatism. When her daughter complains that "Germans are not nice people," Mrs. Kempowski reminds her that they are also German. And as Germans, they comply with rationing, blackouts, and the other indignities of war. Nevertheless the family members feel that they are not otherwise involved in what is occurring around them and therefore they feel no need to oppose it. Fechner portrays the members of the family as, in a sense, wondering what the war and nazism have to do with them. When Mrs. Kempowski goes to a rooftop during a bombing raid, she is horrified as a plane strafes her house. "They were shooting at me," she indignantly remarks. She clearly cannot understand why she should be a target of the shells. And at the end of the film she triumphantly proclaims: "The Nazi scum is gone. We won the war: the church and the good people." The family then brings out champagne to celebrate, and as they turn to go into the house, Mrs. Kempowski asks, "How could it happen?"

Showing "how it could happen" has been the subject of the previous four and a half hours of film. To answer this question, Fechner employs the same nonthreatening, objective style he employs in his oral history documentaries—*Unter Denkmalschutz* (*Historic Building*, 1975), *Der Process von Majdanek* (*The Majdanek Trial*, 1984), *Im Damenstift* (*Home for Ladies*, 1984), and *Klassenphoto: Erinnerungen deutscher Bürger*

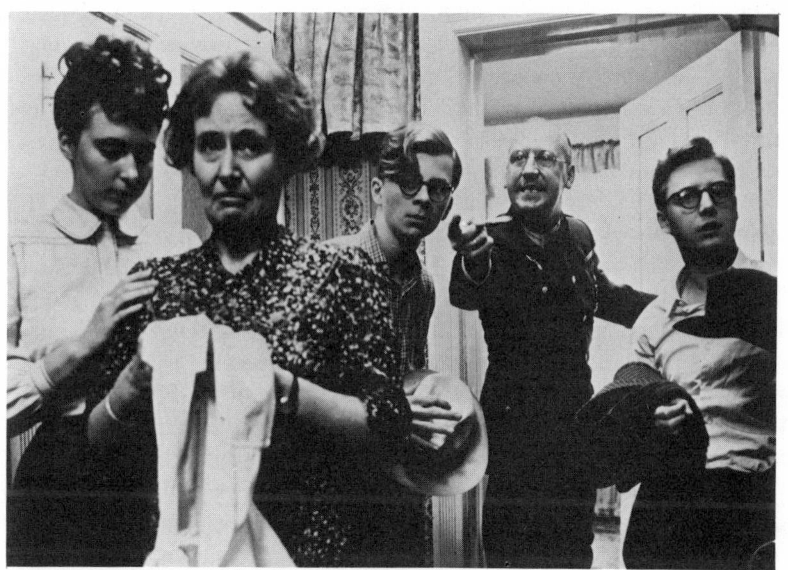

My Country, Right or Wrong (1975). Family tableau. From left: Ulla (Gabriele Michel), Mrs. Kempowski (Edda Seipel), Walter (Michael Poliza), Mr. Kempowski (Karl Liefen), and Robert (Martin Semmelrodde). Courtesy Inter Nationes.

(*Class Photo*, 1970). The stated purpose of these documentaries is to produce narrative history through a series of interviews. They attempt to show the relationship between personal history and public history. In *Historic Building*, for example, an off-camera narrator converses with the various individuals who have lived in a house that is now being declared a historic property. The subjects of the interviews are never distorted, never allowed to become caricatures of historical types. Rather, they are permitted to tell their stories in a simple and straightforward manner to the camera. In this way, viewers begin to understand the motives behind their past actions and learn about the history of individual Germans. At the same time the format of the documentary gives viewers distance from what they are hearing and seeing. Since the narrator brings in political history through his questioning, viewers recognize that the private history of these individuals occurred against a larger political history. Moreover, the distance granted to viewers by the documentary format allows them to weigh the answers (stories) of the individuals against each other in order to arrive at a fuller understanding of history. In other words, the film brings viewers to an understanding of the relationship between individuals in their private spheres and the interaction of those private spheres with political history. By choosing "ordinary individuals" for the interviews, and through the method of the interview itself, Fechner gets viewers to identify with the interviewees' stories and to understand the motivations behind the choices they made.

My Country, Right or Wrong creates the same interplay as the documentaries between the private histories of individuals and the public history of politics and government. Through fiction rather than documentary, the film shows that there is a relationship between the private and public spheres. Although the narrative is told from the perspective of a family that feels it is not a part of what is going on, distancing techniques give viewers a second perspective. The narrative frame of the film establishes viewers' omniscience, which allows them to see that the actions and attitudes of the characters are mistaken. As the film opens, while the screen shows bombed-out buildings, the mother is heard to exclaim, "How beautiful things are." This moment places viewers in a position of superiority from which to judge the members of the family. Even as they identify with the characters, viewers can see that this proclamation on the beauty of life is merely a charm uttered to ward off reality. It is repeated in many forms throughout the movie as the family tries to hide from the worsening situation. Mrs. Kempowski's version of the charm never changes. But her sons prefer to use a personal expression, "*Tadellöser und Wolff*" (couldn't be better), and to lose themselves in American swing music. Mr. Kempowski prefers to focus on his conservative family values, finding life in the home comfortable and safe. The daughter finds a Dane to marry so that she can avoid the turmoil physically as well as spiritually by moving to Denmark. Viewers identify with these sentiments throughout the movie. They understand and sympathize with the desire of the family members to stay uninvolved, to lead normal lives. Nonetheless, the events that prevent them from leading normal lives are always visible, reminding viewers that the characters of *My Country, Right or Wrong* are engaging in self-deception. They may turn away from world events, but they cannot escape them. More important, they cannot escape responsibility for them. Here the film succeeds where *Autumn Milk* and *Heimat* fail: it successfully portrays the average citizen as separate from, and yet a part of, the larger sphere of history. The Kempowski family is both innocent of and responsible for what occurred during the Third Reich. Whereas *Autumn Milk* implies that the Third Reich was caused by an evil spell of unknown origin, *My Country, Right or Wrong* shows that national socialism was aided and abetted by the wish of so-called ordinary people to stay uninvolved.

The Children of No. 67

▲▼▲

Three other films that focus on memory are *Die Kinder aus No. 67* (*The Children of No. 67*, 1979/1980), *Germany, Pale Mother*, and *Katz und Maus* (*Cat and Mouse*, 1966). In their different ways, all three successfully portray the relationship between private lives and the events of history. Usch Barthelmess-Weller and Werner Meyer are able to avoid historical distortion in their children's film, *The Children of No. 67*, by telling the story from the perspective of two 12-year old boys. Made in 1979/1980, the film follows the lives of a group of children who live in apartment complex 67 in Berlin. The film starts shortly before Hitler wins election and ends about six months into the Third Reich. The story is not complex. It tells of the efforts of the two friends to save up money for a leather football during a time when the unemployment lines were growing daily. It follows them through a period of six months during which Hitler comes to power and they drift apart, one joining the Hitler Youth and the other assisting his father in political resistance.

The story is told in two parts. In the first half, although the economic situation is bad, families and friends pull together and help each other through the troubled times. In the second half, once Hilter has taken over the economic situation improves for those who follow the Nazis and deteriorates for those who oppose them. Differing economic fortunes cause the alienation between the friends, who eventually become enemies. Since the intended audience for the film is children, the directors are not always subtle about the political situation. For example, when one of the tenants is carted off to jail, his elderly mother stands in the courtyard crying, "Isn't anyone going to do something?" In a subsequent scene, the father of one of the boys is arrested, beaten, and loses his job. His wife comments on his return home that "the Nazis arrest some, ban others from working, and fire up the war industry; that's how they combat unemployment." Finally, in another scene, a Jewish friend of one of the boys is beaten up, about which the mother remarks, "That's not so bad if they'll only stop there."

Although a children's film, *The Children of No. 67* provides a satisfying film experience for adults as well. Because the film is told from the perspective of children, viewers are prepared for the distortions that arise; historical events become exaggerated or diminished in importance. (A similar phenomenon occurs in Marianne Rosenbaum's *Peppermint Peace* and Volker Schlöndorff's *The Tin Drum*.) Moreover, the problems the children have earning money, and the difficulties they have in getting along with each other once politics enters their relationship, reflect what is occurring in the lives of the parents. The children help give viewers a new perspective on the events that led to the Third Reich: the rise in unemployment; the fights between Nazis and Communists, the compulsion to turn one's back on what was happening to the Jews. Because the movie is meant for children, the world the child-heroes inhabit is nonthreatening. The children are by no means cute or saccharine, but they are appealing, and their problems, whether trying to earn money, arguing with parents, or playing hooky, are the problems of typical adolescents. In addition, a film about, and from, the perspective of adolescents and intended for a youthful audience has an ironic dimension that is not lost on adult viewers. Although many films use adolescents in the years 1938–45, *The Children of No. 67* uses early adolescents in the early years of the Nazis. As some of the young protagonists gradually drift into the Nazi camp, viewers have a sense of foreboding, for these are the young minds and hearts that will later be part of Hitler's war machine. The fathers will, of course, also be fighting seven years later, but it is the children who will have grown up on Nazi propaganda and who, if still alive after the war, will somehow have to readjust the most. The historical counterparts of the film's fictional youngsters are the grandparents of the children for whom the film was made.

Cat and Mouse

▲▼▲

The world that the adolescents in Hansjürgen Pohland's *Katz Und Maus* (*Cat and Mouse*, 1966) inhabit is neither inviting nor familiar. It is set in a twilight zone between past and present. As the movie opens, the figure who will become the narrator of the hero's story is driving into Gdansk (Danzig), Poland, in search of answers about Germany's past. At his old school he begins to tell the story of his friend Mahlke, an outsider who commanded a small but loyal following because of his strangeness: he possessed a large Adam's apple and an equally impressive sexual member. The film created a scandal because of what conservatives considered its outrageous mockery of military virtues. Based on Günter Grass's novella of the same name, *Cat and Mouse* tells Mahlke's story as he grows from adolescence to manhood in Danzig at the start of World War II. The movie contains many of the bizarre and memorable moments that helped make the book notorious and so delighted liberal-minded readers, for example: references to Mahlke's mouse (Adam's apple); Mahlke's fixation

Cat and Mouse (1966). Peter Brandt (older son of Willi Brandt, then mayor of Berlin) as Mahlke. Courtesy Inter Nationes.

on his father's death in a train accident; Mahlke's large penis and a scene of masturbation on the wreck of a ship; the pom-poms and screwdriver that Mahlke wears around his neck; the curious and strange girl Tulla; and finally, Mahlke's apparent suicide at the end of the film as he deserts the military.

That the film created a controversy at its release in 1966 is hardly surprising. Pohland, surely with the intention of provoking reaction from

Germany's conservatives, cast Lars and Peter Brandt, the sons of the then mayor of Berlin, Willi Brandt, as the heroes. The presence of the sons of Brandt—who even at that time, before his chancellorship, was an important national figure—gave a political and semiofficial imprimatur to a film that the conservatives saw as blasphemy. "The underage son of our German foreign minister makes a mockery of Germany's highest military honor. It is easy to imagine, how much importance the Brandt household must place on the German military and German values."[16] Given that one of Brandt's sons bares his bottom and simulates masturbation and the other does a wild dance with the Iron Cross in which he lets it bounce off his crotch and dangles it inside of his swim trunks, it is not surprising that conservatives were angry.[17] While Grass's book had already committed these sacrileges, Pohland's movie gave them visual form and related them to contemporary German politics with his casting. Moreover, the film's style—a cross between the marginalizing techniques of Alexander Kluge and the distancing strategies of Bertolt Brecht—keeps viewers out of the movie and forces them to notice its antimilitary tone and the degree to which the director equates sexual adolescence and German militarism.

Perhaps more disturbing to conservatives than the connection the film makes between sexual immaturity and militarism is the implication that this immature past still influences the present. Pohland blends past and present by cutting freely between Gdansk in 1966, the year in which the narrative frame is set, and Danzig during the Third Reich. He further equates past and present by having the cabaret artist Wolfgang Neuss portray both the middle-aged narrator and the hero Mahlke's schoolboy friend. Pohland at times substitutes mannequins for the actors playing the other youths, an allusion to a number of ideas about German youth in the service of the Third Reich, including loss of soul and loss of life. In one scene, for example, the youths, portrayed by live actors, are on a wrecked ship, along with Mahlke. As the camera pulls away, it reveals that the live actors have been replaced by mannequins. The scene further deconstructs itself by foregrounding the modern speedboat that carries the camera doing the filming. This example is but one of many ways in which Pohland demythologizes the past for the audience. While the film has problems—among them, a certain amateur quality—Pohland's willingness to confront viewers with an unsentimental view of struggle and survival during the Third Reich and his relentless attempt to show that the past was still being played out in the present, are unique for a film made in 1966. *Cat and Mouse* is more than a warning about repeating the past; it implies that the past may never have been overcome.

Germany, Pale Mother

▲▼▲

Early in her film *Deutschland, bleiche Mutter* (*Germany, Pale Mother*, 1979), Helma Sanders-Brahms has her heroine comment about the story she is to narrate, "It is a conventional love story, except that it happened in that time and that place." It is clear from the opening, however, that even if the romance is conventional, the cinematic experience it provides is not, for the story of her parents will be told without sentimentality and from a nonvoyeuristic point of view. It is also clear that history will be more than background to a love story, and that the icons of the period will be more than window dressing. History pervades *Germany, Pale Mother*. It is present to such a great degree in the world of the fictional lovers that it becomes for them an accepted part of their landscape. The first image on the screen is of a Nazi banner; its black swastika and red background are reflected in a river as two men row past a young woman on the river bank. She has been harassed by young Nazis and is now sitting on the bank in a pose resembling that of a wounded Germania, a position that recalls the title of the film and the Brecht poem from which it is taken. In the next scene the two men from the boat discuss the coming war from a male viewpoint. As one covers up Germany on a globe with his thumb, the other remarks that "we will conquer the world—victory or destruction." Again the screen is filled with a huge Nazi banner, and the narrator begins the love story. In the lives of the lovers, nazism is so ubiquitous that it becomes transparent to them, even as they acknowledge its existence. A comment by the heroine, Lene, for example, that she only wants to marry a nonparty member may seem to signify that she is opposed to Nazi ideology. In reality, however, she looks through the dangers of nazism and remains unconcerned with its significance for her welfare. She focuses only on her immediate wants. The viewer, however, cannot look through the Nazi symbols. They are foregrounded to such a degree that the viewer cannot overlook the danger the characters are in when they fail to recognize the threat of national socialism.

Unlike many of the other films discussed in this chapter, *Germany, Pale Mother* does not depict a normal world that is only temporarily dysfunctional. In her film, Sanders-Brahms instead creates a world whose major dislocations in the political sphere are destroying the happiness found in the private sphere. That is, "History"—nazism, the Third Reich, Hitler, the war, the Holocaust—is intertwined with "history"—Lene and her husband, Lene's sister, their friends. Unlike in *Autumn Milk* and *Heimat*, the characters are not separate from the political milieu. And unlike in *My Country, Right or Wrong*, they do not lie to themselves that events are not that bad. Sanders-Brahms differs from the directors of those films in another way also: she forces viewers to experience events and characters from a distance, never letting them get inside to feel what the characters are feeling or to walk in their shoes. Instead of sympathizing with Lene and the others, viewers are asked to judge them and their actions against the political background.

Sanders-Brahms distances viewers with an almost minimalist camera style. The camera frustrates normal viewer curiosity by refusing to probe: it never tracks forward, offers no zooms, and seldom tracks backward. Rather than move forward and pry into the characters' lives and thereby satisfy the audience's urge to know them better and, perhaps, to identify with them more, the camera remains fixed; characters move, or do not move, in relation to *it*. At other times the camera moves from side to side with the characters, and for scenes that depict forward movement the director cuts in rather than track slowly or zoom. Frequently, the camera lingers longer than is necessary to establish the shot and longer than is needed to advance the narrative. The nonprobing style of *Germany, Pale Mother* gives viewers a feminine perspective on war. The gaze that this camera gives viewers is different from the male gaze, as identified by Laura Mulvey in her essay on the three looks of the camera.[18] Sanders-Brahms allows viewers to see with a female "look," one that is patient, observing, calm, and nonvoyeuristic. Her style is noninquisitive and unobtrusive. The only forward-tracking shot—which is noticeable for being the exception to the rule—is an aerial shot showing a city destroyed by bombs. The plane-camera sweeps forward over the landscape, as if showing how war has raped the land, expressing, in form as well as content, the masculine nature of war and destruction.

With the camera work keeping viewers at such a distance from the characters and their problems, there is really no easy point of entry. At times this works well. For example, in a sequence during which Lene is raped by American soldiers, the camera pans away immediately before the assault and focuses on the uncomprehending face of her child. Afterward, Lene calmly tells her daughter that rape is the prerogative of the victor. The camera, as directed by Sanders-Brahms, refuses to exploit the scene, or the act, as might the camera of a male director. At other times, however, the nonprobing camera overly frustrates viewers. Sometimes viewers need to identify with the characters, to get some feeling for why they act as they do. But the static camera prevents viewers from experiencing what the characters experience. Its nonmovement may allow viewers to contemplate the ruined landscapes on the screen, whether these be of a ruined

Germany, the ruined souls of its citizens, or a ruined marriage, but this same nonmovement prevents any bond of recognition from developing between viewers and characters. Even the close-ups do not create identification with Lene and her husband, for the characters are too unemotional for classic identification to take place. Viewers may watch the faces and ponder them intellectually, but they are never allowed inside.

And yet Sanders-Brahms's *Germany, Pale Mother* offers viewers perhaps the fullest experience of any of the Nazi-retro films. It is rich in historical allusions. Its narrative includes most of the themes found in the other movies we have been discussing—coming of age during the Third Reich, the war front, inner immigration, Jewish persecution, fellow travelers. Among the common themes of Nazi-retro films, only that of resistance to Hitler is absent. The topics covered in the last third of the film include all of the major postwar problems. The facial paralysis Lene suffers at the end of the war becomes a symbol for Germany's postwar malaise, a theme also well documented in Staudte's *The Murderers Are among Us*, Lorre's *The Lost One*, Lamprecht's *Somewhere in Berlin*, and finally, Fassbinder's *The Marriage of Maria Braun*, *Lola*, and *Veronika*

Germany, Pale Mother (1979). Lene (Eva Mattes) and her daughter. Courtesy Inter Nationes.

Voss. In addition, Lene becomes a cipher for a divided nation; the veil that covers half of her face symbolizes, of course, the physically divided Germany. But more than that, it symbolizes a people at odds with each other and with themselves as they try to understand defeat and try to come to terms with questions of responsibility and guilt.

In these themes, *Germany, Pale Mother* reflects the overriding concern of Nazi-retro films: the search for answers about Germany's past and how that past relates to the present. Sanders-Brahms does not, however, allow viewers a comfortable escape into fantasy, as do some of the Nazi-retro films, particularly those made in the 1950s—*08/15*, *Professor Mamlock*, *It Doesn't Always Have to Be Caviar*, *Aren't We Wonderful*—and the more recent films *Autumn Milk* and *Heimat*. Nor does her film allow viewers the comfort of seeing the world divided between good and evil, between non-Nazis, represented by the fictional heroes and heroines, and Nazis, represented by the "other." Sanders-Brahms's world of national socialism is not a world based on polarities but one based on dualities. Her heroine and hero are good decent Germans who comply with their legal government. In its honest remembrance, *Germany, Pale Mother* perhaps best accomplishes the goal of the Nazi-retro film: to help viewers experience and thereby gain insight into why they—the film characters, the German people, and, perhaps, viewers in the movie audience—acquiesced so readily to policies that denied humanity.

appendix a

▲▼▲

films cited in text listed by german title

38—Auch das war Wien (*38—Vienna before the Fall*).

An uns glaubt Gott nicht mehr (*God Does Not Believe in Us Anymore*).

Der Attentäter (*The Assassin*).

Das Beil von Wandsbek (*The Axe of Wandsbek*).

Bittere Ernte (*Angry Harvest*).

Die Blechtrommel (*The Tin Drum*).

Die bleierne Zeit (*Marianne and Juliane*).

Das Boot (*The Boat*).

Das Boot ist voll (*The Boat Is Full*).

Die Brücke (*The Bridge*).

Charlotte.

David.

Deutschland, bleiche Mutter (*Germany, Pale Mother*).

Die Ehe der Maria Braun (*The Marriage of Maria Braun*).

Ehe im Schatten (*Marriage in the Shadows*).

Die erste Polka (*The First Polka*).

Es geschah am 20. Juli (*It Happened on the 20th of July*; also, *Jackboot Mutiny*).

Es ging Tag und Nacht, liebes Kind: Zigeuner (Sinti) in Auschwitz (*It Went on Day and Night, Dear Child: Gypsies in Auschwitz*).

Es muss nicht immer Kaviar sein (*It Doesn't Always Have to Be Caviar*).
Fünf letzte Tage (*Five Last Days*).
Der Fussgänger (*The Pedestrian*).
Der gelbe Stern (*The Yellow Star*).
Hanussen.
Heimat.
Herbstmilch (*Autumn Milk*).
Hitlerjunge Salomon (*Europa Europa*).
Hunde, wollt ihr ewig leben? (*Dogs, Do You Want to Live Forever?*).
Ich war neunzehn (*I Was Nineteen*).
Irgendwo in Berlin (*Somewhere in Berlin*).
Katz und Maus (*Cat and Mouse*).
Kennwort: Morituri (*Morituri*).
Die Kinder aus No. 67 (*The Children of No. 67*).
Klassenphoto: Erinnerungen deutscher Bürger (*Class Photo*).
Der Krieg meines Vaters (*My Father's War*).
Land der Väter, Land der Söhne (*Country of the Fathers, Country of the Sons*).
Lili Marleen.
Mädchenkrieg (*Girls' War*).
Mama, ich lebe (*Mama, I Am Alive*).
Mephisto.
Eine Minute Dunkel macht uns nicht blind (*A Minute of Darkness Does Not Blind Us*).
Die Mitläufer (*Fellow Travellers*; also, *Following the Führer*).
Die Mörder sind unter uns (*The Murderers Are among Us*).
Nacht fiel über Gotenhafen (*Night Fell on Gotenhafen*).
08/15, parts 1–3.
Peppermint Frieden (*Peppermint Peace*).
Professor Mamlock.
Regentropfen (*Raindrops*).
Rommel ruft Kairo (*Rommel Calling Cairo*).
"Sansibar oder der letzte Grund" (*Sansibar*).
Schachnovelle (*Brainwashed*).
Das schreckliche Mädchen (*The Nasty Girl*).
Die Sehnsucht der Veronika Voss (*Veronika Voss*).

films cited in text

Das Spinnennetz (*The Spider's Web*).
Tadellöser und Wolff (*My Country, Right or Wrong*).
Ein Tag (*One Day*).
Des Teufels General (*The Devil's General*).
Der Verlorene (*The Lost One*).
Verlorenes Leben (*Lost Life*).
Die Wannseekonferenz (*The Wannsee Conference*).
Die weisse Rose (*The White Rose*).
Welcome in Vienna.
Winterspelt.
Wir Wunderkinder (*Aren't We Wonderful*).
Zwischengleis (*Between the Tracks*).

appendix b

▲▼▲

additional films dealing with the third reich

The following films, most of which are not cited in the text of this book, all deal with some aspect of the Nazi or immediate post-Nazi period. They are included here for the benefit of those who would like to pursue the topic of coming to terms with the Third Reich.

Abrahams Gold (1990), directed by Jörg Graser.

Adolf und Marlene (1977), directed by Ulli Lommel.

Alle Juden raus (1990), directed by Emanuel Rund.

Als Hitler das rote Kaninchen stahl (TV, 1978), directed by Ilse Hofmann.

Am Galgen hängt die Liebe (1960), directed by Edwin Zbonek.

Aus einem deutschen Leben (1976), directed by Theodore Kotulla.

Beil von Wandsbeck (East Germany, 1951), directed by Falk Harnack.

Berlinger (1975), directed by Alf Brustellin and Bernhard Sinkel.

Betrogen bis zum jüngsten Tag (East Germany, 1957), directed by Kurt Jung-Alsen.

Blaue Jungs (1957), directed by Wolfgang Schleif.

Blitzmädels an die Front (1958), directed by Werner Klingler.

Blokade (1991), directed by Thomas Kufus.

Blut und Ehre—Jugend unter Hitler, parts 1 and 2 (Italy, United States, West Germany, 1981), directed by Bernd Fischerauer.

additional films

Der Bockerer (Austria, 1981), directed by Franz Antel and Karl Merkatz.

Bomben auf Berlin: Leben zwischen Furcht und Hoffnung (1984), directed by Irmgard von zur Mühlen.

Bronsteins Kinder (1991), directed by Jerzy Kawalerowicz.

Canaris (1954), directed by Alfred Weidenmann.

Deutscher Frühling (Austria, Switzerland, West Germany, 1980), directed by Dieter Berner.

Deutschstunde, parts 1 and 2 (1971), directed by Peter Beauvais.

Diesmal muss es Kaviar sein (1961), directed by O. W. Fischer.

Eiszeit (1974), directed by Peter Zadek.

Der Engel mit der Posaune (Austria, 1948), directed by Karl Hartl.

Die Erben (Austria, 1983), directed by Walter Bannert.

Er ging an meiner Seite (1958), directed by Peter Pewas.

Ernst Thaelmann—Führer seiner Klasse (1955), directed by Kurt Maetzig.

Erster Verlust (1991), directed by Maxim Dessau.

Es ist kalt in Brandenburg (Hitler töten) (Switzerland, 1981), directed by Hans Stürm, Villi Hermann, and Niklaus Meienberg.

Fabrik der Offiziere (1960), directed by Frank Wisbar.

Fallada—letztes Kapitel (1988), directed by Roland Gräf.

Der Fall Gleiwitz (East Germany, 1961), directed by Gerhard Klein.

Der Fall Ö. (1991), directed by Rainer Simon.

Fast ein Held (also, *Die Abenteuer des braven Kommandanten Kuppes*) (1967), directed by Rainer Erler.

Flamme empor (1979), directed by Eberhard Schubert.

Flucht in den Norden (1985), directed by Ingemo Engström.

Fluchtweg nach Marseille (1977), directed by Ingemo Engström and Gerhard Theuring.

Die Frau am Wege (Austria, 1948), directed by Eduard von Borsody.

Eine Frau fürs ganze Leben (1960), directed by Wolfgang Liebeneiner.

Der Frontgockel (1955), directed by Ferdinand Dorfler.

Der Fuchs von Paris (1957), directed by Paul May.

Die Gegenprobe (TV film, 1965), directed by Johannes Schaaf.

Geheime Reichssache (1979), directed by Jochen Bauer.

Genesung (1956), directed by Konrad Wolf.

Georg Elser (1990), directed by Klaus Maria Brandauer.

Geschwister Oppermann, parts 1 and 2 (TV, 1983), directed by Egon Monk.

Ghetto (TV dramatization of Joshua Sobol's play, 1985), directed by George Moorse.

Das Glück beim Händewaschen (1981), directed by Werner Masten.

Die glücklichen Jahre der Thorwalds (1962), directed by Wolfgang Staudte and John Olden.

Die grünen Teufel von Monte Cassino (1958), directed by Harold Reinl.

Grünstein-Variante (1985), directed by Bernhard Wicki.

Gruppenbild mit Dame (1977), directed by Aleksandar Petrovic.

Gudrun (1991), directed by Hans W. Geissendörfer.

Haie und kleine Fische (1957), directed by Frank Wisbar.

Hanussen (1955), directed by O. W. Fischer and Georg Marischka.

Der Hauptmann und sein Held (1955), directed by Max Nosseck.

Der Hauptmann von Köln (East Germany, 1956), directed by Slatan Dudow.

Das Haus in der Karpfengasse (1965), directed by Kurt Hoffmann.

Das Heimweh des Walerjan Wrobel (1991), directed by Rolf Schübel.

Heldentum nach Ladenschluss (1955), directed by Wolfgang Schleif.

Herrliche Zeiten (1950), directed by Günter Neumann, Fritz Aeckerle, Hans Vietzke, and Erik Ode.

Hitler: Eine Karriere (1977), directed by Joachim Fest and Christian Herrendoerfer.

Hitler, ein Film aus Deutschland (1977), directed by Hans Jürgen Syberberg.

Im Damenstift (TV, 1984), directed by Eberhard Fechner.

Im Land meiner Eltern (1981), directed by Jeanine Meerapfel.

In jenen Tagen (1947), directed by Helmut Käutner.

Jakob der Lügner (1975), directed by Frank Beyer.

Jeder stirbt für sich allein (1976), directed by Alfred Vohrer.

Jetzt nach so viel Jahren (TV documentary, 1981), directed by Harald Lüders and Paul Schnabel.

Kalmenhofkinder (1990), directed by Nikolaus Tscheschner.

Kanonen-Serenade (1958), directed by Wolfgang Staudte.

Ein Kapitel für sich (TV miniseries, 1984), directed by Eberhard Fechner.

Kennwort: Reiher (1963), directed by Rudolf Jugert.

Kieselsteine (Austria, 1983), directed by Lukas Stepanik.

Kinder, Mütter, und ein General (1954), directed by Laslo Benedek.

Kirmes (1980), directed by Wolfgang Staudte.

Küchengespräche mit Rebellinnen (Austria, 1984), directed by Karin Berger, Elisabeth Holzinger, Charlotte Podgornik, and Lisbeth N. Trallori.

Leben für Leben (1991), directed by Krzysztof Zanussi.

Lebenszeichen (1968), directed by Werner Herzog.

Der letzte Akt (Austria, 1955), directed by G. W. Pabst.

Die letzte Brücke (Austria, 1954), directed by Helmut Käutner.

Leute mit Flügeln (East Germany, 1960), directed by Konrad Wolf.

Eine Liebe in Deutschland (1983), directed by Andrzej Wajda.

Ein Lied geht um die Welt (1958), directed by Geza von Bolvary.

Lissy (East Germany, 1957), directed by Konrad Wolf.

Der Majdanek-Prozess (TV, 1984), directed by Eberhard Fechner.

Malou (1981), directed by Jeanine Meerapfel.

Mein Kampf (Sweden, 1959), directed by Erwin Leiser.

Mein Krieg (1990), directed by Harriet Eder and Thomas Kufus.

Mein Schulfreund (1960), directed by Robert Siodmak.

Morituri (1948), directed by Eugen York.

Nach Mitternacht (1979), directed by Wolf Gremm.

Nachts, wenn der Teufel kam (1957), directed by Robert Siodmak.

Nicht versöhnt oder es hilft nur Gewalt: wo Gewalt herrscht (1965), directed by Jean-Marie Straub and Daniele Huillet.

Die papierne Brücke (Austria, 1987), directed by Ruth Beckermann.

Parole Heimat (1955), directed by Hans Fritz Wilhelm

Die Patriotin (1979), directed by Alexander Kluge.

Rama Dama (1991), directed by Joseph Vilsmaier.

Die Reise nach Wien (1973), directed by Edgar Reitz.

Rotation (East Germany, 1948–49), directed by Wolfgang Staudte.

Schlacht um Berlin (documentary, 1969–70), directed by Franz Baake.

Schuss Gegenschuss (1991), directed by Niels Bolbrinker and Thomas Tielsch.

Schtonk (1991), directed by Helmut Dietl.

Sie nannten ihn Amigo (East Germany, 1959), directed by Heiner Carow.

Sie sind frei, Dr. Korczak (1973), directed by Alexander Ford.
So war der deutsche Landser (1955), directed by Albert Baumeister.
Spion für Deutschland (1956), directed by Werner Klingler.
Sterne (East Germany, 1959), directed by Konrad Wolf.
Stern ohne Himmel (1981), directed by Ottokar Runze.
Der Stern von Afrika (1956), directed by Alfred Weidenmann.
Strafbataillon 999 (1959), directed by Harald Phillipp.
Ein Stück Himmel (1982), directed by Franz Peter Wirth.
Stunde Null (1976), directed by Edgar Reitz.
Ein Tag der nie zu Ende geht (1959), directed by Franz Peter Wirth.
Taiga (1958), directed by Wolfgang Liebeneiner.
Das tausendunderste Jahr (TV miniseries, 1984), directed by Eberhard Itzenplitz.
Die Toten bleiben jung (East Germany, 1968), directed by Joachim Kunert.
Der Transport (1961), directed by Jürgen Roland.
U 47 (1958), directed by Harald Reinl.
Und finden dereinst wir uns wieder (1947), directed by Hans Müller.
Unruhige Nacht (1958), directed by Falk Harnack.
Unternehmen Schlafsack (1955), directed by Arthur Maria Rabenalt.
Unversöhnliche Erinnerungen (docudrama, 1979), directed by Klaus Volkenborn, Johannes Feindt, and Karl Siebig.
Urlaub auf Ehrenwort (1955), directed by Wolfgang Liebeneiner.
Verfolgte Wege (1990), directed by Uwe Janson.
Verrat an Deutschland (1954), directed by Veit Harlan.
Von Richtern und anderen Sympathisanten (1982), directed by Axel Engstfeld.
Wallers letzter Gang (1988), directed by Christian Wagner.
Warszawa (1992), directed by Janusz Kijowski.
Die Welt in jenem Sommer (TV, 1979), directed by Ilse Hofmann.
Werwolfe (1973), directed by Werner Klett.
Wie ein Hirschberger Dänisch lernte (TV, 1968), directed by Rolf Busch.
. . . wie einst Lili Marleen (1956), directed by Paul Verhoeven.
Wie ich ein Neger wurde (1969), directed by Roland Gall.
Wien retour (Austria, 1983), directed by Josef Aichholzer and Ruth Beckermann.

additional films

Wir Kellerkinder (1960), directed by Jochen Wiedermann.
Wolfskinder (1991), directed by Eberhard Fechner.
Der 20. Juli (1955), directed by Falk Harnack.
Das zweite Leben (1954), directed by Victor Vicas.
Zwischen Gestern und Morgen (1947), directed by Harald Braun.
Zwischen zwei Kriegen (1978), directed by Harun Farocki.

appendix c

▲▼▲

film sources

U.S. Film Distributors

Atara Releasing, Jewish Film Festival
2600 10th St., #102
Berkeley, CA 94710
(415) 548–0556

Capitol Entertainment
4818 Uma St., NW
Washington, DC 20016
(202) 363–8800
FAX: (202) 363–4680

Castle Hill Productions
1414 Ave. of the Americas
15th Floor
New York, NY 10019
(212) 888–0080
FAX: (212) 644–0956

Cine World
2858 Mendenhall Loop Rd.
P.O. Box 34619
Juneau, AK 99803–4619
(907) 789–3995
(800) 327–9344

East-West Classics
1529 Acton St.
Berkeley, CA 94702
(415) 526–3611
FAX: (415) 526–3428

Films, Inc., Entertainment Division
5547 N. Ravenswood Ave.
Chicago, IL 60640–1199
(800) 323–4222, ext. 42
FAX: (312) 878–8648

Grove Press, Film Division
841 Broadway
New York, NY 10003
(212) 614–7850
FAX: (212) 614–7886

Kino International Corp.
333 W. 39th St.
Suite 503
New York, NY 10018
(212) 629–6880
FAX: (212) 714–0871
TELEX: 221190

Kit Parker Films
P.O. Box 16022
Monterey, CA 93942–6022
(408) 393–0303
(800) 538–5838 (orders only)
FAX: (408) 393–0304

New Yorker Films
16 W. 61st St.
New York, NY 10023
(212) 247–6110
FAX: (212) 307–7855

Roxie Releasing
3110 16th St.
San Francisco, CA 94103
(415) 431–3611
FAX: (415) 431–2822

Swank Motion Pictures
201 S. Jefferson
P.O. Box 231
St. Louis, MO 63166
(800) 876–5577
FAX: (314) 289–2192
Chicago: (800) 876–3330
FAX: (708) 833–0096
New York: (800) 876–3344
FAX: (516) 434–1574

West Glen Films
Attn: German Feature Films
1430 Broadway
New York, NY 10018–3396
(212) 921–2800
FAX: (212) 944–9055

U.S. Video Sources

Facets Multimedia
1517 W. Fullerton Ave.
Chicago, IL 60614
(312) 281–9075
(800) 331–6197
FAX: (312) 929–5437
TELEX: 206701

German Language Video Center
7625 Pendleton Pike
Indianapolis, IN 46226
(317) 547–1257
FAX: (317) 547–1263

Home Vision Cinema, Films, Inc.
5547 N. Ravenswood Ave.
Chicago, IL 60640–1199
(800) 323–4222, ext. 208

Tamarelle's
7900 Hickman Rd.
Des Moines, IA 50322
(515) 254–7254
(800) 356–3577
FAX: (515) 254–7021

German Video Sources

Bertelsmann
Neumarkter Str. 18
P.O. Box 800360
8000 Munich 80
Phone: 089431890
FAX: 0894312877

Mailorder Kaiser
Aachener Str. 11
P.O. Box 401209
8000 Munich 40

Useful Addresses

Austrian Cultural Institute
11 E. 52nd St.
New York, NY 10022
(212) 759–5165

Goethe House
Attn.: Ingrid Scheib-Rothbart
Program Dept.
1014 Fifth Ave., #5
New York, NY 10028
(212) 439–8700
Library: (212) 439–8688 (opens at noon)

Library of Congress
Motion Picture, Broadcasting, and Record Sound Division
10 First St., SW
Washington, DC 20540
(202) 707–5840

notes and references

▲▼▲

Chapter 1

1. Robert Stam, *Subversive Pleasures: Bakhtin, Cultural Criticism, and Film* (Baltimore: Johns Hopkins University Press, 1989), 41, hereafter cited in text.

2. Christian Metz, *The Imaginary Signifier: Psychoanalysis and the Cinema*, trans. Celia Britton, et al. (Bloomington: Indiana University Press, 1982), 54, hereafter cited in text.

3. Hans Robert Jauss, *Toward an Aesthetic of Reception*, trans. Timothy Bahti, Theory and History of Literature, vol. 2 (Minneapolis: University of Minnesota Press, 1982), 24.

4. Tony Pipolo, "German Filmmakers and the Nazi Legacy," *International Herald Tribune*, 6 August 1982, hereafter cited in text; Margarethe von Trotta is quoted in Pipolo's article.

5. Amos Vogel, *Film as a Subversive Art* (New York: Random House, 1974), 9–10, hereafter cited in text.

6. Kristin Thompson, "Concepts of Cinematic Excess," in *Narrative, Apparatus, Ideology: A Film Reader*, ed. Philip Rosen (New York: Columbia University Press, 1986), 131–32, hereafter cited in text.

7. Thomas Elsaesser, "Primary Identification and the Historical Subject: Fassbinder and Germany," in Rosen, *Narrative, Apparatus, Ideology*, 539.

8. Martin Osterland, *Gesellschaftsbilder in Filmen: Eine soziologische Untersuchung des Filmangebots der Jahre 1949 bis 1964*, Göttinger Abhandlungen zur Soziologie und ihrer Grenzgebiete, vol. 19 (Stuttgart: Ferdinand Enke, 1970), 209, n. 317.

9. Quoted in Friedrich P. Kahlenberg, *Starting Towards Freedom: The German Experience, 1945–1950: A Retrospective with Documentary Films from the Federal Republic of Germany* (Munich: Goethe-Institut München, 1987), 7.

Chapter 2

1. Quoted in Joe Hembus and Christa Bandmann, *Klassiker des deutschen Tonfilms, 1930–1960* (Munich: Goldmann, 1980), 154, hereafter cited in text.

2. Quoted in Frederick W. Ott, *The Great German Films* (Secaucus, N.J.: Citadel, 1986), 242, hereafter cited in text.

3. Thomas Elsaesser, *New German Cinema: A History* (New Brunswick, N.J.: Rutgers University Press, 1989), 250.

4. Anton Kaes, *From Hitler to Heimat: The Return of History as Film* (Cambridge: Harvard University Press, 1989), 12, hereafter cited in text; Eric Rentschler, "Germany: The Past That Would Not Go Away," in *World Cinema since 1945*, ed. William Luhr (New York: Ungar, 1987), 212.

5. Roger Ebert, "*Lost One* Expands View of Lorre," *Chicago Sun-Times*, 5 April 1985.

6. Jay Carr, "Peter Lorre's *Lost One* a Fascinating Find," *Boston Globe*, 26 June 1985.

7. Wolf Donner, "Zurück in die Zukunft," *Tip Magazine*, October 1989, hereafter cited in text.

8. Carla Rhode, "Alle Strömungen dieser Zeit Aufgegriffen," *Tagesspiegel* (Berlin), 17 September 1989.

9. Siegfried Kracauer, *Theory of Film: The Redemption of Physical Reality* (New York: Oxford University Press, 1960), 78, hereafter cited in text.

10. Klaus Mann, *Mephisto: Roman einer Karriere* (Berlin: Aufbau-Verlag, 1956), 353.

11. Quoted in György Fenyves, "Leider kann man einen Film nur einmal drehen," *Film und Fernsehen* 9, no. 9 (1981): 45, hereafter cited in text.

12. Vincent Canby, "Film: Sweetheart of the Third Reich," *New York Times*, 10 July 1981.

13. Louis Skorecki, "L'Amour n'est pas plus fait que l'argent," *Cahiers du Cinéma* 322 (April 1981): 12.

14. *MacNeil-Lehrer News Hour*, 14 August 1990.

15. Fred Gehler, "Porträt eines Amateurhenkers," *Film und Fernsehen* 9, no. 12 (1981): 6.

16. Horst Knietzsch, "Auf Halben Wege," *Film und Fernsehen* 3, no. 6 (1975): 45.

17. Evan Pattak, "Walking to the Sounds of Different Drummers: Responses to *The Pedestrian*," *Jump Cut* 7 (May–July 1975): 26.

18. Quoted in Charles Champlin, "The Real 'Nasty Girl,' " *Los Angeles Times*, 3 January 1991.

19. Anna [Anja] Elisabeth Rosmus, "Should German Movies Look Back?" *New York Times*, 21 October 1990. Rosmus reports that, "since *The Nasty Girl* began running in theaters, I've become the target of widespread hostility again."

Chapter 3

1. Curt Riess, *Das gab's nur einmal: Die grosse Zeit des deutschen Films*, 3 vols. (Frankfurt am Main: Ullstein Sachbuch, 1985), 2: 157–58.

2. To be fair to Paul May, it must be noted that most films from the period, and even those from Hollywood—with the exception of *The Stranger* (1946), starring Edward G. Robinson and Orson Welles—also avoided this topic. Not until the 1960s was the theme of the Holocaust explored, in *The Pawnbroker* (1965).

3. John Sandford, *The New German Cinema* (Totowa, N.J.: Barnes and Noble, 1980), 11, hereafter cited in text.

4. All quoted in "*Die Brücke* am Regen," *Spiegel*, no. 45 (4 November 1959): 189, hereafter cited in text as *Spiegel* 1959.

5. Werner Birkenmaier, "Fünf Stunden lang tobt U-Boot-Krieg im Fernsehen," *Stuttgarter Zeitung*, 22 February 1985, hereafter cited in text.

6. "Ein 'noch echteres' Boot kreuzt auf," *Stuttgarter Zeitung*, 2 March 1985.

7. Carrie Rickey, "In Which We Sink," *Village Voice* 27 (10–16 February 1982): 60.

8. The film in this regard reflects the intentions of Lothar Günther Buchheim, the author of the book on which the movie is based. On 1 March 1985, Buchheim narrated a German television program, "Zu Tode gesiegt—Vom Untergang der U-Boote," on the background to *The Boat*. On the program, produced by Bavaria Atelie Productions, presented on Westdeutscher Rundfunk, the author related how the arrogance of Dönitz, commander of the Nazi navy, kept the navy from utilizing the latest innovations on its boats and insisted that the German submarine fleet was the best in the world as it was.

9. David Ansen, "Going Under," *Newsweek*, 1 March 1982, 7.

10. Jon Gartenberg, "*Das Boot*," *Films in Review* 33 (April 1982): 242.

11. Janet Maslin, "The Screen: *Das Boot*, The Fortunes of a U-Boat," *New York Times*, 10 February 1982.

12. Jo Ann Rhetts, "W. German Film, *Das Boot*, Coming to Charlotte," *Charlotte Observer*, 9 September 1982.

13. Douglas Fowler, "*Alien, The Thing* and the Principle of Terror, " *Studies in Popular Culture* 4 (1981): 16–19.

14. I. C. Jarvie, *Movies as Social Criticism: Aspects of Their Social Psychology* (Metuchen, N.Y.: Scarecrow, 1978), 15.

15. D. J. R. Bruckner, Seymour Chwast, and Steven Heller, *Art against War: 400 Years of Protest in Art* (New York: Abbeville Press, 1984), 106.

Chapter 4

1. Arthur Knight, *The Liveliest Art: A Panoramic History of the Movies* (New York: Macmillan, 1957; New York: New American Library/Mentor Books, 1959), 181.

2. Philipp Jenninger, "Many Were 'Blinded and Seduced' by Nazis," excerpts from speech before the West German parliament, 10 November 1988, *Charlotte Observer*, 12 November 1988.

3. Hans Rothfels, *The German Opposition to Hitler: An Assessment*, trans. Lawrence Wilson, German History Series, vol. 2 (1961; reprint, London: Oswald Wolff, 1970), 14, hereafter cited in text.

4. Bavaud's attempt is portrayed in the film, *Es ist kalt in Brandenburg (Hitler töten)* (*It Is Cold in Brandenburg [Kill Hitler]*, 1981), directed by Hans Stürm, Villi Hermann, and Niklaus Meienberg. Elser's attempt was first made into a television film, *Der Attentäter* (*The Assassin*, 1969), directed by Rainer Erler, and has since been made into a movie, *Georg Elser* (*Sevèn Minutes*, 1990), directed by and starring Klaus Maria Brandauer.

5. Michael Balfour, *Withstanding Hitler in Germany, 1933–1945* (New York: Routledge, 1988), hereafter cited in text. In his preface (x), Balfour suggests using the German word *Widerstand* so as not to conjure up the organized activity one associates with the English words *resistance* and *opposition.*

6. Verhoeven returns periodically to themes of history and dealing with the past. Besides *The Nasty Girl*, Verhoeven made an earlier film on this theme, *Sonntagskinder* (*Sunday Children*, 1979), which focuses on the experiences of an adolescent girl and her family during the war.

7. H. G. Pflaum, "Deutliche Spuren von Genre-Kino?" *Süddeutsche Zeitung*, 29 September 1982.

8. Ruprecht Skasa-Weiss, "Das Typische, das Fassliche," *Stuttgarter Zeitung*, 25 September 1982.

9. Vicky Elliot, "In Germany, a Late Blooming of the Anti-Nazi *White Rose*," *International Herald Tribune*, 18 February 1983.

10. Gordon Craig, "Facing up to the Nazis," *New York Review of Books* 36, no. 1 (2 February 1989): 12, hereafter cited in text.

11. Percy Adlon, " 'Sprich, ich höre dir zu,' " *Süddeutsche Zeitung*, 2 October 1982.

12. H. G. Pflaum, "Fast betulich unverbindlich," *Süddeutsche Zeitung*, 8 October 1982.

13. Prince Hubert zu Löwenstein, *What Was the German Resistance Movement?* (Bad Godesberg: Grafes, 1965), 54, hereafter cited in text.

14. Eric Rentschler, *West German Film in the Course of Time: Reflections on the Twenty Years since Oberhausen* (Bedford Hills, N.Y.: Redgrave, 1984), 150.

15. Walther Schmieding, "Les Généraux du diable," *Cahiers de la Cinémathéque* 32 (Spring 1981): 128.

16. Quoted in Robert Fischer and Joe Hembus, *Der neue deutsche Film, 1960–1980* (Munich: Goldmann, 1981), 244.

Chapter 5

1. William Paul, *Ernst Lubitsch's American Comedy* (New York: Columbia University Press, 1983), 227.

2. Barbara Hyams, "' . . . so grausam, dass sie fast schon wieder komisch war': Humor in Rainer Werner Fassbinder's *Die Ehe der Maria Braun*," paper presented at the Fourth Hollins Colloquium on German Film: Humor in German Films, Roanoke, Va., 27 April 1990.

3. Henri Bergson, *Laughter: An Essay on the Meaning of the Comic*, trans. Cloudesley Brereton and Fred Rothwell (New York: Macmillan, 1911), 168–69.

4. Jerry Palmer, *The Logic of the Absurd: On Film and Television Comedy* (London: BFI, 1987), 199.

5. Viola Herms Drath, ed., *"Wir Wunderkinder": Eine Filmkomödie über Deutschland und die Deutschen* (screenplay by Heinz Pauch and Günter Neumann), Blaisdell Book in the Modern Languages (Waltham, Mass.: Blaisdell, 1969), x.

6. "Gypsies in a green wagon" is a leitmotiv in Thomas Mann's novella *Tonio Kröger*, (1903), with which German audiences would have been familiar.

7. Nicholas Wapshott, "The Winning of Oskar's Oscar," *London Times*, 10 May 1980.

8. Quoted in Jonathan Kandell, "A German Obsessed with Germany," *International Herald Tribune*, 25 January 1980.

9. Quoted in James Franklin, *New German Cinema: From Oberhausen to Hamburg*, Twayne's Filmmakers Series, ed. Warren French (Boston: Twayne, 1983), 106.

10. Helmut Schmitz, "Bilder aus einer deutschen Kindheit," *Frankfurter Rundschau*, 17 May 1979.

11. Volker Schlöndorff, Die Blechtrommel: *Tagebuch einer Verfilmung*, 3d ed. (Darmstadt: Luchterhand, 1979), 39.

12. Andrew Sarris, "Banging the Tin Drum Slowly," *Village Voice* 25 (21 April 1980): 47.

13. Eleanor Ringel, "*Tin Drum* Marches to Frantic, Creepy Beat," *Atlantic Constitution*, 25 July 1980.

14. Joy Gould Boyum, "Günter Grass on Screen: An Allegory of Nazism," *Wall Street Journal*, 11 April 1990.

Chapter 6

1. Yehuda Bauer, *A History of the Holocaust* (New York: Franklin Watts, 1982), 334–35.

2. "Mit Gestrigen in die Zukunft," *Spiegel*, no. 15 (10 April 1989): 150–51.

3. Ilan Avisar, *Screening the Holocaust: Cinema's Images of the Unimaginable*, Jewish Literature and Culture series, ed. Alan Rosenfeld (Bloomington: Indiana University Press, 1988), 16.

4. Lawrence L. Langer, *The Holocaust and the Literary Imagination* (New Haven: Yale University Press, 1975), 77. Some of the romanticism in the film may be due to elements present in the book, of which the Holocaust scholar Langer writes: "But her *Diary*, cherished since its appearance as a celebration of human courage in the face of impending disaster, is in actuality a conservative and even old-fashioned book which appeals to nostalgia".

5. Serge Schmemann, "85 Minutes That Scarred History," *New York Times*, 22 November 1987.

6. Raul Hilberg, "Is It History or Is It Drama?" *New York Times*, 13 December 1987, hereafter cited in text.

7. Janet Maslin, "Film: *David*, Jewish Lad in Germany," *New York Times*, 21 January 1982.

8. Judith Crist, "The Flowers (and Weeds) of Spring," *Saturday Review* 9 (March 1982): 55.

9. Carlos Clarens, "*David:* A Film by Peter Lilienthal," *Soho News*, 19 January 1982.

10. Quoted in Judy Stone, "True Tale of Jew 'Adopted' by Nazi Soldiers in '*Europa*,' " *San Francisco Chronicle*, 5 July 1991.

11. Quoted in Peter Buchka "A Simple Complication: No Oscar for this Film," *German Tribune*, no. 1501 (31 January 1992): 10; reprinted from *Süddeutsche Zeitung*, 1992.

12. "Kulturnachrichten: Golden Globe für *Europa Europa*," *Deutschland Nachrichten*, 24 January 1992, 7.

13. Quoted in Rebecca Lieb, "German Panel Stands by *Europa* Decision," *Variety*, 10 February 1992, 15.

14. Lotte H. Eisner, *Ich hatte einst ein schönes Vaterland: Memoiren*, written by Martje Grohmann (Heidelberg: Wunderhorn, 1984).

15. The third film of Corti's trilogy, *Welcome in Vienna* (1985), is discussed in chapter 2. The second film, *Santa Fe* (1985), focuses on the problems of immigrant Jews in the United States.

16. Markus Imhoof, "Die Unerwüschten: Wie die Schweiz ihren guten Ruf als Asylland verspielte; Das traurige Los deutscher Emigranten" (How the Swiss squandered away their good reputation as a country for asylum seekers; the sad fate of German emigrants), *Die Zeit*, 19 March 1982, hereafter cited in text. *Die*

Zeit noted that this was the first censored article it ever published. Imhoof was required to submit his article, in which he quotes from secret police files and censored government dossiers, to Swiss authorities for approval before it could be published.

17. Brigitte Jeremias, "Ans Leben geklammert," *Frankfurter Allgemeine*, 18 December 1981.

18. Louis L. Snyder, *Louis L. Snyder's Guide to World War II* (Westport, Conn.: Greenwood Press, 1982), 228; *New Encyclopædia Britannica*, 15th ed., s.v. "World Wars."

Chapter 7

1. George Santayana, *The Life of Reason, or, The Phases of Human Progress*, 1-vol. ed., rev. (New York: Charles Scribner's Sons, 1953), 82.

2. Wilfried Wiegand, "Interview" in *Rainer Werner Fassbinder*, ed. Peter W. Jansen and Wolfram Schütte, Reihe Film, vol. 2, 5th ed., enl. (Munich: Carl Hanser, 1985), 92.

3. Rainer Werner Fassbinder, director, *The Marriage of Maria Braun*, ed. Joyce Rheuban, Rutgers Films in Print, vol. 4 (New Brunswick, N.J.: Rutgers University Press, 1986), 12.

4. Tom Noonan, review of *The Marriage of Maria Braun*, *Film Quarterly* 33, no. 3 (Spring 1980): 44, hereafter cited in text.

5. Frank Rich, "High Camp: *The Marriage of Maria Braun*," *Time* 114 (22 October 1979): 86, hereafter cited in text; Vincent Canby, "Film: *Maria Braun* from Fassbinder," *New York Times*, 14 October 1979.

6. Hellmuth Karasek, "Kraut und Rüben," *Spiegel*, no. 38 (12 September 1977): 233, hereafter cited in text.

7. Anna Wimschneider, *Herbstmilch: Lebenserinnerungen einer Bäuerin* (Munich: Piper, 1987).

8. *Heimat* is difficult to translate into English since "home," "home country," and "homeland" do not carry the nostalgic but also sociopolitical connotations of the German word.

9. For a detailed discussion and insightful analysis of history in *Heimat*, see Kaes (163–98).

10. Gideon Bachman, "The Reitz Stuff" (an interview with Edgar Reitz) *Film Comment* 21 (July-August 1985): 18.

11. Quoted in John Curtin, "Germany Unfolds in a 16-Hour Film," *New York Times*, 31 March 1985.

12. For a definitive reading of how the photos in *Heimat* function to create tension between present and past, see Kaes (178–82).

13. Charles S. Maier, in *The Unmasterable Past: History, Holocaust, and German National Identity* (Cambridge: Harvard University Press, 1988), writes:

"Historical ethnography tempts the historian to abandon his detachment and to become a folklorist. *Alltagesgeschichte* [everyday history] begins by showing how partially or how subtly power works. It can end by having power and domination disappear into an ether of popular culture" (119).

14. Stanley Cavell, *The World Viewed: Reflections on the Ontology of Film*, enl. ed. (Cambridge: Harvard University Press, 1979), 154.

15. Quoted in Rolf Becker, "Tadellos, primig," *Spiegel*, no. 18 (28 April 1975): 152.

16. Letter to the editor, *Spiegel*, no. 4 (16 January 1967): 5. This is one of a number of angry letters *Spiegel* received after printing a news article on the making of the film (no. 53 [26 December 1966]: 22–23).

17. Reinstated at various times by different German governments, the Iron Cross, in its several grades, is Germany's highest military honor.

18. Laura Mulvey, "Visual Pleasure and Narrative Cinema," in Rosen, *Narrative, Apparatus, Ideology*, 198–209.

selected bibliography

▲▼▲

The books and articles below fall into three categories: those that give readers a general introduction to postwar German film; those that offer more detailed analysis of the films treated; and those that orient readers to various aspects of German history between 1933 and 1945.

Adlon, Percy. " 'Sprich, ich höre dir zu.' " *Süddeutsche Zeitung*, 2 October 1982. Essay by the director on his film *Five Last Days*.

Ash, Timothy Garton. "The Life of Death." *New York Review of Books* (19 December 1985): 26–39. Essay review of *Heimat* and Claude Lanzman's film *Shoah* (1985).

Avisar, Ilan. *Screening the Holocaust: Cinema's Images of the Unimaginable.* Jewish Literature and Culture, edited by Alan Rosenfeld. Bloomington: Indiana University Press, 1988. Readings of films from *Night and Fog* (1955) to *Mr. Klein* (1976) using postmodern theories. Includes an excursus on Chaplin's *The Great Dictator*.

Bachmann, Gideon. "The Reitz Stuff." *Film Comment* 21 (July-August 1985): 16–18. Informative interview with the director Edgar Reitz.

Balfour, Michael. *Withstanding Hitler in Germany, 1933–1945*. New York: Routledge, 1988. The most comprehensive study of resistance in Germany currently available.

Bauer, Yehuda. *A History of the Holocaust*. New York: Franklin Watts, 1982. Includes a review of Jewish history, a treatment of anti-Semitism in Europe, a description of ghetto life, a history of resistance, and statistics on Europe's Jewish population before the war.

Blum, Heiko R. *30 Jahre danach: Dokumentation zur Auseinandersetzung mit dem Nationalsozialismus im Film 1945 bis 1975*. 2d ed., enl. Cologne: Horst May, 1975. Annotated filmography of movies made between 1945 and 1975 in which nazism plays a major or secondary role. Not limited to German films.

Blum, Heiko R., et al. *Film in der DDR*. Reihe Film, edited by Peter W. Jansen and Wolfram Schütte, vol. 13. Munich: Carl Hanser, 1977. Introduction to the major directors of the former German Democratic Republic.

Bruckner, D. J. R., Seymour Chwast, and Steven Heller. *Art against War: 400 Years of Protest in Art*. New York: Abbeville Press, 1984.

Brunette, Peter. "Lessons from the Past: An Interview with Agnieszka Holland." *Cineaste* 15, no. 1 (1986): 15–17. Interview with the director of *Angry Harvest*, conducted at the Montreal Film Festival.

Buchheim, Lothar-Günther. *Der Film "Das Boot": Ein Journal*. Munich: Goldmann, 1981. Background information on submarine warfare by the author of the novel upon which the film is based.

Cavell, Stanley. *The World Viewed: Reflections on the Ontology of Film*. Enl. ed. Cambridge: Harvard University Press, 1979. Philosophical treatise on how films are remembered.

Christie, Ian. "Syberberg Statement." *Framework* 6 (August 1977): 12–18. Includes an extract from a letter Hans Jürgen Syberberg sent the German press, a compilation of opinions that the director expressed about his film both before and after its release, and an interview conducted by Christie in Cannes.

Craig, Gordon. "Facing up to the Nazis." *New York Review of Books*, 2 February 1989, 12.

Drath, Viola Herms, ed. *"Wir Wunderkinder": Eine Filmkomödie über Deutschland und die Deutschen*. Screenplay by Heinz Pauch and Günter Neumann. A Blaisdell Book in the Modern Languages, edited by H. H. Henry Remark. Waltham, Mass.: Blaisdell, 1969. Textbook script of the movie.

Elsaesser, Thomas. *New German Cinema: A History*. New Brunswick, N.J.: Rutgers University Press, 1989. Exhaustive history of the topic. Particularly suited for those with some knowledge of cinema in general and German cinema in particular. Excellent bibliography.

_____. "Primary Identification and the Historical Subject: Fassbinder and Germany." In *Narrative, Apparatus, Ideology: A Film Reader*, edited by Philip Rosen, 535–49. New York: Columbia University Press, 1986. Discusses the concept of the double in New German Cinema. The second part analyzes Fassbinder's characters and suggests that the people in his movies are not so much individuals being spied upon by a voyeuristic camera as narcissists consciously performing to an audience (the camera).

Erkkila, Betsy. "Hans-Jürgen Syberberg: An Interview." *Literature Film Quarterly* 10, no. 4 (1982): 206–18. Conducted in San Francisco, July 1979.

selected bibliography

Fassbinder, Rainer Werner. *The Marriage of Maria Braun.* Rutgers Films in Print, edited by Mirella Jona Affron, Robert Lyons, and E. Rubinstein, vol. 4. New Brunswick, N.J.: Rutgers University Press, 1986. Screenplay of film. Also includes excellent essays on film.

Fischer, Robert, and Joe Hembus. *Der neue deutsche Film, 1960–1980.* Munich: Goldmann, 1981. Detailed critical reviews of over 50 films and brief critical reviews of over 700 others. Introduction by Douglas Sirk.

Fenyves, György. "Leider kann man einen Film nur einmal drehen . . .: Gespräch mit István Szabó." *Film und Fernsehen* 9, no. 3 (1981): 43–45.

Franklin, James. *New German Cinema: From Oberhausen to Hamburg.* Twayne's Filmmakers Series, edited by Warren French. Boston: Twayne, 1983. Excellent introduction to New German Cinema. Chapters on Kluge, Straub-Huillet, Schlöndorff, Herzog, Fassbinder, Wenders, and Syberberg.

Gambaccini, Peter. "The New German Film Makers." *Horizon* 23, no. 6 (June 1980): 22–33. Summary introduction to the topic.

Grenier, Richard. "Fassbinder and the Bloomingdale's Factor." *Commentary* 74 (October 1982): 53–62. An unflattering but nonetheless informative and insightful analysis of Fassbinder's popularity in America.

Helt, Richard C., and Marie E. Helt. *West German Cinema since 1945: A Reference Handbook.* Metuchen, N.J.: Scarecrow, 1987. Thumbnail sketches and film statistics on West German films, including some made for television.

Hembus, Joe, and Christa Bandmann. *Klassiker des deutschen Tonfilms, 1930–1960.* Munich: Goldmann, 1980. Brief critical reviews of over 500 German films made between 1930 and 1960, with more detailed reviews of the 70 most important.

Hoberman, J. "Hard to Be a Jew." *Village Voice* 27 (20–26 January 1982): 48. Excellent review of the film *David*, including background information on European Jewry.

Honickel, Thomas. "Mit geringem Aufwand zu grösstmöglicher Wirkung." *Film und TV Kameramann* 35 (May 1986): 418–24. Interview with Gernot Roll, the cameraman for Axel Corti's trilogy *Whereto and Back.*

Iden, Peter, et al. *Rainer Werner Fassbinder.* 5th ed., rev. and enl. Reihe Film, edited by Peter W. Jansen and Wolfram Schütte, vol. 2. Munich: Carl Hanser, 1985. Contains articles on Fassbinder and analyses of all his movies. Includes a full filmography.

Imhoof, Markus. *"Das Boot is voll": Ein Filmbuch.* Zurich: Ammann, 1983. Screenplay plus background information.

_____. "Die Unerwüschten: Wie die Schweiz ihren guten Ruf als Asylland verspielte; Das traurige Los deutscher Emigranten." *Die Zeit,* 19 March 1982. Article by the director of *The Boat Is Full* that describes anti-Semitism in Switzerland.

Insdorf, Annette. *Indelible Shadows: Film and the Holocaust.* 2d ed. New York: Cambridge University Press, 1989. Survey of major films dealing with the Holocaust. Includes U.S. and Western and Eastern European films.

Jarvie, I. C. *Movies as Social Criticism: Aspects of Their Social Psychology.* Metuchen, N.J.: Scarecrow, 1978. Excellent introduction for readers interested in the sociology of film.

Jauss, Hans Robert. *Toward an Aesthetic of Reception.* Translated by Timothy Bahti. Theory and History of Literature, edited by Wlad Godzich and Jochen Schulte-Sasse, vol. 2. Minneapolis: University of Minnesota, 1982. The focus is on literature, but the theories of reception that the work develops can be applied to film as well.

Kaes, Anton. *From Hitler to Heimat: The Return of History as Film.* Cambridge: Harvard University Press, 1989. Postwar German history on film. After an informative introduction to the way in which history has been handled in film since 1945, the book discusses critical reception and gives close readings of individual films, including *Heimat*, *Germany, Pale Mother*, and *Hitler, a Film from Germany* (*Hitler, ein Film aus Deutschland* [1977]; also known in English as *Our Hitler*). Includes excellent bibliography on German film.

Karasek, Hellmuth. "Kindertraum von der Burg." *Spiegel*, no. 43 (23 October 1989): 230–40. Interview with Klaus Maria Brandauer on his film *Georg Elser* (*Seven Minutes*, 1990), a remake of the 1969 television film, *Der Attentäter* (*The Assassin*), based on the life of Georg Elser.

Kracauer, Siegfried. *Theory of Film: The Redemption of Physical Reality.* New York: Oxford University Press, 1960. Definitive study of realism in film. Although much of the text has been superseded by the formalist theories of the 1950s and the postmodern theories of present-day studies, this book provides insight into the power film has because of the way it captures everyday reality.

Large, David Clay, ed. *Contending with Hitler: Varieties of German Resistance in the Third Reich.* Publications of the German Historical Institute, edited by Hartmut Lehmann. Washington, D.C.: German Historical Institute; Cambridge: Cambridge University Press, 1991.

Löwenstein, Prince Hubert zu. *What Was the German Resistance Movement?* Bad Godesberg: Grafes, 1965.

Maier, Charles S. *The Unmasterable Past: History, Holocaust, and German National Identity.* Cambridge: Harvard University Press, 1988. Excellent introduction to postwar German history, focusing on the Historikerstreit.

Metz, Christian. *The Imaginary Signifier: Psychoanalysis and the Cinema.* Translated by Celia Britton, et al. Bloomington: Indiana University Press, 1982. The pioneer work on semiology and film.

"Die Mörder sind noch unter uns" parts 1–4. *Spiegel*, nos. 25–28 (1988): 112–22, 100–112, 102–115, 90–108. Fascinating survey on the echoes of nazism in postwar Germany.

Mulvey, Laura. "Visual Pleasure and Narrative Cinema." In *Narrative, Apparatus, Ideology: A Film Reader*, edited by Philip Rosen, 198–209. New York: Columbia University Press, 1986. Oft-cited study on the theory of the three looks of the camera.

Osterland, Martin. *Gesellschaftsbilder in Filmen: Eine soziologische Untersuchung des Filmangebots der Jahre 1949 bis 1964*. Göttinger Abhandlungen zur Soziologie und ihrer Grenzgebiete, edited by H. Plessner and H. P. Bahrdt, vol. 19. Stuttgart: Ferdinand Enke, 1970. Well-documented study of sociology and film.

Ott, Frederick W. *The Great German Films*. Secaucus, N.J.: Citadel, 1986. Genesis, reception, and review of over 40 films, from *The Cabinet of Dr. Caligari* (1919) to *Celeste* (1981).

Palmer, Jerry. *The Logic of the Absurd: On Film and Television Comedy*. London: BFI, 1987. Detailed analysis of the phenomenology of humor in film.

Pattak, Evan. "Walking to the Sounds of Different Drummers: Responses to *The Pedestrian*." *Jump Cut* 7 (May–July 1975): 24–26. Fascinating survey of the responses of a Pittsburgh audience after viewing Schell's movie.

Phillips, Klaus, ed. *New German Filmmakers: From Oberhausen through the 1970s*. New York: Unger, 1984. Informative essays on the top German filmmakers at the time of the book's publication.

Pipolo, Tony. "German Filmmakers and the Nazi Legacy." *International Herald Tribune*, 6 August 1982. Informative essay on the degree to which German filmmakers avoided treating the Third Reich critically in the first three decades after the war.

Ranvaud, Don. "Heimat: Edgar Reitz at Venice." *Sight and Sound* 54, no. 2 (1985): 124–26. Background information on the director and the film.

Reimer, Robert, and Carol Reimer. "Nazi-retro Filmography." *Journal of Popular Film and Television* 14 (Summer 1986): 80–92. Includes thumbnail sketches and sources for 60 postwar movies set in Nazi Germany and lists an additional 80 films not available in the United States, giving title, director, and year of release.

Reitz, Edgar, and Peter Steinbach. *Heimat: Eine deutsche Chronik*. Nördlingen: Greno, 1985. Screenplay plus background information.

Rentschler, Eric. *West German Filmmakers on Film: Visions and Voices*. Modern German Voices series. New York: Holmes & Meier, 1988. Valuable source of essays by major directors.

_____. "Germany: The Past That Would Not Go Away." In *World Cinema since 1945*, edited by William Luhr, 208–51. New York: Ungar, 1987. Insightful essay on how German filmmakers treat history in their films.

_____. *West German Film in the Course of Time: Reflections on the Twenty Years since Oberhausen*. Bedford Hills, N.Y.: Redgrave, 1984. Excellent study of its topic from one of the leading American scholars on German film.

Reynaud, Berenice. " 'Impure Cinema' Adaptation and Quotation at the 1985 New York Film Festival." *Afterimage* 13 (January 1986): 9–11. Excellent essay on *Angry Harvest*.

Riess, Curt. *Das gab's nur einmal: Die grosse Zeit des deutschen Films*. 3 vols. Frankfurt am Main: Ullstein Sachbuch, 1985. Gossipy survey of Germany's golden age of film, 1918–33.

Riley, Brooks. "Rainer Werner Fassbinder, 1946–82." *Film Comment* 18 (September-October 1982): 19–23. Laudatory but insightful obituary.

Root, Jane. "Women in Jeopardy: 2." *Monthly Film Bulletin* (British Film Institute) 52 (February 1985): 41–42. Interview with Marianne Rosenbaum, director of *Peppermint Peace*. The movie is one of the few films about the past directed by a woman.

Rothfels, Hans. *The German Opposition to Hitler: An Assessment*. Translated by Lawrence Wilson. German History Series, vol. 2. 1961. Reprint. London: Oswald Wolff, 1970. Although superseded by Balfour's work, this book gives a good, brief introduction to the subject of resistance in Germany.

Sanders-Brahms, Helma. *"Deutschland, bleiche Mutter": Film-Erzählung*. Reinbek bei Hamburg: Rowohlt, 1980. Screenplay plus background information.

Sandford, John. *The New German Cinema*. Totowa, N.J.: Barnes and Noble, 1980. General introduction to New German Cinema.

Santner, Eric L. *Stranded Objects: Mourning, Memory, and Film in Postwar Germany*. Ithaca, N.Y.: Cornell University Press, 1990. Postmodern readings of Edgar Reitz's *Heimat* and Hans Jürgen Syberberg's *Our Hitler*.

Schlöndorff, Volker. *"Die Blechtrommel": Tagebuch einer Verfilmung*. 3d ed. Darmstadt: Luchterhand, 1979. Diary of the filming of *The Tin Drum*.

Schlöndorff, Volker, and Günter Grass. *"Die Blechtrommel" als Film*. Frankfurt am Main: Zweitausendeins, 1979. Screenplay and background information.

Schmitt, Sigrid, and Heiko R. Blum. " . . . um Erkenntnis zu zeigen, ist es meistens zu spät: Ein Interview mit Peter Lilienthal zu seinem Film *David*." *Medium* 9 (March 1979): 35–37. An interview with Peter Lilienthal conducted 15 November 1978 and 16–17 January 1979.

"Schrei, was du kannst," parts 1–3. *Spiegel*, nos. 37–39 (1988): 134–58, 142–58, 142–59. Essays on the history of the events leading to the concentration camps.

Stam, Robert. *Subversive Pleasures: Bakhtin, Cultural Criticism, and Film*. Baltimore: Johns Hopkins University Press, 1989. Applies Bakhtin's theories of literature—carnivalesque, hyperglossia, tact—to film analysis. Particularly useful for alternative readings of comedic films.

"Tanz auf dem Vulkan." *Spiegel*, no. 40 (28 September 1981): 228–38. Fascinating comparison of Gustaf Gründgens's life, Klaus Mann's novel, *Mephisto*, and Szabó's movie, *Mephisto*, based on the novel.

Thompson, Kristin. "Concepts of Cinematic Excess." In *Narrative, Apparatus, Ideology: A Film Reader*, edited by Philip Rosen, 130–42. New York: Columbia University Press, 1986. Suggests that often material in a film will influence viewers in ways not intended by the director and thus lead to alternative readings.

Verhoeven, Michael, and Mario Krebs. *Der Film "die weisse Rose": das Drehbuch.* Karlsruhe: Von Loeper, 1982. Screenplay.

_____. *"Die weisse Rose": Der Widerstand Münchner Studenten gegen Hitler: Informationen zum Film.* Frankfurt am Main: Fischer Taschenbuch, 1982. Background information on the film.

Vilsmaier, Joseph. *Die Verfilmung des Lebens der Anna Wimschneider: Eine Dokumentation über den Film "Herbstmilch."* Berlin: Ullstein, 1990. Background information on the film.

Vogel, Amos. *Film as a Subversive Art.* New York: Random House, 1974. Good analysis of the hypnotic effects of film and the willingness of viewers to suspend disbelief and become a part of the illusory world of the narrative.

selected filmography

▲▼▲

The following films are primarily productions of the Federal Republic of Germany. A few are DEFA productions, the film production company of the former German Democratic Republic (East Germany). Others were produced in Austria and German-speaking Switzerland. The filmography also includes films by non-German directors that were made in the German language and/or made as co-productions between German and non-German production companies.

A recent source is given for all films that are available in the United States either in 16mm or 35mm or on video. All rental information is for nontheatrical showings. Unless otherwise noted, these copies are in German with English subtitles. We have also included information on videos in the PAL format (German standard) for those who have the special equipment needed to play them. Finally, we recommend contacting the production companies directly to obtain copies of those films for which no U.S. source is available; they will often have prints or videos for sale or rent. Current addresses for many of these production companies can be found in the *Variety International Film Guide*, an annual edited by Peter Cowie and published by Samuel French.

Angry Harvest [*Bittere Ernte*] (CCC Filmkunst/Admiral Film, 1984)
Director: Agnieszka Holland
Screenplay: Agnieszka Holland, Paul Hengge
Camera: Josef Ort-Snep (color)
Music: Jörg Strassburger
Cast: Armin Mueller-Stahl, Elisabeth Trissenaar, Käthe Jaenicke, Hans Beerhenke, Isa Haller, Margit Carstensen, Kurt Raab

Running time: 102 minutes
16mm and 35mm rental: Capitol Entertainment, classroom rates available. VHS video also available for purchase from Capitol Entertainment.
American standard VHS video available. Contact video sources for purchase or rental.

Aren't We Wonderful [*Wir Wunderkinder*] (Filmaufbau, 1958)
Director: Kurt Hoffmann
Screenplay: Heinz Pauck, Günter Neumann; based on a novel by Hugo Hartung
Camera: Richard Angst (b/w)
Sound: Walter Rühland
Cast: Hansjörg Felmy, Robert Graf, Johanna von Koczian, Wera Frydtberg, Elisabeth Flickenschildt, Jürgen Goslar, Liesl Karlstadt, Michl Lang, Wolfgang Neuss, Wolfgang Müller
Running time: 108 minutes
No U.S. source

The Assassin [*Der Attentäter*] (Bavaria, 1969)
Director: Rainer Erler
Cast: Fritz Hollenbeck, Ulrich Matschoss, Ingeborg Lapsien
Running time: 90 minutes
No U.S. source

Autumn Milk [*Herbstmilch*] (Perathon Film/Zweites Deutsches Fernsehen, 1988)
Director: Joseph Vilsmaier
Screenplay: Peter Steinbach; based on the memoir of Anna Wimschneider
Camera: Joseph Vilsmaier (color)
Music: Norbert Jürgen Schneider
Cast: Dana Vavrova, Werner Stocker, Claude Oliver Rudolph, Eva Mattes, Ilona Mayer, Renate Grosser, Hertha Schwarz, Julius Mitterer, Albert Wimschneider, Anna Wimschneider
Running time: 111 minutes
No U.S. source
German PAL standard VHS video available (German language only). Contact German video sources.

The Axe of Wandsbek [*Das Beil von Wandsbek*] (Norddeutscher Rundfunk/Westdeutscher Rundfunk, 1981)
Director: Horst Königstein, Heinrich Breloer
Screenplay: Horst Königstein, Heinrich Breloer; based on a novel by Arnold Zweig
Camera: Klaus Brix (b/w and color)
Music: Annette Humpe
Cast: Erwin Geschonneck, Käthe Braun, Willy A. Kleinau

Running time: 149 minutes
16mm rental: West Glen Films, catalog no. 12290.

Between the Tracks [*Zwischengleis*] (Artus/BR, 1978)
Director: Wolfgang Staudte
Screenplay: Dorothea Dhan
Camera: Igor Luther (color)
Music: Eugen Illin
Cast: Mel Ferrer, Pola Kinski, Martin Lüttge, Hannelore Schroth
Running time: 110 minutes
16mm rental: West Glen Films, catalog no. 12108.

The Boat [*Das Boot*] (Bavaria/Radiant/WDR/SDR, 1981)
Director: Wolfgang Petersen
Screenplay: Wolfgang Petersen; based on a novel by Lothar-Günther Buchheim
Camera: Jost Vacano (color)
Music: Klaus Doldinger
Cast: Jürgen Prochnow, Herbert-Arthur Grönemeyer, Klaus Wennemann, Hubertus Bengsch, Martin Semmelrogge
Running time: 149 minutes
16mm rental: Films, Inc. VHS video also available for rental through Films, Inc. Classroom rates available for all formats.
American standard VHS video available. Contact video sources for purchase or rental. Dubbed English also available from a few sources.
German PAL standard VHS video available (German language only). Contact German video sources.

The Boat Is Full [*Das Boot ist voll*] (Limbo/SRG/Zweites Deutsches Fernsehen/Österreichischer Rundfunk, 1980) (Switzerland)
Director: Markus Imhoof
Screenplay: Markus Imhoof
Camera: Hans Liechti (color)
Cast: Tina Engel, Curt Bois, Renate Steiger, Mathias Gnadinger
Running time: 110 minutes
Language: Swiss-German dialect with English subtitles
16mm and 35mm rental: Castle Hill Productions. One-inch tape, TV and cable rights, and sales also available from Castle Hill.
American standard VHS video available. Contact video sources for purchase or rental.

Brainwashed [*Schachnovelle*] (Roxy, 1960) (Austria)
Director: Gerd Oswald
Screenplay: Harold Medford, Gerd Oswald, Herbert Reinecker; based on the novella by Stefan Zweig
Camera: Günther Senftleben (b/w)

Music: Hans-Martin Majewski
Cast: Curd Jürgens, Claire Bloom, Hansjörg Felmy, Mario Adorf
Running time: 103 minutes
Available for research in the film archives of the U.S. Library of Congress.

The Bridge [*Die Brücke*] (Fono-Film, 1959)
Director: Bernhard Wicki
Screenplay: Michael Mansfeld, Karl-Wilhelm Vivier, Bernhard Wicki; based on a novel by Manfred Gregor
Camera: Gerd von Bonin (b/w)
Music: Hans-Martin Majewski
Cast: Volker Bohnet, Fritz Wepper, Michael Hinz, Frank Glaubrecht, Karl Michael Balzer, Volker Lechtenbrink, Günther Hoffmann
Running time: 105 minutes
16mm rental: Cine World (also available dubbed in English); West Glen Films, catalog no. 12382 (dubbed English only).
German PAL standard VHS video available (German language only). Contact German video sources.

Cat and Mouse [*Katz und Maus*] (Modern Art Film, Berlin/Zespol Rytm, Warsaw, 1966)
Director: Hansjürgen Pohland
Screenplay: Hansjürgen Pohland; based on a novella by Günter Grass
Camera: Wolf Wirth (b/w)
Music: Attila Zoller
Cast: Lars Brandt, Peter Brandt, Wolfgang Neuss, Michael Hinz, Claudia Bremer
Running time: 88 minutes
16mm rental: Grove Press Film Division, classroom rates available; West Glen Films, catalog no. 12368.

Charlotte (CCC-Filmkunst/Concorde Film, 1981) (Netherlands-Germany)
Director: Frans Weisz
Screenplay: Judith Herzberg, Frans Weisz; based on the life and works of Charlotte Salomon
Camera: Jerzy Lipman, Theo van de Sande (color)
Music: Egisto Macchi
Cast: Birgit Doll, Derek Jacobi, Elisabeth Trissenaar, Max Croiset, Brigitte Horney
Running time: 90 minutes
Language: English
35mm rental: Atara Releasing, Jewish Film Festival.

The Children of No. 67 [*Die Kinder aus No. 67*] (Road Movies/Zweites Deutsches Fernsehen, 1979/80)
Director: Usch Bartelmess-Weller, Werner Meyer

Screenplay: Usch Bartelmess-Weller, Werner Meyer; based on a novel by Lisa Tetzner
Camera: Jürgen Jürges (color)
Music: Andi Brauer
Cast: Bernd Riedel, René Schaaf, May Buschke, Elfriede Irrall, Tilo Prückner, Martina Krauel
Running time: 103 minutes
No U.S. source
German PAL standard VHS video available (German language only). Contact German video sources.

Class Photo [*Klassenphoto: Erinnerungen deutscher Bürger*] (parts 1 and 2) (Norddeutscher Rundfunk, 1970)
Director: Eberhard Fechner
Screenplay: Eberhard Fechner
Camera: Rudolf Körösi and Ursula Hofmann (b/w)
Music: Werner Kuck
Sound: Dieter Schulz and Horst Faahs
Running time: 195 minutes
16mm rental: West Glen Films, catalog no. 12170 (German language only). Dubbed English also available, catalog no. 12171.

Country of the Fathers, Country of the Sons [*Land der Väter, Land der Söhne*] (NHF Nico Hofmann Filmproduktion/B.A. Bob Arnold Filmproduktion/SWF/BR, 1988)
Director: Nico Hofmann
Screenplay: Nico Hofmann
Camera: Laszlo Kadar (color)
Cast: Karl-Heinz von Liebezeit, Katharina Meinecke, Lieselotte Rau, Adolf Laimböck, Thomas Ott, Wolfgang Preiss, Eva Kotthaus, Wolf-Dietrich Sprenger, Günther Ziessler
Running time: 85 minutes
No U.S. source

David (von Vietinghoff/Pro-ject/Zweites Deutsches Fernsehen, 1978)
Director: Peter Lilienthal
Screenplay: Peter Lilienthal; based on a novel by Joel König
Camera: Al Ruban (color)
Music: Wojciech Kilar
Cast: Mario Fischl, Valter Taub, Irena Vrkljan, Eva Mattes, Dominique Horwitz
Running time: 125 minutes
16mm and 35mm rental: Kino International, classroom rates available. For sales, inquire Kino International. Purchase of VHS video also available through Kino on Video.

American standard VHS video available. Contact video sources for purchase or rental.
German PAL standard VHS video available (German language only). Contact German video sources.

Death Mills [*Die Todesmühlen*] (Zeit im Film, U.S. Office of Military Government, 1945)
Director: Hanns Burger
Screenplay: Hanns Burger
Editor: Sam Winston
Cast: commentary by Oskar Seidlin, narration by Anton Reimer
Running time: 22 minutes
No U.S. source

The Desert Fox (Twentieth Century-Fox, 1951) (U.S.)
Director: Henry Hathaway
Screenplay: Nunnally Johnson
Camera: Norbert Brodine (b/w)
Music: Daniele Amfitheatrof
Cast: James Mason, Cedric Hardwicke, Jessica Tandy, Luther Adler
Running time: 88 minutes
Language: English
16mm rental: Films, Inc., classroom rates available.
American standard VHS video available. Contact video sources for purchase or rental.

The Devil's General [*Des Teufels General*] (Real-Film, 1955)
Director: Helmut Käutner
Screenplay: Georg Hurdalek, Helmut Käutner; based on a play by Carl Zuckmayer
Camera: Albert Benitz (b/w)
Music: Archiv
Cast: Curd Jürgens, Viktor de Kowa, Karl John, Eva-Ingeborg Scholz, Marianne Koch
Running time: 115 minutes
16mm rental: West Glen Films, catalog no. 12166 (dubbed English only).

Dogs, Do You Want to Live Forever? [*Hunde, wollt ihr ewig leben?*] (Deutsche Film Hansa, 1958)
Director: Frank Wisbar
Screenplay: Frank Wisbar, Frank Dimen, Heinz Schröter; based on a novel by Fritz Wöss and the books *Stalingrad-bis zur letzten Patrone* (*Stalingrad—To the Last Bullet*) and *Letzte Briefe aus Staningrad* (*Last Letters from Stalingrad*) by Heinz Schröter
Camera: Helmut Ashley (b/w)
Music: Herbert Windt

Cast: Joachim Hansen, Wilhelm Borchert, Peter Carsten, Armin Dahlen, Horst Frank, Karl John, Sonja Ziemann
Running time: 97 minutes
No U.S. source
American standard VHS video available (German language only). Contact German Language Video Center for purchase or rental.
German PAL standard VHS video available (German language only). Contact German video sources.

Europa Europa [*Hitlerjunge Salomon*] (CCC Filmkuns/Margaret Menegoz/Les Films Du Losange, 1991)
Director: Agnieszka Holland
Screenplay: Agnieszka Holland; based on the autobiography of Salomon Perel
Camera: Jacek Petrycki (color)
Music: Zbigniew Preisner
Cast: Marco Hofschneider, Julie Delpy, Hans Zischler, Klaus Abramowsky, Rene Hofschneider
Running time: 115 minutes
16 mm and 35 mm rental: New Yorker Films, classroom rates available.
American standard VHS video available. Contact video sources.

Fellow Travellers (also, *Following the Führer*) [*Die Mitläufer*] (EML-Film/Zweites Deutsches Fernsehen, 1984)
Director: Erwin Leiser, Eberhard Itzenplitz, Oliver Storz
Screenplay: Oliver Storz
Camera: Gerard Vandenberg, Jochen Radermacher (b/w)
Narrator: Günther Sauer
Cast: Giesela Fritsch, Klaus Jepsen, Gottfried John, Barbara Klein, Armin Mueller-Stahl, Walter Schultheiss
Running time: 94 minutes
No U.S. source

The First Polka [*Die erste Polka*] (Norddeutsches Fernsehen/Bavaria, 1978)
Director: Klaus Emmerich
Screenplay: Helmut Krapp; based on a novel by Horst Bienek
Camera: Michael Ballhaus (color)
Music: Edward Aniol
Cast: Maria Schell, Erland Josephson, Guido Wieland, Ernst Stankowski, Claus Theo Gärtner, René Schell, Marco Kröger
Running time: 105 minutes
16mm rental: West Glen Films, catalog no. 12205. German language also available, catalog no. 12204.

Five Last Days [*Fünf letzte Tage*] (Pelemele/BR, 1982)
Director: Percy Adlon

Screenplay: Percy Adlon
Camera: Horst Lermer (color)
Music: Franz Schubert
Cast: Lena Stolze, Irm Hermann, Will Spindler, Hans Hirschmüller, Philipp Arp
Running time: 112 minutes
16mm rental: West Glen Films, catalog no. 12279.

Germany, Pale Mother [*Deutschland, bleiche Mutter*] (Helma Sanders-Brahms/Literarisches Colloquium Berlin, 1979)
Director: Helma Sanders-Brahms
Screenplay: Helma Sanders-Brahms
Camera: Jürgen Jürges (color)
Music: Jürgen Knieper
Cast: Eva Mattes, Ernst Jacobi, Elisabeth Stepanek, Angelika Thomas, Rainer Friedrichsen, Giesela Stein, Fritz Lichtenhahn
Running time: 145 minutes
16mm rental: New Yorker Films, classroom rates and sales (institutions only) available; West Glen Films, catalog no. 12262.

Girls' War [*Mädchenkrieg*] (Independent/ABS/Maran/Terra, 1977)
Director: Alf Brustellin, Bernhard Sinkel
Screenplay: Alf Brustelling, Bernhard Sinkel; based on a novel by Manfred Bieler
Camera: Dietrich Lohmann (color)
Music: Nicos Mamangakis
Cast: Adelheid Arndt, Katherine Hunter, Antonia Reinighaus, Matthias Habich, Hans Christian Blech, Dominik Graf, Christian Berkel, Valter Taub
Running time: 145 minutes
16mm rental: West Glen Films, catalog no. 12145.

God Does Not Believe in Us Anymore [*An uns glaubt Gott nicht mehr*] (team-film produktion/Österreichischer Rundfunk, 1982) (Austria)
Director: Axel Corti
Screenplay: Georg Stefan Troller
Camera: Wolfgang Treu (b/w)
Music: Hans Georg Koch, Archival Music
Cast: Johannes Silberschneider, Barbara Petritsch, Armin Mueller-Stahl, Fritz Muliar
Running time: 110 minutes
16mm rental: contact the Austrian Cultural Institute for availability.

Hanussen (Objektiv Filmstúdió Vállalat/Mafilm, 1989) (Germany-Hungary)
Director: István Szabó
Screenplay: István Szabó, Péter Dobai
Camera: Gyula Kovács (color)
Music: György Vukán

Cast: Klaus Maria Brandauer, Erland Josephson, Bánsági, Walter Schmidinger, Károly Eperjes, Grazyna Szapolowska
Running time: 110 minutes
American standard VHS video available. Contact video sources for purchase or rental.

Heimat (Edgar Reitz Film/Sender Freies Berlin/Westdeutscher Rundfunk, 1984)
Director: Edgar Reitz
Screenplay: Edgar Reitz, Peter Steinbach
Camera: Gernot Roll (b/w and color)
Music: Nicos Mamangakis
Cast: Gertrud Bredel, Rüdiger Weigang, Karin Rasenack, Marita Breuer, Michael Lesch, Dieter Schaad, Jörg Richter
Running time: 924 minutes
Video rental: West Glen Films, 11 episodes available only as a complete set and for a maximum of two weeks, VHS catalog no. 13721–13724; also available in 3/4" U-matic, catalog no. 13715–13720.

It Doesn't Always Have to Be Caviar [*Es muss nicht immer Kaviar sein*] (CCC/CEC, 1961)
Director: Geza von Radvanyi
Screenplay: Henri Jeanson; based on a novel by Mario Simmel
Camera: Friedl Behn-Grund (b/w)
Music: Wolf Wilhelm
Cast: O. W. Fischer, Eva Bartok, Senta Berger
Running time: 106 minutes
No U.S. source
German PAL standard VHS video available (German language only). Contact German video sources.

It Happened on the 20th of July [*Es geschah am 20. Juli*] (Ariston/Arca, 1955)
Director: G. W. Pabst
Screenplay: Werner P. Zibaso, Gustav Machaty
Camera: Kurt Hasse (b/w)
Music: Johannes Weissenbach
Cast: Bernhard Wicki, Karl Ludwig Diehl, Carl Wery, Kurt Meisel, Erik Frey, Albert Hehn, Jochen Hauer
Running time: 107 minutes
No U.S. source

It Went on Day and Night, Dear Child: Gypsies in Auschwitz (*Es ging Tag und Nacht, liebes Kind: Zigeuner [Sinti] in Auschwitz*) (Katrin Seybold/SDF, 1981–82)
Director: Katrin Seybold, Melanie Spitta
Screenplay: Melanie Spitta

Camera: Alfred Tichawsky, Heiner Stadler (color)
Music: Duo Z, Rudko Kawczynski, Tornado Rosenberg
Running time: 78 minutes
No U.S. source

I Was Nineteen [*Ich war neunzehn*] (DEFA, 1967)
Director: Konrad Wolf
Screenplay: Wolfgang Kohlhaase, Konrad Wolf
Camera: Werner Bergmann (b/w)
Music: "Am Rio Jarama," sung by Ernst Busch
Cast: Jaecki Schwarz, Wassili Liwanow, Alexej Ejboshenko, Galina Polskih, Jenn Gröllmann, Rolf Hoppe
Running time: 119 minutes
No U.S. source

Lili Marleen (Roxy/CIP/Rialto, 1980)
Director: Rainer Werner Fassbinder
Screenplay: Manfred Purzer; based on the memoir of Lale Andersen
Camera: Xaver Schwarzenberger (color)
Music: Peer Raben
Cast: Hanna Schygulla, Giancarlo Giannini, Mel Ferrer, Hark Bohm, Karl-Heinz von Hassel, Christine Kaufmann
Running time: 121 minutes
16mm and 35mm rental: Swank Motion Pictures, classroom rates available.
German PAL standard VHS video available (German language only). Contact German video sources.

Lost Life [*Verlorenes Leben*] (Ottokar Runze, 1976)
Director: Ottokar Runze
Screenplay: Peter Hirche
Camera: Michael Epp (b/w)
Music: Hans-Martin Majewski
Cast: Gerhard Olschewski, Marius Müller-Westernhagen, Gerd Haucke
Running time: 92 minutes
16mm rental: West Glen Films, catalog no. 12105.

The Lost One [*Der Verlorene*] (Arnold Pressburger, 1951)
Director: Peter Lorre
Screenplay: Peter Lorre, Benno Vigny, Axel Eggebrecht
Camera: Vaclav Vich (b/w)
Music: Willy Schmidt-Gentner
Cast: Peter Lorre, Karl John, Helmut Rudolf, Renate Mannhardt, Johanna Hofer, Lotte Rausch, Giesela Trowe
Running time: 98 minutes
No U.S. source

Mama, I Am Alive [*Mama, ich lebe*] (DEFA, 1976)
Director: Konrad Wolf
Screenplay: Wolfgang Kohlhaase
Camera: Werner Bergmann (b/w)
Music: Rainer Böhm
Cast: Peter Prager, Uwe Zerbst, Eberhard Kirhberg, Detlef Giess, Donatas Banionis, Margarita Terechowa
Running time: 103 minutes
No U.S. source

Marriage in the Shadows [*Ehe im Schatten*] (DEFA, 1947)
Director: Kurt Maetzig
Screenplay: Kurt Maetzig; based on the novella *Es wird schon nicht so schlimm sein* (*It Won't Be That Bad*) by Hans Schweikart
Camera: Friedl Behn Grund (b/w)
Music: Wolfgang Zeller
Cast: Paul Klinger, Ilse Steppat, Alfred Balthoff, Claus Holm
Running time: 105 minutes
No U.S. source

The Marriage of Maria Braun [*Die Ehe der Maria Braun*] (Albatros/Trio/Westdeutscher Rundfunk, 1978)
Director: Rainer Werner Fassbinder
Screenplay: Peter Märthesheimer, Pea Fröhlich, Rainer Werner Fassbinder
Camera: Michael Ballhaus (color)
Music: Peer Raben
Cast: Hanna Schygulla, Klaus Löwitsch, Ivan Desny, Gottfried John, Giesela Uhlen, Günter Lamprecht, George Byrd, Elisabeth Trissenaar, Isolde Barth, Volker Spengler, Michael Ballhaus, Hark Bohm, Günther Kaufmann, Rainer Werner Fassbinder
Running time: 120 minutes
16mm and 35mm rental: New Yorker Films, classroom rates available. For sales (institutions only), inquire New Yorker.
American standard VHS video available. Contact video sources for purchase or rental.
German PAL standard VHS video available (German language only). Contact German video sources.

Mephisto (Mafilm/Manfred Durniok/Österreichischer Rundfunk, 1981) (Germany-Hungary)
Director: István Szabó
Screenplay: István Szabó, Péter Dobai; based on a novel by Klaus Mann
Camera: Lajos Koltai (color)
Music: Zdenko Tamassy

Cast: Klaus Maria Brandauer, Rolf Hoppe, Krystyna Janda, Karin Boyd, Ildiko Bansagi
Running time: 145 minutes
16mm rental: Kit Parker (ALMI/Kypton Library) (German with English subtitles), classroom rates available. For sales, including purchase of subtitled video, contact Kit Parker.
American standard VHS video available (dubbed English only). Contact video sources for purchase or rental.
German PAL standard VHS video available (German language only). Contact German video sources.

A Minute of Darkness Does Not Blind Us [*Eine Minute Dunkel macht uns nicht blind*] (Thalia-Film/Österreichischer Rundfunk, 1986)
Director: Susanne Zanke
Screenplay: Susanne Zanke; based on the memoir of Grete Schütte Luhotzky
Camera: Tamás Ujlaki (b/w)
Music: Anka Hauter
Cast: Gertrud Roll, Hanne Rohrer, Günter Einbrodt, Daniela Graf
Running time: 110 minutes
No U.S. source

Morituri [*Kennwort: Morituri*] (Arcola/Colony/Twentieth-Century Fox, 1965) (U.S.)
Director: Bernhard Wicki
Screenplay: Daniel Taradash; based on a novel by Werner Jörg Lüddecke
Camera: Conrad Hall (b/w)
Cast: Marlon Brando, Yul Brynner, Trevor Howard, Janet Margolin, Wally Cox, William Redfield, Martin Benrath
Running time: 123 minutes
Language: English
16mm rental: Films, Inc., classroom rates available.

The Murderers Are among Us [*Die Mörder sind unter uns*] (DEFA, 1946)
Director: Wolfgang Staudte
Screenplay: Wolfgang Staudte
Camera: Friedl Behn-Grund, Eugen Klagemann (b/w)
Music: Ernst Roters
Cast: Ernst Wilhelm Borchert, Hildegard Knef, Erna Sellmer, Arno Paulsen, Robert Forsch, Albert Johannes
Running time: 88 minutes
Available for research in the film archives of the U.S. Library of Congress.

My Country, Right or Wrong [*Tadellöser und Wolff*], parts 1 and 2 (Polyphon/Zweites Deutsches Fernsehen, 1975)
Director: Eberhard Fechner

Screenplay: Eberhard Fechner; based on the autobiographical novel of Walter Kempowski
Camera: Gero Erhardt (b/w and color)
Cast: Edda Seippel, Karl Lieffen, Martin Semmelrogge, Gabriele Michel, Martin Kollewe, Jesper Christensen
Running time: 205 minutes
16mm rental: West Glen Films, catalog no. 12139.

My Father's War [*Der Krieg meines Vaters*] (Hochschule für Fernsehen und Film/Novoskop Filmproduktion/Südwestfunk, 1984)
Director: Nico Hofmann
Screenplay: Nico Hofmann
Camera: Ernst Kubitza (b/w)
Sound: Winfried Leyh
Running time: 60 minutes
No U.S. source

The Nasty Girl [*Das schreckliche Mädchen*] (1990)
Director: Michael Verhoeven
Screenplay: Michael Verhoeven
Camera: Axel De Roche (color)
Cast: Lena Stolze, Hans-Reinhard Muller
Running time: 92 minutes
16mm and 35mm rental: Films, Inc. VHS video rental also available through Films, Inc. Classroom rates available for all formats.

Night Fell on Gotenhafen [*Nacht fiel über Gotenhafen*] (DFH, 1959)
Director: Frank Wisbar
Screenplay: Victor Schuller, Frank Wisbar
Camera: Willy Winterstein (b/w)
Cast: Sonja Ziemann, Gunnar Möller, Brigitte Horney
Running time: 99 minutes
No U.S. source

08/15, part 1 (Divina, 1954)
Director: Paul May
Screenplay: Ernst von Salomon; based on the novels by Hans Helmut Kirst
Camera: Kurt Hasse (b/w)
Music: Rolf Wilhelm
Cast: Joachim Fuchsberger, Eva Ingeborg Scholz, Paul Bösinger
Running time: 95 minutes
No U.S. source

08/15, part 2 (Divina, 1955)
Director: Paul May

Screenplay: Ernst von Salomon; based on the novels by Hans Helmut Kirst
Camera: Kurt Hasse (b/w)
Music: Rolf Wilhelm
Cast: Joachim Fuchsberger, Hans Christian Blech, O. E. Hasse
Running time: 110 minutes
No U.S. source

08/15, part 3 (Divina, 1955)
Director: Paul May
Screenplay: Ernst von Salomon; based on the novels by Hans Helmut Kirst
Camera: Kurt Hasse (b/w)
Music: Rolf Wilhelm
Cast: O. E. Hasse, Gustav Knuth, Hans Christian Blech
Running time: 96 minutes
No U.S. source

One Day [*Ein Tag*] (1965)
Director: Egon Monk
Screenplay: Egon Monk, Claus Hubalek, Günther R. Lys
Camera: Walther Fehmder (b/w)
Sound: Hans Diestel
Cast: Achim Dünnwald, Eberhard Fechner, Ernst Jacobi, Josef Frölich, Josef Schafer, Ludwig Wühr
Running time: 97 minutes
16mm rental: West Glen Films, catalog no. 12394.

The Pedestrian [*Der Fussgänger*] (Franz Seitz/Alfa/MFG/Zev Braun, 1973)
Director: Maximilian Schell
Screenplay: Maximilian Schell
Camera: Wolfgang Treu, Klaus König (color)
Music: Manos Hadjidakis
Cast: Gustav Rudolf Sellner, Peter Hall, Gila von Weitershausen, Maximilian Schell, Ruth Hausmeister, Lil Dagover, Walter Schmidinger, Elsa Wagner
Running time: 98 minutes
Language: dubbed English
American standard VHS video available. Contact video sources for purchase or rental.
Available for research in the film archives of the U.S. Library of Congress.

Peppermint Peace [*Peppermint Frieden*] (Nourfilm, 1982)
Director: Marianne S. W. Rosenbaum
Screenplay: Marianne S. W. Rosenbaum
Camera: Alfred Tichawsky
Music: Konstantin Wecker

Cast: Saskia Tyroller, Gesine Strempel, Hans Peter Korff, Peter Fonda, Cleo Kretschmer
Running time: 110 minutes
16mm rental: West Glen Films, catalog no. 12366

Professor Mamlock (DEFA, 1960–61)
Director: Konrad Wolf
Screenplay: Karl Georg Egel, Konrad Wolf; based on a play by Friedrich Wolf
Camera: Werner Bergmann, Günter Ost (b/w)
Music: Hans-Dieter Hosalla, Ludwig von Beethoven
Cast: Wolfgang Heinz, Ursula Burg, Hilmar Thate, Liss Tempelhof, Doris Abesser, Ulrih Thein
Running time: 100 minutes
No U.S. source

Raindrops [*Regentropfen*] (Tellux/Zweites Deutsches Fernsehen, 1981)
Director: Michael Hoffmann, Harry Raymon
Screenplay: Michael Hoffmann, Harry Raymon
Camera: Jürgen Grundmann (b/w)
Music: Louis Bloom
Cast: Elfriede Irrall, Walter Renneisen, Jack Geula, Gloria Swoboda, Giovanni Früh
Running time: 90 minutes
16mm rental: West Glen Films, catalog no. 12288.

Rommel Calling Cairo [*Rommel ruft Kairo*] (Omega, 1958)
Director: Wolfgang Schleif
Screenplay: K. H. Turner, Heinz Oskar Wuttig; based on a novel by John Eppler
Camera: Manfred Ensinyer (b/w)
Cast: Adrian Hoven, Elisabeth Müller, Peter van Eyck
Running time: 105 minutes
No U.S. source

Sansibar [*"Sansibar oder der letzte Grund"*] (DEFA, 1987)
Director: Bernhard Wicki
Screenplay: Wolfgang Kirchner, Bernhard Wicki; based on a novel by Alfred Andersch
Camera: Klaus Neumann, Edward Kosinski, Jürgen Lenz (color)
Music: Günter Fisher
Cast: Gregor Peter Kremer, Cornelia Schmaus, Giesela Stein, Michel Gwisdek, Elisabeth Endriss, Peter Sodann, Frank Hessenland, Ulrich Mühe
Running time: 87 minutes
No U.S. source

Somewhere in Berlin [*Irgendwo in Berlin*] (DEFA, 1946)
Director: Gerhard Lamprecht

Screenplay: Gerhard Lamprecht
Camera: Werner Krien (b/w)
Music: Erich Einegg
Cast: Harry Hindemith, Hedda Sarrow, Charles Kentschke
Running time: 85 minutes
Available for research in the film archives of the U.S. Library of Congress.

The Spider's Web [*Das Spinnennetz*] (Provobis/Zweites Deutsches Fernsehen/Österreichischer Rundfunk/Csekoslovensk Filmexport/K Betafilm, 1989)
Director: Bernhard Wicki
Screenplay: Wolfgang Kirchner, Bernhard Wicki; based on a novel by Joseph Roth
Camera: Gerard Vandenberg (color)
Music: Günther Fischer
Cast: Ulrich Mühe, Klaus Maria Brandauer, Corinna Kirchhoff, Ulrich Haupt, Armin Mueller-Stahl, Andrea Jonasson
Running time: 195 minutes
No U.S source

38—Vienna before the Fall [*38—Auch das war Wien*] (Crocus, 1986) (Austria)
Director: Wolfgang Glück
Screenplay: Wolfgang Glück, Lida Winiewiz; based on the novel *Auch das war Wien* (*This Too Was Vienna*) by Friedrich Torberg
Camera: Gerard Vandenberg (color)
Music: Bert Grund
Cast: Tobias Engel, Sunnyi Melles, Heinz Trixner, Ingrid Burkhard
Running time: 97 minutes
35mm rental: East-West Classics, classroom rates available. VHS video also available for purchase through East-West Classics.
American standard VHS video available. Contact video sources for purchase or rental.

The Tin Drum [*Die Blechtrommel*] (Franz Seitz/Bioskop/Artemis/Hallelujah/Argos, 1979)
Director: Volker Schlöndorff
Screenplay: Jean-Claude Carrière, Volker Schlöndorff, Franz Seitz; based on a novel by Günter Grass
Camera: Igor Luther (color)
Music: Maurice Jarre
Cast: David Bennent, Angela Winkler, Mario Adorf, Daniel Olbrychski, Katharina Thalbach, Charles Aznavour, Heinz Bennent, Ernst Jakobi, Fritz Hakl, Mariella Oliveri
Running time: 144 minutes
16mm rental: Films, Inc., classroom rates available; West Glen Films, catalog no. 12362.

American standard VHS video available. Contact video sources for purchase or rental.
German PAL standard VHS video available (German language only). Contact German video sources.

Veronika Voss [*Die Sehnsucht der Veronika Voss*] (Laura/Tango/Rialto/Trio/Maran, 1982)
Director: Rainer Werner Fassbinder
Screenplay: Peter Märthesheimer, Pea Fröhlich
Camera: Xaver Schwarzenberger (b/w)
Music: Peer Raben
Cast: Rosel Zech, Armin Mueller-Stahl, Hilmar Thate, Annemarie Düringer, Doris Schade, Cornelia Froboess
Running time: 104 minutes
16mm and 35mm rental: Swank Motion Pictures, classroom rates available. VHS video rental also available through Swank.

The Wannsee Conference [*Die Wannseekonferenz*] (Infafilm/Österreichischer Rundfunk/Bavarian Broadcasting Co., 1984)
Director: Heinz Schirk
Screenplay: Paul Mommertz
Camera: Horst Schier (color)
Cast: Robert Artzhorn, Friedrich Beckhaus, Gerd Bockmann, Jocchen Busse, Hans Bussinger, Harald Dietl, Peter Fritz, Martin Lüttge, Dietrich Mattausch, Günter Spoerrle
Running time: 85 minutes
16mm and 35mm rental: Films, Inc. VHS video rental also available through Films, Inc. Classroom rates available for all formats.
American standard VHS video available. Contact video sources for purchase or rental.

Welcome in Vienna (THALIA-Film/Österreichischer Rundfunk, 1985)
Director: Axel Corti
Screenplay: Georg Stefan Troller, Axel Corti
Camera: Gernott Roll (b/w)
Music: Hans Georg Koch, Franz Schubert
Cast: Gabriel Barylli, Nicolas Brieger, Claudia Messner, Hubert Mann, Kurt Sowinwetz, Karlheinz Hackl, Joachim Kemmer
Running time: 121 minutes
35mm rental: Roxie Releasing, classroom rates available.

The White Rose [*Die weisse Rose*] (Sentana/CCC Filmkunst, 1982)
Director: Michael Verhoeven
Screenplay: Michael Verhoeven, Mario Krebs
Camera: Axel de Roche (color)

Music: Konstantin Wecker
Cast: Lena Stolze, Wulf Kessler, Oliver Siebert, Ulrich Tukur, Werner Stocker
Running time: 123 minutes
16mm rental: New Line Cinema, distributed by Films, Inc., classroom rates available.
American standard VHS video available. Contact video sources for purchase or rental.
German PAL standard VHS video available (German language only). Contact German video sources.

Winterspelt (Ullstein AV/SFB/HR, 1977)
Director: Eberhard Fechner
Screenplay: Eberhard Fechner; based on a novel by Alfred Andersh
Camera: Rudolf Körösi, Kurt Weber (color)
Music: Görgy Ligeti
Cast: Ulrich von Dobschütz, Katharina Thalbach, Hans Christian Blech, Henning Schlüter, Georg Roubicek
Running time: 110 minutes
16mm rental: West Glen Films, catalog no. 12186.

The Yellow Star [*Der gelbe Stern*] (Chronos-Film, 1980)
Director: Dieter Hildebrandt
Screenplay: Dieter Hildebrandt
Historical adviser: Gerhard Schoenberner
Camera: Nicolas Joray (b/w)
Running time: 90 minutes
No U.S. source
German PAL standard VHS video available (German language only). Contact German video sources.

index

▲▼▲

the authors

▲▼▲

Robert C. Reimer studied at the University of Wisconsin at Milwaukee, the University of Wisconsin at Madison (B.A., 1965), the Technical University at Stuttgart, and the University of Kansas (M.A., 1968, Ph.D., 1971). He has taught German language, literature, and film courses since 1971 at the University of North Carolina at Charlotte. In 1984–85 he was a Fulbright professor at the Pädagogische Hochschule in Ludwigsburg, where he started researching Nazi-retro film. He is a member of the board of the Charlotte Film Society and has written articles on drama, pedagogy, and film for *Unterrichtspraxis, USF Language Quarterly, Foreign Language Annals,* and *Journal of Popular Film and Television.*

Carol J. Reimer studied at the University of Wisconsin at Madison, the University of North Carolina at Charlotte (B.A., 1976), and the University of Wisconsin at Milwaukee (M.L.S., 1981). She spent 1984–85 in Stuttgart, Germany. During her stay she began watching and analyzing some of the films discussed in this book. She is head of monograph and audio-visual ordering at the J. Murrey Atkins Library, University of North Carolina at Charlotte, and has published in *Sightlines* and *Journal of Popular Film and Television.*

Colaiste Mhuire Gan Smal
Luimneach

WITHDRAWN
FROM STOCK